McGraw-Hill's

500
Macroeconomics
Questions

Also in McGraw-Hill's 500 Questions Series

McGraw-Hill's

500

Macroeconomics
Questions

Ace Your College Exams

Eric R. Dodge, PhD, and Melanie E. Fox, PhD

New York   Chicago   San Francisco   Lisbon   London   Madrid   Mexico City
Milan   New Delhi   San Juan   Seoul   Singapore   Sydney   Toronto

1 2 3 4 5 6 7 8 9 10 11 12 13 14 15   QFR/QFR   1 9 8 7 6 5 4 3 2

ISBN   978-0-07-178034-6
MHID   0-07-178034-3

e-ISBN   978-0-07-178047-6
e-MHID   0-07-178047-5

Library of Congress Control Number 2012933635

McGraw-Hill products are available at special quantity discounts to use as premiums and sales promotions or for use in corporate training programs. To contact a representative, please e-mail us at bulksales@mcgraw-hill.com.

This book is printed on acid-free paper.

CONTENTS

INTRODUCTION

Congratulations! You've taken a big step toward achieving your best grade by purchasing *McGraw-Hill's 500 Macroeconomics Questions*. We are here to help you improve your grades on classroom, midterm, and final exams. These 500 questions will help you study more effectively, use your preparation time wisely, and get the final grade you want.

This book gives you 500 multiple-choice questions that cover the most essential course material. Each question has a detailed answer explanation. These questions give you valuable independent practice to supplement your regular textbook and the groundwork you are already doing in the classroom.

You might be the kind of student who needs to study extra questions a few weeks before a big exam for a final review. Or you might be the kind of student who puts off preparing until right before a midterm or final. No matter what your preparation style is, you will surely benefit from reviewing these 500 questions that closely parallel the content, format, and degree of difficulty of the questions found in typical college-level exams. These questions and their answer explanations are the ideal last-minute study tool for those final days before the test.

Remember the old saying "Practice makes perfect." If you practice with all the questions and answers in this book, we are certain that you will build the skills and confidence that are needed to ace your exams. Good luck!

—Editors of McGraw-Hill Education

CHAPTER 1

Basic Economic Concepts

1. Which of the following would be the best definition of the study of economics?
    - (A) Economics is the study of how to profit from the stock market.
    - (B) Economics is the study of how to make money.
    - (C) Economics is the study of labor decisions.
    - (D) Economics is the study of how individuals, households, and societies choose to allocate limited resources to unlimited wants.
    - (E) Economics is the study of government debts and deficits.

2. The economic system of the United States is best described as a
    - (A) pure market system
    - (B) pure command and control system
    - (C) strictly public system
    - (D) strictly private system
    - (E) a mix of market and command

3. Normative analysis can best be shortened to _____, while positive analysis is best shortened to _____.
    - (A) the next best alternative; the way things ought to be
    - (B) the way things should be; the way things were meant to be
    - (C) the way things should be; the way things actually are
    - (D) the way things should be; the next best alternative
    - (E) the way things actually are; the next best alternative

4. A market-based system would be characterized by _____, but a planned system would be characterized by _____.

    (A) prices that effectively allocate resources; markets that allocate goods

    (B) firms that have the ultimate choice on what and how much they produce; a central agency that decides on what and how much should be produced

    (C) a government that decides the best allocation of resources; individual decision makers that decide on the best allocation of resources

    (D) the presence of economic resources; the absence of economic resources

    (E) private ownership of resources, which ensures that they are distributed equally; public ownership of resources, which ensures that they are distributed equally

5. Which of the following best describes a microeconomic question?

    (A) What is the optimal amount of health insurance that a family should buy?

    (B) Should a nation fix the price of its currency?

    (C) Is the economy of Italy in a recession?

    (D) What is the value of the goods and services that the United States produces every year?

    (E) What is the aggregate price level in an economy?

6. Fabiola is asked by her teacher to write a paper based on a macroeconomic topic. Which of the following titles would be appropriate for a macroeconomics paper?

    (A) Are Inflation and Unemployment Related?

    (B) Does a Woman's Marriage Outcome Reflect Dating Time?

    (C) Does a Mother's Level of Education Influence Purchasing Decisions?

    (D) How Do Farmers Decide on Technology Adoption?

    (E) Does Your College Roommate's GPA Influence Your Own?

7. The idea of _____ in economics is that we have unlimited wants but limited resources.

    (A) opportunity costs

    (B) scarcity

    (C) marginal analysis

    (D) specialization

    (E) normative economics

8. The president of Karlonia is deciding whether or not to increase government spending. Which of the following statements would be considered positive analysis?

   (A) Government is already too large to be effective, and government involvement should be decreased.
   (B) Government is too small and should have a larger role in the economy.
   (C) The unemployment rate may decrease if government spending is increased.
   (D) Government should intervene when an economy is in a recession.
   (E) The government should not incur a deficit to increase government spending.

9. The nation of Kittyania is moving from a centralized planning system to a market-based economy. Which of the following are most likely to be part of the country's move to a market economy?

   (A) Resources will no longer be rationed, because there is no more scarcity.
   (B) Kittyania will require that the government own all factors of production.
   (C) Production decisions will be made by bureaucrats rather than entrepreneurs.
   (D) Firms will consult government agencies for which resources they should use in production.
   (E) Resources will begin to be rationed by markets.

10. Which of the following would be counted in the category of resources called labor?

    (A) Money raised by firms through issuing bonds
    (B) The factory that a firm uses to produce goods
    (C) The ability of a business owner to combine resources
    (D) The set of skills that workers possess
    (E) The common stock that a family owns in a firm

11. The four economic resources are

    (A) natural resources, capital, land, and money
    (B) natural resources, entrepreneurial ability, physical capital, and labor
    (C) land, income, capital, and entrepreneurial ability
    (D) land, labor, capital, and money
    (E) income, inflation, capital, and land

12. In the production of bread, which of the following would be considered the economic resource of capital?

(A) The wheat flour used in the bread dough
(B) The bowl you use to mix the bread dough
(C) The work of the person mixing the cookie dough
(D) The recipe to mix the cookie dough
(E) The energy used to bake the bread

13. Amanda is considering going to art school to become a graphic artist. Which of the following considerations captures the idea of her opportunity costs?

(A) How much income she will forgo when she quits her current job as a teacher
(B) How much money she can borrow to pay tuition
(C) How many hours per week she will work as a graphic artist once she graduates
(D) Whether or not her friends think it is a good idea to go to art school
(E) How much she spends on groceries while in school

14. The total opportunity cost of X is best described as the

(A) combined value of all superior alternatives to X that must be given up
(B) inefficiency in a free market system
(C) combined value of all inferior alternatives to X
(D) price of X plus the value of the next-best alternative to X
(E) cost of scarcity

15. President Hass is considering several construction projects: build roads, build a university, or create a national science program. Costs for each project are the same, but she can choose only one of them. If she builds roads, the country will receive an additional $120,000,000 in revenue. If she builds a university, the nation will receive an additional $110,000,000 in revenue. However, if she creates a national science program, this will generate an additional $100,000,000 in revenue. What is the implicit opportunity cost of building roads?

(A) $110,000,000, the forgone earnings from the university
(B) $210,000,000, the forgone earnings from the science program and university
(C) $20,000,000, the earnings from the roads less the forgone earnings from the science program
(D) $100,000,000, the forgone earnings from the science program
(E) There is no opportunity cost, since all projects cost the same.

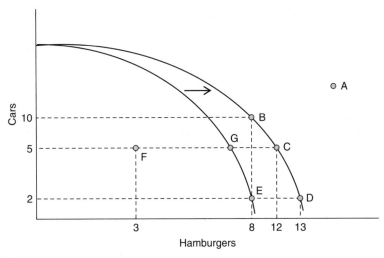

Figure 1.1

16. Refer to Figure 1.1. Suppose a nation wanted to move from producing a combination of cars and hamburgers represented by point B to production represented by point C. Which of the following is true?

(A) An economy would need to require more resources to move from point B to point C.

(B) An economy currently producing at a point represented by point B could not move to point C unless it experienced economic growth.

(C) An economy currently producing at point B is already producing an unattainable amount and will have to decrease the production of either hamburgers or cars.

(D) An economy currently producing at point B could produce more of both goods and increase production to point C.

(E) An economy currently producing at point B would need to reduce the amount of cars it produced to produce more hamburgers to get to point C.

17. According to Figure 1.1, what would be necessary for this economy to shift from producing at point E to point D?
    (A) The country would need to reallocate all of its existing resources to producing hamburgers.
    (B) The country would need to become better at producing only cars.
    (C) The country would need to become better at producing only hamburgers.
    (D) The country would need to reallocate resources away from producing cars to producing hamburgers.
    (E) The country would need to reallocate resources away from producing hamburgers to producing cars.

18. Suppose the production possibilities frontier of a nation has moved outward as shown in Figure 1.1. Which of the following is definitely true?
    (A) Points A, F, and B are allocatively efficient.
    (B) Points B, C, and D are productively efficient.
    (C) Points A, F, and B are productively efficient.
    (D) Points B, C, and D are allocatively efficient.
    (E) All points would be productively efficient, but not allocatively efficient.

19. In Figure 1.1, what information would we need to have to determine whether point B or point D is allocatively efficient?
    (A) None, since B is roughly halfway between the two axes, we know it is allocatively efficient.
    (B) The dollar price of each good
    (C) Whether or not we could move from B to D without a loss of productive efficiency
    (D) Whether or not the marginal benefit of hamburgers exceeded the marginal cost of hamburgers at point B or point D
    (E) Whether or not the marginal cost of a car is equal to the marginal cost of a hamburger at point B or point D

20. In Figure 1.1, which of the following movements would be considered economic growth?

(A) A to B
(B) G to B
(C) F to G
(D) G to E
(E) E to G

21. In a single day, Crabtown can produce 15 boats or 10 hush puppies. Their potential trading partner, Lobstertown, can produce 15 boats or 5 hush puppies. Who has the comparative advantage in producing what?

(A) Crabtown has comparative advantage in producing hush puppies, and Lobstertown has comparative advantage in producing boats.
(B) Crabtown has comparative advantage in producing both goods, and Lobstertown has comparative advantage in producing both goods.
(C) Crabtown has comparative advantage in producing boats, and Lobstertown has comparative advantage in producing hush puppies.
(D) Neither town has comparative advantage in producing either of the goods.
(E) Crabtown has comparative advantage in producing hush puppies, but neither town has comparative advantage in producing boats.

22. In a single day, Crabtown can produce 12 boats or 10 hush puppies. Their potential trading partner, Lobstertown, can produce 15 boats or 5 hush puppies. Which of the following statements is true?

(A) Both Crabtown and Lobstertown have absolute advantage in producing boats.
(B) Neither Crabtown nor Lobstertown have absolute advantage in producing boats.
(C) Crabtown has absolute advantage in producing boats, and Lobstertown has absolute advantage in producing hush puppies.
(D) Crabtown has absolute advantage in producing hush puppies, and Lobstertown has absolute advantage in producing boats.
(E) Neither has absolute advantage in producing either good.

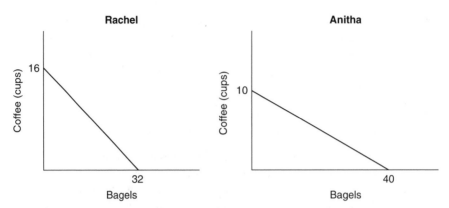

Figure 1.2

23. Refer to Figure 1.2. Rachel has absolute advantage in producing
_____, and Anitha has comparative advantage in producing

_____.

    (A) bagels; coffee
    (B) coffee; bagels
    (C) both goods; bagels
    (D) bagels; neither good
    (E) both goods; neither good

24. Refer to Figure 1.2. Which of the following would be an efficient level
of production for Rachel?
    I.   16 cups of coffee and 0 bagels
    II. 13 cups of coffee and 6 bagels
    III. 12 cups of coffee and 12 bagels

    (A) I only
    (B) II only
    (C) III only
    (D) I and II only
    (E) II and III only

25. Refer to Figure 1.2. What is Rachel's opportunity cost of bagels?
    (A) 1 cup of coffee
    (B) ½ cup of coffee
    (C) 2 cups of coffee
    (D) 16 cups of coffee
    (E) ¼ cups of coffee

26. Refer to Figure 1.2. Which of the following trading terms would both Anitha and Rachel find acceptable?

(A) 1 bagel trades for $\frac{1}{10}$ cup of coffee.
(B) 1 bagel trades for $\frac{1}{16}$ cup of coffee.
(C) 1 bagel trades for 3 cups of coffee.
(D) 1 bagel trades for $\frac{1}{3}$ cup of coffee.
(E) 1 bagel trades for 1 cup of coffee.

27. Refer to Figure 1.2. Anitha and Rachel currently split their time equally between producing coffee and bagels. If the trading price is 1 bagel for $\frac{5}{16}$ of a cup of coffee, which of the following describes the result of specialization and trade?

(A) Anitha would be unwilling to trade at this price, so there would be no gains from trade.
(B) Rachel will specialize in bagels, and Anitha will specialize in coffee. Rachel could sell 5 cups of coffee for 16 bagels produced by Anitha. Rachel will end up with 4 cups of coffee and 16 bagels, and Anitha will end up with 5 cups of coffee and 12 bagels.
(C) Rachel will specialize in coffee and Anitha will specialize in bagels. Rachel could sell 5 cups of coffee for 16 bagels produced by Anitha. Rachel will end up with 11 cups of coffee and 16 bagels, and Anitha will end up with 5 cups of coffee and 16 bagels.
(D) Rachel will specialize in coffee, and Anitha will specialize in bagels. Rachel could sell 5 cups of coffee for 16 bagels produced by Anitha. Rachel will end up with 11 cups of coffee and 16 bagels, and Anitha will end up with 5 cups of coffee and 24 bagels.
(E) Rachel will be unwilling to trade at this price, so there would be no gains from trade.

28. Refer to Figure 1.2. Every time Anitha produces a cup of coffee, she gives up making _____ bagels.

(A) 4
(B) 2
(C) $\frac{1}{4}$
(D) 40
(E) 10

29. Refer to Figure 1.2. Suppose Anitha wanted to consume 4 bagels and 10 cups of coffee. Which of the following could allow that to occur?
   I. Anitha gets better at producing bagels but not coffee.
   II. Anitha gets better at producing both goods.
   III. Anitha trades with Rachel.

   (A) I only
   (B) II only
   (C) III only
   (D) I and III only
   (E) II and III only

30. On Monday Oscar baked 3 loaves of bread and 18 cupcakes. On Tuesday Oscar baked 4 loaves of bread and 18 cupcakes. Assuming Oscar is efficient and has constant costs, which of the following statements is true about what changed between Monday and Tuesday?
   I. Oscar has more resources to produce both goods.
   II. Oscar has moved along his production possibilities frontier.
   III. Oscar's production possibilities frontier has rotated out.

   (A) I only
   (B) II only
   (C) III only
   (D) I and II only
   (E) I and III only

31. Max is always efficient and has constant costs. On Friday Max edited 10 papers and had 4 meetings. On Thursday Max edited 5 papers and attended 6 meetings. Which of the following statements is true about Max?
   I. Max would be willing to go to 2 meetings for Patti if she edits 6 papers for him.
   II. Max can attend 8 meetings in a day and edit no papers.
   III. Max can attend 3 meetings and edit 10 papers in a day.

   (A) I only
   (B) II only
   (C) III only
   (D) I and III only
   (E) II and III only

32. Zoe can bake 5 pasta bakes or 10 quiches in an hour, and Elmo can bake 3 pasta bakes or 15 quiches in an hour. Which of the following statements regarding the possibility for trade between Zoe and Elmo is true?

    (A) Zoe should specialize in making pasta bakes, and Elmo should specialize in making quiches. They would both be willing to trade at a price of 4 quiches for every pasta bake.
    (B) Zoe should specialize in making pasta bakes, and Elmo should specialize in making quiches. They would both be willing to trade at a price of 6 quiches for every pasta bake.
    (C) Zoe should specialize in making quiches, and Elmo should specialize in making pasta bakes. They would both be willing to trade at a price of 4 quiches for every pasta bake.
    (D) Zoe should specialize in making quiches, and Elmo should specialize in making pasta bakes, and they would both be willing to trade, at a price of 6 quiches for every pasta bake.
    (E) They should not specialize and trade, since Elmo has absolute advantage in producing quiches.

33. Jane can grow 100 bales of cotton or 50 tons of lumber on her land. Clark can grow 120 bales of cotton or 80 tons of lumber on his land. What terms of trade would both agree to if they specialize and trade?

    (A) They trade 1 bale of cotton for ⅔ of a ton of lumber.
    (B) They trade 3 bales of cotton for 1 ton of lumber.
    (C) They trade 1 bale of cotton for ¼ of a ton of lumber.
    (D) They trade 1 bale of cotton for ⅝ of a ton of lumber.
    (E) No terms of trade can be agreed on, since Clark has absolute advantage in producing both goods.

CHAPTER **2**

Supply and Demand

34. The demand for cookies will increase if

(A) the price of cookies decreases
(B) the population increases
(C) the price of crackers, a substitute for cookies, decreases
(D) the supply of cookies increases
(E) the price of milk, a complement to cookies, increases

35. The demand for airplane tickets will increase if

(A) the supply of airplane tickets decreases
(B) the price of jet fuel increases
(C) the price of an airplane ticket increases
(D) the price of hotel rooms decreases
(E) consumers believe air travel is becoming unsafe

36. Which of the following is a demand determinant for chocolate milk?

(A) The price of regular milk, which is often used instead of chocolate milk
(B) The price of chocolate milk
(C) The cost of the corn that feeds the dairy cows that produce the milk
(D) The number of milk producers in the market
(E) The price of land used to raise the dairy cows

37. Suppose we are told that fewer cartons of cigarettes are being demanded, regardless of the price of a carton of cigarettes. One explanation for this trend may be that

(A) consumers have a stronger preference for cigarettes
(B) the number of smokers in the market has increased
(C) the cost of producing cigarettes has decreased
(D) the number of firms that produce cigarettes has increased
(E) educational efforts have succeeded in convincing consumers that cigarettes cause cancer

38. Select the choice that would cause a rightward shift in the demand for good X.

(A) A higher price of good X
(B) Stronger consumer tastes and preferences for good X
(C) Improved technology used to produce good X
(D) A lower price of an input used in the production of good X
(E) A lower price of a substitute for good X

39. The demand for pie will increase if

(A) the price of sugar used to make the pie increases
(B) income increases and pie is an inferior good
(C) income increases and pie is a normal good
(D) the medical community reveals that pie is harmful to our health
(E) the price of pie rises

40. The supply of houses is likely to increase if

(A) the number of home builders decreases
(B) the price of houses increases
(C) consumer incomes increase
(D) the cost of building materials decreases
(E) the wages paid to carpenters increases

41. If the supply curve for good Z is known to have shifted to the right, we might conclude that

(A) consumer tastes for good Z have diminished
(B) the technology used in producing good Z has improved
(C) there are fewer producers of good Z
(D) the price of good Z has fallen
(E) the cost of producing good Z has risen

42. Which of the following is considered a determinant of supply curves?

(A) Consumer income
(B) Tastes and preferences
(C) The number of consumers
(D) Consumer income expectations
(E) Number of suppliers

43. Suppose that many producers of furniture can produce both couches and recliners. All else equal, if recliners become a more trendy piece of furniture and the price of recliners begins to rise, what would we expect to happen to the supply of recliners and the supply of couches?

	Market for Recliners	**Market for Couches**
(A)	An increase in supply	An increase in supply
(B)	An increase in supply	A decrease in supply
(C)	An increase in quantity supplied	An increase in quantity supplied
(D)	An increase in quantity supplied	A decrease in supply
(E)	A decrease in quantity supplied	An increase in supply

44. Which of the following would likely decrease the current supply of cars?

(A) The price of gasoline has decreased.
(B) The cost of the robotics used to produce cars has decreased.
(C) Car producers expect future car prices to increase.
(D) The technology used to produce cars has improved.
(E) The price of new cars has increased.

45. Which of the following statements describes a leftward shift in the supply of good W?

(A) At any price the quantity supplied of good W has fallen.
(B) At any price the quantity demanded of good W has fallen.
(C) At any price the quantity supplied of good W has risen.
(D) At a higher price the quantity supplied of good W has fallen.
(E) At a higher price the quantity supplied of good W has risen.

Use Table 2.1 to answer questions 46 and 47.

Table 2.1

Price per Pound	Quantity Demanded (pounds)	Quantity Supplied (pounds)
$1	5,000	1,000
$2	4,500	1,300
$3	4,000	1,600
$4	3,500	1,900
$5	3,000	2,200
$6	2,500	2,500
$7	2,000	2,800
$8	1,500	3,100
$9	500	3,400

46. Table 2.1 shows the quantity of beef demanded and supplied at a variety of prices. If the market is in equilibrium, the price would be _____ per pound and _____ pounds would be exchanged.

(A) $4; 1,900
(B) $5; 800
(C) $6; 5,000
(D) $7; 2,000
(E) $6; 2,500

47. Table 2.1 shows the quantity of beef demanded and supplied at a variety of prices. Suppose the price of beef is currently $3 per pound. At this price, there exists a _____ equal to _____ pounds of beef. The price must _____.

(A) surplus; 800; rise
(B) shortage; 2,400; rise
(C) shortage; 5,600; rise
(D) surplus; 2,400; fall
(E) surplus; 1,600; fall

48. Suppose the market demand for a quirk is represented by the equation: $P = 50 - Q_d$, and the market supply of quirks is represented by the equation: $P = 10 + Q_s$. The market equilibrium price and equilibrium quantity are

	Price	Quantity
(A)	$20	20
(B)	$20	30
(C)	$30	30
(D)	$30	20
(E)	$25	25

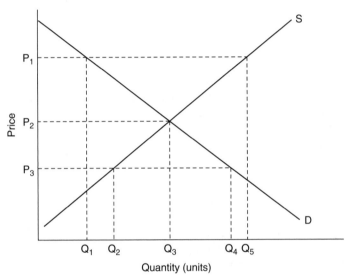

Figure 2.1

49. Figure 2.1 shows the market for a good. At market equilibrium, the price is _____ and the quantity is _____.

(A) P_2; Q_3
(B) P_1; Q_5
(C) P_3; Q_2
(D) P_3; Q_4
(E) P_1; Q_1

50. Figure 2.1 shows the market for a good. If the current price is P_1, there exists a _____ in the market equal to _____ units of the good. The price must eventually _____.

(A) surplus; $Q_5 - Q_3$; fall
(B) shortage; $Q_4 - Q_2$; rise
(C) surplus; $Q_5 - Q_1$; fall
(D) shortage; $Q_5 - Q_1$; rise
(E) surplus; $Q_4 - Q_2$; fall

51. Market equilibrium occurs when

(A) the quantity of the good supplied is greater than the quantity of the good demanded
(B) the quantity of the good supplied is less than the quantity of the good demanded
(C) the marginal cost of the last unit supplied is greater than the marginal benefit of the last unit demanded
(D) the marginal cost of the last unit supplied is less than the marginal benefit of the last unit demanded
(E) the quantity of the good supplied equals the quantity of the good demanded

52. If a market is in equilibrium,

(A) there is pressure on the price to fall
(B) there is no pressure on the price to rise or fall
(C) there is pressure on the price to rise
(D) quantity demanded is greater than quantity supplied
(E) quantity supplied is greater than quantity demanded

53. The market for cheese is currently in equilibrium. If the demand for cheese decreases, what will happen to the market price and quantity of cheese?

	Market Price	Market Quantity
(A)	Decreases	Decreases
(B)	Decreases	Increases
(C)	Increases	Remains constant
(D)	Increases	Increases
(E)	Increases	Decreases

54. The market for gasoline is currently in equilibrium. If the demand for gasoline increases, what will happen to the market price and quantity of gasoline?

	Market Price	Market Quantity
(A)	Decreases	Decreases
(B)	Decreases	Increases
(C)	Increases	Remains constant
(D)	Increases	Increases
(E)	Increases	Decreases

55. You are told that the market price of tea has increased and more tea is being purchased in the market. Of the following choices, which of the following would definitely cause these changes in the tea market?

(A) The supply of tea increased.
(B) The demand for tea increased.
(C) The demand for tea decreased.
(D) The supply of tea decreased.
(E) The demand for tea and the supply of tea both decreased.

56. You are told that the market price of lumber has decreased and less lumber is being sold in the market. Of the following choices, which is the most likely cause of these changes in the lumber market?

(A) The supply of lumber increased.
(B) The demand for lumber increased.
(C) The demand for lumber decreased.
(D) The supply of lumber decreased.
(E) The demand for lumber and the supply of lumber both increased.

57. You are told that the market price of butter has decreased and more butter is being sold in the market. Of the following choices, which is the cause of these changes in the butter market?

(A) The supply of butter increased.
(B) The demand for butter increased.
(C) The demand for butter decreased.
(D) The supply of butter decreased.
(E) The demand for butter and the supply of butter both decreased.

58. You are told that the market price of carpet has increased and less carpet is being sold in the market. Of the following choices, which is the most likely cause of these changes in the carpet market?

(A) The supply of carpet increased.
(B) The demand for carpet increased.
(C) The demand for carpet decreased.
(D) The supply of carpet decreased.
(E) The demand for carpet and the supply of carpet both increased.

59. The market for wine is currently in equilibrium. If the supply of wine increases, what will happen to the market price and quantity of wine?

	Market Price	**Market Quantity**
(A)	Decreases	Decreases
(B)	Decreases	Increases
(C)	Remains constant	Remains constant
(D)	Increases	Decreases
(E)	Increases	Increases

60. If the market supply of houses increases, we expect

(A) fewer houses sold at lower prices
(B) more houses sold and no change in the price
(C) fewer houses sold at higher prices
(D) no change in quantity of houses sold at lower prices
(E) more houses sold at lower prices

61. The market for rental housing is currently in equilibrium. If the demand for rental housing decreases and the supply of rental housing increases, what will happen to the market price and quantity of rental housing?

	Market Price	**Market Quantity**
(A)	Uncertain change	Decreases
(B)	Decreases	Uncertain change
(C)	Increases	Uncertain change
(D)	Uncertain change	Increases
(E)	Decreases	Decreases

62. The market for sugar is currently in equilibrium. If the demand for sugar increases and the supply of sugar decreases, what will happen to the market price and quantity of sugar?

	Market Price	Market Quantity
(A)	Uncertain change	Decreases
(B)	Decreases	Uncertain change
(C)	Increases	Uncertain change
(D)	Uncertain change	Increases
(E)	Increases	Increases

63. You are informed that the demand for a good has increased and the supply of that good has also increased. You know that the market quantity must have _____, while the market price could have _____ if the change in demand was _____ than the change in supply.

(A) increased; increased; greater
(B) increased; increased; less
(C) increased; decreased; greater
(D) decreased; increased; less
(E) decreased; decreased; greater

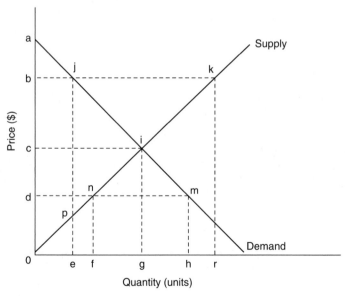

Figure 2.2

64. Which of the following choices would represent the height of an effective price floor in the market shown in Figure 2.2, on the previous page?

(A) 0d

(B) 0e

(C) 0c

(D) 0b

(E) 0r

65. Which of the following choices would be an effective price ceiling in the market shown in Figure 2.2?

(A) 0e

(B) 0b

(C) 0c

(D) 0r

(E) 0d

66. Suppose that an effective price ceiling has been imposed on the market portrayed in Figure 2.2. This price ceiling will create a _____ equal to _____.

(A) surplus; $(r - e)$ units

(B) shortage; $(r - g)$ units

(C) shortage; $(h - f)$ units

(D) surplus; $(h - f)$ units

(E) shortage; zero units

67. Suppose that an effective price floor has been imposed on the market portrayed in Figure 2.2. This price floor will create a _____ equal to _____ units.

(A) shortage; $(r - e)$ units

(B) surplus; $(r - e)$ units

(C) shortage; $(h - f)$ units

(D) surplus; $(h - f)$ units

(E) surplus; $(m - n)$ units

68. Refer to the market portrayed in Figure 2.2. Suppose that the equilibrium level of output in this market is believed to be too large. If a quota is imposed at e units of output, the quota rent for producers will be equal to

(A) $\$(j - p)$

(B) $\$j$

(C) $\$p$

(D) $\$(j - c)$

(E) $\$c$

69. When government imposes a restriction on the quantity that can be produced in a market because the market equilibrium quantity is deemed to be too many units, the policy is labeled a(n)

(A) regressive tax
(B) price ceiling
(C) quota
(D) excise tax
(E) price floor

70. A production quota in a market will usually create

(A) a surplus of the good
(B) an increase in total welfare
(C) a more efficient outcome than market equilibrium
(D) deadweight loss in the market
(E) lower prices to the consumer

71. All else equal, the _____ a price floor is set _____ the equilibrium price, the _____ deadweight loss created by the policy.

(A) further; below; less
(B) further; above; more
(C) further; below; more
(D) closer; above; more
(E) closer; below; more

72. A competitive market produces the equilibrium quantity that maximizes total surplus because for the last unit exchanged, the _____ is equal to the _____.

(A) total utility consumers receive; total profit producers earn
(B) total revenue producers earn; total cost producers incur
(C) marginal utility consumers receive; price consumers pay
(D) consumer surplus; producer surplus
(E) price consumers are willing to pay; marginal cost producers incur

73. Which of the following statements are correct?
  I. Price controls create deadweight loss because for the last unit exchanged, willingness to pay exceeds marginal cost.
  II. A competitive market produces an equilibrium price that inefficiently allocates resources to the market.
  III. Price and quantity controls both create deadweight loss in markets.
  (A) I only
  (B) II only
  (C) III only
  (D) I and II only
  (E) I and III only

CHAPTER 3

General Macroeconomic Issues

74. The _____ is the short-run alternation between economic downturns and economic upturns.

(A) aggregate demand curve
(B) economic growth rate
(C) business cycle
(D) product life cycle
(E) circular flow model

75. Since the Great Depression, most economists believe that economic policy can smooth out the volatile fluctuations of

(A) the business cycle
(B) the national debt
(C) tax rates
(D) government spending
(E) international trade

76. As the business cycle is rising, the economy is experiencing

(A) a depression
(B) the peak
(C) an expansion
(D) a recession
(E) the trough

77. When the business cycle is in the _____ stage, the unemployment rate is _____.

(A) contraction; falling
(B) expansion; falling
(C) trough; at its lowest
(D) peak; at its highest
(E) expansion; equal to zero

78. When the business cycle is in the _____ stage, the unemployment rate is _____.
- (A) contraction; falling
- (B) expansion; rising
- (C) trough; at its lowest
- (D) trough; at its highest
- (E) trough; equal to zero

79. Typically the rate of inflation begins to increase at what stage of the business cycle?
- (A) Depression
- (B) Contraction
- (C) Trough
- (D) Expansion
- (E) Peak

80. Usually when the business cycle is in the _____ stage, the inflation rate is _____.
- (A) contraction; falling
- (B) expansion; falling
- (C) peak; at its lowest
- (D) trough; at its highest
- (E) peak; negative

81. A nation's measure of national output is typically weakest during which stage of the business cycle?
- (A) The peak stage
- (B) The trough stage
- (C) The expansion stage
- (D) The growth stage
- (E) The inflationary stage

82. Suppose the economy is experiencing a very strong expansionary stage of the business cycle. Which of the following is likely true?
- (A) National income is falling.
- (B) The employment rate is falling.
- (C) Gross domestic product is rising.
- (D) The unemployment rate is rising.
- (E) The inflation rate is falling.

83. Economic growth is
    (A) the long-run increase in national output
    (B) the same as an expansion in the business cycle
    (C) achieved only when the unemployment rate reaches zero
    (D) experienced at the peak of the business cycle
    (E) the natural result of the end of a recession

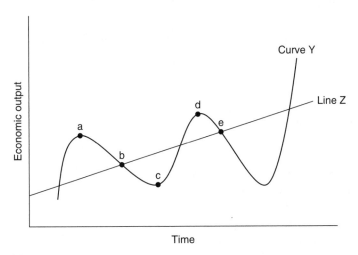

Figure 3.1

84. Which of the following movements in Figure 3.1 represents economic growth over time?
    (A) Point b to point c
    (B) Point a to point b
    (C) Point c to point d
    (D) Point c to point a
    (E) Point b to point e

85. In Figure 3.1, we can see economic growth as
    (A) the ups and downs of economic output represented by Curve Y
    (B) the long-term upward trend in economic output represented by Line Z
    (C) the movement from point c to point d on Curve Y
    (D) point d on Curve Y
    (E) the movement from point a to point c on Curve Y

86. Refer to Figure 3.1. Which range of points would define the length of a recession?

(A) Point b to point c
(B) Point a to point c
(C) Point c to point d
(D) Point c to point a
(E) Point b to point e

87. Refer to Figure 3.1. Which range of points would define the length of a complete business cycle?

(A) Point b to point c
(B) Point a to point c
(C) Point c to point d
(D) Point a to point d
(E) Point b to point e

88. Refer to Figure 3.1. An economic expansion is seen as _____, and economic growth is seen as _____.

(A) point a to point d; point b to point e
(B) point b to point c; point a to point d
(C) point c to point d; point b to point e
(D) point c to point d; point a to point d
(E) point a to point d; point a to point d

89. Which of the following statements is accurate about economic growth and expansion?
    I. Economic growth is a long-term upward trend in a nation's ability to produce goods and services.
    II. Economic expansion is a short-term increase in economic output as an economy recovers from a recession.
    III. An economy's business cycle rises and falls around the long-term economic path of growth.

(A) I only
(B) II only
(C) III only
(D) I and III only
(E) I, II, and III

CHAPTER 4

National Income Accounts

90. Which model is used to show the flows of money, factors of production, and goods and services in the economy?

    (A) The Phillips curve model
    (B) The model of production possibilities
    (C) The circular-flow model
    (D) The aggregate demand and aggregate supply model
    (E) The rational expectations model

91. A household spends money on _____ and in exchange sells _____ to firms.

    (A) revenue; services
    (B) goods and services; factors of production
    (C) imports and exports; taxes and transfers
    (D) bonds; stocks
    (E) goods and services; revenue

92. In a closed economy with no government sector, all money paid by firms to households in the _____ is returned to firms as consumption spending in the _____.

    (A) foreign sector; domestic sector
    (B) product markets; factor markets
    (C) stock market; bond market
    (D) factor markets; product markets
    (E) export market; import market

93. In the circular-flow diagram for the nation of Portlandyburg, which of the following would be considered a monetary leakage?
    (A) Household saving in the Portlandyburg financial sector
    (B) Firms hiring citizens of Portlandyburg in the labor markets
    (C) Household spending on imported goods
    (D) Households paying taxes to the government of Portlandyburg
    (E) Government selling bonds to firms and households of Portlandyburg

94. In the circular-flow diagram of a private closed economy, private savings ends up as
    (A) wages paid to labor
    (B) export spending
    (C) revenue earnings for firms
    (D) government borrowing
    (E) investment spending by firms

95. The sum of all wages, interest, rent, and profit is called
    (A) national income
    (B) the budget balance
    (C) net exports
    (D) government spending
    (E) national savings

96. When computing the value of a nation's domestic output of goods and services, we can add up all of the income earned by the factors of production in the economy. In this way we are calculating national output with the
    (A) expenditure approach
    (B) value-added approach
    (C) income approach
    (D) public sector approach
    (E) national savings approach

97. Which of the following would be included in the income approach to calculation of national income?
    (A) Government lending to a foreign country
    (B) Wages
    (C) Import spending
    (D) Savings
    (E) Government borrowing

98. In the circular-flow diagram, wages and salaries represent

  (A) factor income earned by capital
  (B) interest earned from lending money to firms
  (C) rental income earned from the leasing of land to the government
  (D) factor income earned by labor in labor markets
  (E) factor income earned by firms when hiring labor

99. In an economy with a public sector, household disposable income is equal to

  (A) gross labor income
  (B) interest plus rent plus profit
  (C) transfer payments from the government minus taxes paid
  (D) consumption spending
  (E) gross labor income plus transfer payments from the government minus taxes paid

100. When computing the value of a nation's domestic output of goods and services, we can add up all of the spending done by all sectors in the economy. In this way we are calculating national output with the

  (A) expenditure approach
  (B) value-added approach
  (C) income approach
  (D) public sector approach
  (E) national savings approach

101. A nation's gross domestic product (GDP) can be determined with which simple formula?

  (A) $GDP = C + I + G$
  (B) $GDP = C + I + G + X$
  (C) $GDP = C + I + G + (X - M)$
  (D) $GDP = C - I + G + (M - X)$
  (E) $GDP = S + I$

102. In a specified period of time, a nation's gross domestic product (GDP) is the

(A) total value of government spending, minus taxes collected
(B) total value of all final goods and services produced within the nation's borders
(C) total value of all intermediate goods and services produced within the nation's borders
(D) total disposable income earned by households in the nation
(E) total value of all final goods and services produced by a nation's citizens, regardless their geographic location

103. Suppose we know that gross domestic product (GDP) is $10,000 and that consumption spending is $7,000, investment spending is $1,500, and government spending is $2,500. We can determine that

(A) net exports are equal to −$100
(B) export spending is $1,000 and import spending is $0
(C) export spending is $1,000 and import spending is $1,000
(D) net exports are equal to −$1,000
(E) net exports are equal to $1,000

Use Table 4.1 for question 104.

Table 4.1 GDP in 2011

Consumption spending	$50
Wages and salaries	$30
Government spending	$12
Exports	$8
Investment spending	$14
Imports	$2
Interest	$12
Rents	$8
Profits	$32

104. Using the data in Table 4.1, what is GDP in 2011?

(A) $162
(B) $100
(C) $164
(D) $84
(E) $82

105. Which of the following would be an intermediate good?

    (A) A visit to the doctor before a tropical vacation

    (B) Your vacation to the island of Yap

    (C) A new skateboard your brother bought

    (D) Gasoline purchased for your car

    (E) Coal used in generating electricity

106. A wealthy owner of the local soccer team pays a construction company to build a new stadium for the team. The stadium would count in GDP as

    (A) investment spending

    (B) government spending

    (C) consumption spending

    (D) export spending

    (E) import spending

107. Which of the following would be classified as consumption spending (C)?

    (A) The state of Oklahoma buys some police cars.

    (B) Ellie enrolls in some classes at the University of Oklahoma.

    (C) A firm in Canada buys some cattle raised in Oklahoma.

    (D) A cattle rancher in Oklahoma builds a new barn.

    (E) The US Air Force builds a new base in Oklahoma.

108. Cans of chili are produced in December 2011 but not sold to a grocery store until January 2012. These unsold cans of chili count

    (A) in 2011 gross domestic product (GDP) as inventories and are part of consumption spending

    (B) in 2011 GDP as consumption spending

    (C) in 2011 GDP as inventories and are part of investment spending

    (D) in 2012 GDP as inventories and are part of investment spending

    (E) in 2011 GDP as intermediate goods and in 2012 GDP as final goods

109. A laptop computer purchased by you is _____, and the same laptop computer purchased by the US Department of Agriculture is _____.

    (A) import spending; export spending

    (B) consumption spending; investment spending

    (C) consumption spending; consumption spending

    (D) consumption spending; government spending

    (E) export spending; import spending

110. An American furniture company sells cedar tables to a store in Canada. In Canada this transaction will be recorded as _____, and in the United States this will be recorded as _____.

    (A) import spending; export spending
    (B) import spending; consumption spending
    (C) consumption spending; export spending
    (D) consumption spending; consumption spending
    (E) export spending; import spending

111. In tabulating gross domestic product (GDP), which component of spending is subtracted from the total?

    (A) Exports
    (B) Imports
    (C) Consumption
    (D) Investment
    (E) Government

112. A consumer in the United States buys a truck built in South Korea. Is the production of this truck added or subtracted in the gross domestic product (GDP) of the United States and of South Korea? In what categories of GDP is this transaction included?

	From the United States	Added or Subtracted	From South Korea	Added or Subtracted
(A)	Imports	Subtracted	Investment	Added
(B)	Imports	Subtracted	Imports	Added
(C)	Investment	Added	Exports	Added
(D)	Consumption	Added	Consumption	Added
(E)	Imports	Subtracted	Exports	Added

113. To adjust nominal gross domestic product (GDP) to real GDP, we must adjust for changes in

    (A) interest rates
    (B) the population
    (C) prices
    (D) the balance of trade
    (E) government spending

114. Suppose that nominal gross domestic product (GDP) increased from $2,000 to $2,100 from year 1 to year 2. Which of the following scenarios would explain why real GDP neither increased nor decreased between year 1 and year 2?

    (A) The aggregate price level decreased by 5%.
    (B) The aggregate price level increased by 1%.
    (C) The aggregate price level decreased by 2.5%.
    (D) The aggregate price level increased by 5%.
    (E) The aggregate price level remained constant.

Use Table 4.2 for questions 115–117.

Table 4.2   GDP in a Peaches and Herbs Economy

Year	Price of Peaches	Quantity of Peaches Produced	Price of Herbs	Quantity of Herbs Produced
2006 (base year)	$1	10	$0.50	20
2007	$2	10	$0.50	24
2008	$3	5	$1	30
2009	$3	15	$2	40

115. Table 4.2 shows the prices and outputs of an economy that produces only two goods, peaches and herbs. What is nominal gross domestic product (GDP) in 2007?

    (A) $32
    (B) $20
    (C) $24
    (D) $75
    (E) $44

116. Table 4.2 shows the prices and outputs of an economy that produces only two goods, peaches and herbs. What is real gross domestic product (GDP) in 2007, using 2006 as a reference year?

    (A) $32
    (B) $22
    (C) $24
    (D) $20
    (E) $44

117. Table 4.2 shows the prices and outputs of an economy that produces only two goods, peaches and herbs. Between 2006 and 2008, real gross domestic product (GDP) increased by

    (A) 5%
    (B) 45%
    (C) 0%
    (D) 125%
    (E) 25%

118. Nominal gross domestic product (GDP) is

    (A) current year output measured in current year prices
    (B) current year output measured in base year prices
    (C) base year output measured in current year prices
    (D) base year output measured in base year prices
    (E) current year output measured in future year prices

119. During a typical business cycle, the rate of real gross domestic product (GDP) growth is negative

    (A) at the peak
    (B) during an expansion
    (C) during an economic boom
    (D) at full employment
    (E) during a contraction

120. Suppose that in year 1 real gross domestic product (GDP) was growing by 2% per year. In year 2, real GDP was growing by 3% per year. And in year 3, real GDP was growing by 4% per year. Knowing this, what can we say about the business cycle from year 1 to year 3?

    (A) The economy was in a recession from year 1 to year 3.
    (B) The economy was at a peak in year 1, and in recession from year 2 to year 3.
    (C) The economy was in an expansion from year 1 to year 3.
    (D) The economy was in a recession from year 1 to year 2, and at a trough in year 3.
    (E) The economy was at a peak in year 1, and in a depression from year 2 to year 3.

121. Which of the following statements is true?
   I. Steve mows his lawn twice a month, and the value of this service is included in GDP.
   II. Becky irons her own clothes, and the value of this service is included in GDP.
   III. Ayda is 12 years old and works as a babysitter for her neighbor and gets paid in cash. This service is not included in GDP.
   (A) I only
   (B) II only
   (C) III only
   (D) I and II only
   (E) I, II and III

122. Which of the following acts are included in official gross domestic product (GDP) calculations?
   (A) Dan is a volunteer coach for his daughter's soccer team.
   (B) Sue is a mother of two who has decided to withdraw from the labor force to care for the children until they are teenagers.
   (C) Linda sees that her gutters are clogged with leaves and spends her Saturday cleaning out the gutters.
   (D) Kathy is paid to be the assistant soccer coach at the local high school.
   (E) Eric spends his Tuesday afternoons volunteering to read books to the children at the public library.

123. In 2008 Jackie bought a 1968 Ford Mustang for $40,000. When it was new, the Mustang sold for $5,000. How much did the Ford Mustang contribute to GDP in 2008?
   (A) $35,000
   (B) $0
   (C) $5,000
   (D) $45,000
   (E) $40,000

124. Suppose that a lawyer pays for a cell phone at $30 per hour and pays $10 per hour for office space. The lawyer charges $150 per hour for her legal advice. If the lawyer provides 4 hours of legal advice, how much gross domestic product (GDP) has been created?
   (A) $600
   (B) $480
   (C) $400
   (D) $760
   (E) $160

125. Which of the following transactions would be included in the nation's gross domestic product (GDP)?

(A) Dave sells his used economics textbook to his girlfriend.

(B) Becky rakes her grandfather's leaves in exchange for a cold glass of iced tea.

(C) Melanie decides to save $500 in the bank for an emergency fund.

(D) Pam goes to the public library to read romance novels.

(E) Stan buys a new romance novel at the local bookstore.

126. Gross domestic product (GDP) in 2011 would include which of the following transactions?

(A) The purchase of a 1993 Chevrolet pickup truck

(B) The purchase of 1,939 shares of General Motors stock

(C) The purchase of a movie ticket to a screening of the classic 1939 movie *Gone with the Wind*

(D) Margaret receiving a Social Security check of $1,939 from the US government

(E) Eli selling Max his old golf clubs for $193

127. Within the circular-flow diagram, transfer payments are

(A) counted in gross domestic product (GDP)

(B) a redistribution of money from one person to another person in the economy

(C) another form of taxation

(D) a way of reducing consumer spending

(E) a leakage from the economy

128. The conventional way of calculating gross domestic product (GDP) tends to underestimate the total economic well-being because it

(A) includes the value of do-it-yourself projects

(B) values $100 of bullets more than it values $100 of diapers

(C) includes the value of a parent who drops out of the labor force to care for children

(D) excludes the value of leisure time and volunteerism

(E) includes the value of healthcare costs due to excessive tobacco use

129. During 2010 the country of Ericksburg had government spending of $3 billion, consumption spending of $9 billion, investment spending of $3.5 billion, and net exports of −$1 billion. Gross domestic product (GDP) in 2010 is equal to

(A) $14.5 billion
(B) $15.5 billion
(C) $16.5 billion
(D) $9 billion
(E) $12.5 billion

CHAPTER 5

Inflation

130. In the United States, inflation is most often measured by changes in the

   (A) gross domestic product (GDP) deflator
   (B) produce price index (PPI)
   (C) consumer price index (CPI)
   (D) real interest rate
   (E) exchange rate between the dollar and other currencies

131. The purpose of the consumer price index is to capture changes in

   (A) the cost of all goods produced in an economy
   (B) the average of the prices of goods a typical urban consumer purchases
   (C) the cost of goods consumers spend the greatest portion of their income on
   (D) the cost of the inputs used to produce consumer goods
   (E) the total change in consumer incomes

132. When wages are adjusted for the effects of inflation, we can determine

   (A) nominal wages
   (B) real wages
   (C) real interest rates
   (D) the natural rate of unemployment
   (E) the exchange rate between the dollar and other currencies

133. The rate of inflation is the

   (A) percentage change in an aggregate price index
   (B) the growth in the money supply
   (C) the percentage change in housing prices
   (D) the percentage change in economic output
   (E) value of the consumer price index (CPI)

134. Which of the following is true of the consumer price index (CPI)?

   (A) It is calculated using the same prices for the different goods that consumers buy each year.

   (B) It is calculated using different prices for a different bundle of goods that consumers buy each year.

   (C) It is calculated using prices from the 3-year period 1982–1984, using different goods for each year.

   (D) It contains the same bundle of goods every year, a bundle that is adjusted periodically, but adjusts prices for the goods in the bundle each time it is calculated.

   (E) It is calculated using a bundle of goods based on consumption patterns from 1982–1984 using different prices for each year.

135. Which of the following goods are not included in the consumer price index (CPI)?

   (A) Goods that consumers rarely purchase such as funeral services

   (B) Goods that consumers purchase only sporadically, such as prescription drugs for illnesses

   (C) Investment by households such as stocks and bonds

   (D) Services such as college tuition

   (E) Sales taxes on consumer goods

136. Which of the following is the formula for calculating the rate of inflation between two years, year 1 and year 2?

   (A) $100 \times (CPI_{base\ year} - CPI_{year\ 1} - CPI_{year\ 2})$

   (B) $100 \times (CPI_{year\ 1} - CPI_{year\ 2})/CPI_{base\ year}$

   (C) $100 \times (CPI_{year\ 2} - CPI_{year\ 1})$

   (D) $100 \times (CPI_{year\ 2} - CPI_{year\ 1})/CPI_{year\ 1}$

   (E) $100 \times (CPI_{year\ 2} - CPI_{year\ 1}) \times CPI_{year\ 1}$

Use Table 5.1 for questions 137–139.

Table 5.1

Year	Price Index
2005	95
2006	99
2007	100
2008	104
2009	110

137. Table 5.1 shows a hypothetical price index for 5 years. Which year is the base year?

(A) 2005
(B) 2006
(C) 2007
(D) 2008
(E) 2009

138. Table 5.1 shows a hypothetical price index for 5 years. Between 2008 and 2009 the rate of inflation was

(A) 5.5%
(B) 4%
(C) 1.1%
(D) 5.8%
(E) 10%

139. Table 5.1 shows a hypothetical price index for 5 years. If nominal wages increased by 4% between 2007 and 2008, we can determine that

(A) real wages fell 1%
(B) real wages rose by 1%
(C) real wages fell by 4%
(D) real wages rose by 4%
(E) real wages remained constant

140. The consumer price index (CPI) measures

(A) the cost of intermediate products used to make final goods and services
(B) the cost of the market basket of a typical urban family
(C) the cost of producing capital equipment used by a typical manufacturer
(D) the cost of housing for a typical urban family
(E) the cost of grocery items typically purchased by a urban family

141. If you hear that the 2011 consumer price index (CPI) is currently 210, you can determine that the same market basket costs

(A) 10% more than it did in 2010
(B) 10% more than it did in the base year
(C) 210% more than it did in the base year
(D) 210% more than it did in 2010
(E) 110% more than it did in the base year

142. What is the interpretation of a consumer price index (CPI) of 122 in year X?

    (A) A bundle of goods in year X costs $22 more than in the base year.

    (B) A bundle of goods in year X costs $122 more than in the previous year.

    (C) A bundle of goods in year X costs 122% more than in the base year.

    (D) A bundle of goods in year X costs 22% more than the previous year.

    (E) A bundle of goods in year X costs 22% more than in the base year.

Use Table 5.2 to answer questions 143–146.

Table 5.2   Annual Price of Goods in a Consumer's Basket

Year	Grubs	Snars	Jems	Pols
2000	$2	$1.50	$2.10	$1.00
2001	$3	$2.50	$2.10	$1.75
2002	$4	$4.90	$2.12	$2.00

143. Refer to the data presented in Table 5.2. The bundle of goods that is purchased by a typical consumer in any given year is 5 Grubs, 10 Snars, 3 Jems, and 2 Pols. What is the cost of a bundle of goods in 2001?

    (A) $9.35

    (B) $7.64

    (C) $49.80

    (D) $79.36

    (E) $16.50

144. Refer to the data presented in Table 5.2. The bundle of goods that is purchased by a typical consumer in any given year is 5 Grubs, 10 Snars, 3 Jems, and 2 Pols. If 2000 is the base year, what is the consumer price index (CPI) in 2001?

    (A) 33.30

    (B) 49.80

    (C) 16.50

    (D) 66.87

    (E) 149.55

145. Refer to the data presented in Table 5.2. The bundle of goods that is purchased by a typical consumer in any given year is 5 Grubs, 10 Snars, 3 Jems, and 2 Pols, and 2000 is the reference year. What is the rate of inflation between 2001 and 2002?

(A) 59.36%
(B) 23.77%
(C) 49.80%
(D) 138.32%
(E) 88.77%

146. Refer to the data presented in Table 5.2. The bundle of goods that is purchased by a typical consumer in any given year is 5 Grubs, 10 Snars, 3 Jems, and 2 Pols, and 2000 is the reference year. What is the rate of inflation between 2000 and 2001?

(A) 16.5%
(B) 49.55%
(C) 149.55%
(D) −16.5%
(E) −49.55%

147. In 2007 the consumer price index (CPI) of Maxistan was 345, in 2008 the CPI of Maxistan was 370, and in 2009 the CPI of Maxistan was 400. What was the total amount of inflation in Maxistan between 2007 and 2009?

(A) The inflation rate of Maxistan cannot be determined using the information given.
(B) −315%
(C) 55%
(D) −13.75%
(E) 15.94%

148. In 2006 the consumer price index (CPI) of Maxistan was 290, and in 2007 the CPI of Maxistan was 320. If nominal gross domestic product (GDP) grew by 6%, which of the following statements is true?
  I. Real GDP declined between 2006 and 2007.
  II. Households whose incomes rose by 6% maintained the same standard of living.
  III. Households earning 6% in nominal interest in their savings accounts had a decline in the value of their savings.

  (A) I only
  (B) II only
  (C) III only
  (D) I and III only
  (E) II and III only

149. Consumers in the nation of Xela paid $500 for a bundle of goods in 2001, the reference year for Xela's consumer price index (CPI). For the same bundle of goods, they paid $700 in 2008, $750 in 2009, and $810 in 2010. What was the CPI in 2009?

  (A) 300
  (B) 150
  (C) 116
  (D) 110
  (E) 108

150. In Erinia the cost of a basket of goods was $500 in 1979, $600 in 1980, $700 in 1981, $800 in 1982, and $900 in 1983. If the consumer price index (CPI) in 1983 is 150, what year is the base year?

  (A) 1979
  (B) 1980
  (C) 1981
  (D) 1982
  (E) 1983

151. Whenever there is inflation, firms must frequently change the prices they offer. This cost of inflation is known as

  (A) menu costs
  (B) shoe leather costs
  (C) distraction costs
  (D) production costs
  (E) misperception costs

152. When Bill goes to fill up his car with gasoline, he notices that the price of gas at his corner store has increased by $0.50 per gallon. He drives to four different stations before he realizes that the price of gas has gone up at all gas stations, not just his corner store. This is an illustration of the idea of

(A) menu costs
(B) shoe leather costs
(C) distraction costs
(D) production costs
(E) misperception costs

153. Which of the following parties is most likely to benefit from unexpected inflation?

(A) A person who owes money at a variable rate of interest
(B) A person who lends money at a variable rate of interest
(C) A person who owes money at a fixed rate of interest
(D) A person who lends money at a fixed rate of interest
(E) It is not possible for anyone to benefit from inflation.

154. Deflation is

(A) a decline in the overall price level
(B) a decrease in the rate of inflation
(C) an increase in the overall price level
(D) an increase in the rate of inflation
(E) a rapid decline in the rate of inflation

155. From 2000 to 2005 the annual rate of inflation in Ile averaged 6%. However, in 2006 the annual rate of inflation in Ile was 3%. Which of the following statements is true?

  I. Ile experienced deflation in 2006.
  II. Ile experienced disinflation in 2006.
  III. Ile experienced inflation in 2006.

(A) I only
(B) II only
(C) III only
(D) I and II only
(E) II and III only

156. Which of the following is considered a cost of inflation?
    I. Menu costs
    II. Shoe leather costs
    III. Money printing costs

    (A) I only
    (B) II only
    (C) III only
    (D) I and II only
    (E) II and III only

157. Barb receives a retirement pension that is indexed annually for inflation. This means that
    (A) her pension payments are adjusted for inflation to maintain her purchasing power
    (B) her pension payments are adjusted for inflation to increase her purchasing power
    (C) her pension payments are unadjusted for inflation
    (D) her pension payments are adjusted for inflation to decrease her real income
    (E) her pension payments are adjusted for inflation to increase her real income

158. In 2009 Janet earned a salary of $40,000 per year and the consumer price index (CPI) was 210. In 2010 Janet earned a salary of $42,000 and the CPI was 225. Which of the following statements is true?
    (A) Janet has experienced a decrease in real earnings of about 2.14%.
    (B) Janet has experienced an increase in real earnings of about 5%.
    (C) Janet has experienced a decrease in real earnings of about 5%.
    (D) Janet has experienced an increase in real earnings of about 2.14%.
    (E) Janet's real earnings are essentially the same in both years.

159. Which of the following do economists generally consider the least desirable?
    (A) Modest inflation
    (B) Modest disinflation
    (C) Significant disinflation
    (D) Significant inflation
    (E) Significant deflation

160. Andrew has a student loan that he pays a fixed 5% annual interest on. If all prices in the economy decline by 10%, Andrew is

(A) better off, since he can now purchase 5% more goods and services
(B) better off, since he can now purchase 10% more goods and services
(C) worse off, since he now effectively pays 10% interest
(D) worse off, since he now effectively pays 15% interest
(E) unaffected, since he is not a lender of money

161. Which of the following will change significantly if the base year is changed?

I. The values of the CPI in each year
II. The values of the cost of the basket of goods in each year
III. The rate of inflation in each year

(A) I only
(B) II only
(C) III only
(D) I and III only
(E) I and II only

162. EliCo created a new gadget in 2002 that most consumers were purchasing by 2004. However, it was not included in the consumer price index (CPI) until 2009. This creates a problem known as

(A) unexpected inflation
(B) expected inflation
(C) quality bias
(D) substitution bias
(E) introduction of new goods bias

163. The consumer price index (CPI) in Kayleestan assumes that households buy 10 pounds of chicken per week and 10 pounds of beef per week. If the price of chicken suddenly doubles and households shift their purchases to buy more beef, this leads to a problem in calculating the CPI known as

(A) unexpected inflation
(B) expected inflation
(C) quality bias
(D) substitution bias
(E) introduction of new goods bias

164. Which of the following are important when considering whether inflation is problematic or not?
  I. The current level of prices
  II. Whether or not the rate of inflation is very high
  III. Whether or not inflation is expected
  (A) I only
  (B) II only
  (C) III only
  (D) II and III only
  (E) I, II, and III

165. Which of the following statements is true?
  (A) Unexpected inflation can lead to distortions in economic activity.
  (B) Deflation is a desirable alternative to inflation.
  (C) Deflation is a desirable alternative to disinflation.
  (D) Lenders who loan at fixed rates benefit when there is inflation.
  (E) Volatility in inflation rates encourages lenders to loan more money.

166. Sarah anticipates that the consumer price index (CPI) will increase by 5% in 2009. She believes that her performance at her job in 2008 warrants a 2% increase in salary in 2009. In 2008 she made $30,000 per year. What is the minimum she should accept in 2009 to get a 2% increase in her real salary?
  (A) $30,000
  (B) $32,100
  (C) $30,600
  (D) $31,500
  (E) $32,130

167. First Bank of Thereading loaned out money at 6% annual interest last year believing that inflation would be 2%. However, the actual rate of inflation was 3.5%. Which of the following did First Bank of Thereading experience?
  (A) Unexpected inflation
  (B) Expected inflation
  (C) Quality bias
  (D) Substitution bias
  (E) Introduction of new goods bias

168. The term *hyperinflation* refers to a period when
    I. the rate of inflation is very high
   II. the rate of disinflation is very high
  III. the rate of deflation is very high

(A) I only
(B) II only
(C) III only
(D) I and II only
(E) I, II, and III

CHAPTER **6**

Unemployment

169. The labor force is best defined as

    (A) the total number of employed persons
    (B) the total number of unemployed persons
    (C) the ratio of employed persons to unemployed persons
    (D) the ratio of unemployed persons to employed persons
    (E) the total number of employed persons plus the total number of unemployed persons

170. Eric is 12 years old and is paid to sweep the floor at his dad's shop 10 hours each week. According to the official employment statistics, Eric is

    (A) not counted in the labor force
    (B) counted as employed part-time
    (C) counted as unemployed
    (D) counted as underemployed
    (E) counted as employed full-time

171. To be counted as unemployed, one must be

    (A) working at least 1 hour per week
    (B) out of work and actively seeking work
    (C) working more than 40 hours per week
    (D) out of work
    (E) working for one job, but actively seeking a better job

172. Sven works at the Burger Village for 10 hours each week but is looking for a better job at the Taco Plaza where he hopes he can work 40 hours each week. Officially, Sven is considered

(A) unemployed
(B) out of the labor force
(C) employed
(D) a discouraged worker
(E) marginally attached to the labor force

173. The sum of the employed persons and the unemployed persons is referred to as

(A) the employment rate
(B) the unemployment rate
(C) the labor force participation rate
(D) the labor force
(E) those out of the labor force

174. A nation has a working-age population of 100 million, with 80 million working and 5 million unemployed and seeking work. The labor force participation rate is

(A) 85%
(B) 80%
(C) 75%
(D) 5%
(E) 100%

175. A nation has a working-age population of 100 million, with 85 million working and 10 million unemployed but not seeking work. The labor force participation rate is

(A) 85%
(B) 90%
(C) 10%
(D) 95%
(E) 11.1%

176. Frank is a recent college graduate but is currently not working. In the last week he has had several phone interviews and continues to distribute his résumé to potential employers. Officially Frank is counted as

(A) out of the labor force
(B) a discouraged worker
(C) employed part time
(D) underemployed
(E) unemployed

177. The labor force participation rate is computed as

(A) (employed)/(working-age population)
(B) (unemployed)/(working-age population)
(C) (unemployed)/(employed + unemployed)
(D) (employed + unemployed)/(working-age population)
(E) (working-age population)/(employed + unemployed)

178. A nation has a working-age population of 200 million, with 14 million not working and not looking for work and 170 million employed. The labor force participation rate is

(A) 7%
(B) 93%
(C) 85%
(D) 92%
(E) 8%

179. You are told that the unemployment rate is 8%. This means that

(A) 92% of the working-age population is employed
(B) 8% of the working-age population is unemployed and seeking work
(C) 8% of the labor force is unemployed and seeking work
(D) 92% of the population is employed
(E) 8% of the population is unemployed and seeking work

180. Jermaine is 50 years old and works third shift at the steel mill in Gary, Indiana. Every year in March the mill, for routine maintenance, does not employ a third shift. The following week the mill resumes employment of Jermaine's shift. During the week when Jermaine is not working, he is not seeking another job, because he knows he will resume work in a few days. Jermaine is considered

   (A) employed
   (B) unemployed
   (C) out of the labor force
   (D) retired
   (E) a discouraged worker

181. A nation has a working-age population of 200 million, with 14 million not working and not looking for work and 170 million employed. The unemployment rate is

   (A) 7%
   (B) 93%
   (C) 85%
   (D) 92%
   (E) 8.6%

182. A nation has a working-age population of 95 million, with 81 million working and 5 million not working and not looking for work. The unemployment rate is

   (A) 10%
   (B) 88%
   (C) 14.7%
   (D) 93%
   (E) 5.2%

Use Table 6.1 to answer questions 183–185.

Table 6.1   The 2011 Population and Employment Status of Costa Erica

Total population	300 million
Population 15 years old and younger	50 million
Total working age population	250 million
Working at least 1 hour per week	200 million
Not working and seeking work	10 million
Not working and not seeking work	40 million

183. Table 6.1 describes the population of Costa Erica in 2011. The labor force participation rate (LFPR) is equal to
    (A) 75%
    (B) 84%
    (C) 80%
    (D) 67%
    (E) 70%

184. Table 6.1 describes the population of Costa Erica in 2011. The unemployment rate (UR) is equal to
    (A) 25%
    (B) 16%
    (C) 10%
    (D) 4.8%
    (E) 20%

185. Table 6.1 describes the population of Costa Erica in 2011. Suppose that the nation's 2012 economy improves and 10 million citizens, who were not looking for work in 2011, begin to look for jobs in 2012. If we hold employment levels constant, how will this affect the labor force participation rate (LFPR) and unemployment rate (UR) in 2012?
    (A) LFPR stays constant and UR decreases.
    (B) Both stay constant.
    (C) Both increase.
    (D) LFPR increases and UR stays constant.
    (E) Both decrease.

186. The proportion of the labor force that is unemployed is called the
    (A) natural rate of employment
    (B) employment to population rate
    (C) discouraged worker rate
    (D) labor force participation rate
    (E) unemployment rate

187. Roxie was fired from her job a year ago. For a year she unsuccessfully looked for work. Last month she gave up looking, and she has no plans to resume her job search. Roxie is classified as
    (A) out of the labor force
    (B) employed
    (C) unemployed
    (D) underemployed
    (E) unable to work due to disability

188. The official unemployment rate excludes _____, and this causes the official unemployment rate to _____ the amount of unemployment in the economy.

(A) part-time workers; understate

(B) unemployed workers; overstate

(C) retired workers; overstate

(D) discouraged workers; understate

(E) underemployed workers; overstate

189. Which of the following is typically true in recessions?

(A) Employment increases.

(B) Unemployment increases.

(C) Unemployment decreases.

(D) Wages rise.

(E) There is no change in employment.

190. Which of the following is typically true in expansions?

(A) Employment decreases.

(B) Unemployment increases.

(C) Employment increases.

(D) Labor force participation decreases.

(E) There is no change in unemployment.

191. Which of the following is an example of an unemployed worker?

(A) Alex is an artist who sells paintings at his own gallery.

(B) Eli is in high school and doesn't have time to hold down a job.

(C) Eric quit his job at the movie theater and has since applied for a job opening at the ballpark.

(D) Melanie is a retired cheese-maker who now enjoys gardening.

(E) Max is an aspiring author of children's books but hasn't yet finished his first book.

192. Oscar recently quit his job at the city sanitation office and is applying for openings in the parks department. Oscar is currently

(A) structurally unemployed

(B) seasonally unemployed

(C) cyclically unemployed

(D) frictionally unemployed

(E) out of the labor force

193. Grover was released from his sales job at the auto dealership when the economy slipped into a recession. Grover is classified as

(A) structurally unemployed
(B) seasonally unemployed
(C) out of the labor force
(D) frictionally unemployed
(E) cyclically unemployed

194. Ros is a ski instructor during the winter but finds herself without a job when the ski resort closes for the summer. Ros is currently

(A) structurally unemployed
(B) seasonally unemployed
(C) cyclically unemployed
(D) frictionally unemployed
(E) out of the labor force

195. When unemployed workers are seeking positions that are a better fit for the skills of those workers, it is called _____ unemployment

(A) frictional
(B) seasonal
(C) structural
(D) operational
(E) cyclical

196. When workers lose their jobs because there is no longer a demand for their particular skills, it is called _____ unemployment.

(A) frictional
(B) seasonal
(C) structural
(D) operational
(E) cyclical

197. When workers lose their jobs because the economy is experiencing a recession, it is called _____ unemployment.

(A) seasonal
(B) frictional
(C) structural
(D) cyclical
(E) political

198. Burgin worked at the Tennessee textile mill for 20 years, but when the mill moved its production to Mexico, he lost his job. Burgin is currently

(A) structurally unemployed
(B) seasonally unemployed
(C) cyclically unemployed
(D) frictionally unemployed
(E) out of the labor force

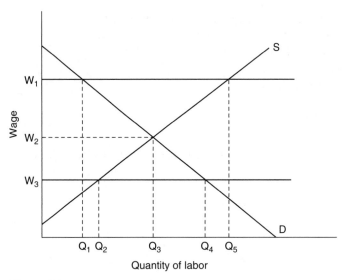

Figure 6.1

199. Figure 6.1 shows a competitive labor market in equilibrium. If a binding minimum wage was instituted, the quantity of labor supplied would

(A) increase from Q_3 to Q_5
(B) increase from Q_3 to Q_5
(C) decrease from Q_3 to Q_2
(D) increase from Q_1 to Q_5
(E) decrease from Q_3 to Q_1

200. Figure 6.1 shows a competitive labor market in equilibrium. If a binding minimum wage was instituted, the quantity of labor demanded would

(A) increase from Q_3 to Q_4
(B) increase from Q_3 to Q_5
(C) decrease from Q_3 to Q_2
(D) increase from Q_1 to Q_5
(E) decrease from Q_3 to Q_1

201. Figure 6.1 shows a competitive labor market in equilibrium. If a binding minimum wage was instituted, how many units of labor would be unemployed?

(A) $Q_5 - Q_3$
(B) $Q_4 - Q_2$
(C) $Q_5 \div Q_1$
(D) $Q_5 - Q_1$
(E) Q_5

202. Figure 6.1 shows a competitive labor market in equilibrium. If a binding minimum wage was instituted, what is the unemployment rate in this market?

(A) $(Q_5 - Q_1) \div Q_5$
(B) $Q_4 - Q_2$
(C) $Q_5 \div Q_3$
(D) $(Q_5 - Q_1) \div Q_3$
(E) Q_5

203. A firm might pay an efficiency wage if it

(A) wanted to lower worker productivity
(B) wanted to decrease absenteeism and turnover
(C) wanted to decrease hours worked
(D) wanted to increase waste and inefficiency
(E) wanted workers to seek alternative jobs

204. The natural rate of unemployment is the level of unemployment

(A) at the trough of a recession
(B) where structural unemployment is zero
(C) when the unemployment rate is zero
(D) where cyclical unemployment is zero
(E) where frictional unemployment is zero

205. The natural rate of unemployment is equal to

(A) zero unemployment
(B) frictional unemployment plus structural unemployment plus cyclical unemployment
(C) frictional unemployment
(D) structural unemployment
(E) frictional unemployment plus structural unemployment

206. When the economy is operating at full employment, the unemployment rate is

(A) equal to the rate of cyclical unemployment
(B) zero
(C) equal to the rate of frictional plus structural unemployment
(D) equal to the rate of frictional unemployment
(E) equal to the rate of structural unemployment

207. A binding minimum wage can lead to

(A) cyclical unemployment
(B) structural unemployment
(C) full employment
(D) frictional unemployment
(E) zero unemployment

208. Suppose a labor union successfully negotiates a wage that exceeds the market equilibrium wage. This contract may _____ the level of _____ unemployment.

(A) increase; structural
(B) decrease; frictional
(C) increase; cyclical
(D) decrease; natural rate of
(E) decrease; cyclical

CHAPTER 7

Aggregate Demand

209. In the United States, the largest component of aggregate demand is

    (A) government spending
    (B) consumption spending
    (C) investment spending
    (D) export spending
    (E) import spending

210. A nation's aggregate demand is

    (A) $S + I$
    (B) $DI + \text{Transfers} - \text{Taxes}$
    (C) $\text{Wages} + \text{Interest} + \text{Profit}$
    (D) $C + I + G + (X - M)$
    (E) $G - \text{Taxes}$

211. The component of aggregate demand that is the most sensitive to changes in the interest rate is

    (A) investment spending
    (B) consumption spending
    (C) government spending
    (D) export spending
    (E) import spending

212. If Congress approved billions of dollars to improve public education in the United States, this would directly affect the _____ component of aggregate demand.

    (A) investment spending
    (B) consumption spending
    (C) government spending
    (D) export spending
    (E) import spending

213. A more open trade agreement between the United States and the European Union will directly affect the _____ component of aggregate demand.

(A) investment spending
(B) consumption spending
(C) government spending
(D) financial spending
(E) net export spending

214. A nation's private sector _____ component of aggregate demand comes from domestic individuals and households, rather than firms and the public sector.

(A) import spending
(B) financial spending
(C) government spending
(D) consumption spending
(E) net export spending

215. As the aggregate price level falls, the real value of assets rises, and consumers increase consumption spending along the aggregate demand curve. This _____ effect partially explains why the aggregate demand curve is downward sloping.

(A) wealth
(B) interest rate
(C) crowding out
(D) substitution
(E) foreign exchange

216. Inflation reduces the real value of assets, including money checking accounts and retirement savings accounts. Because of this, when inflation is high, consumers and firms reduce spending. This _____ effect helps explain why the _____ is downward sloping.

(A) crowding out; aggregate demand curve
(B) interest rate; short-run aggregate supply curve
(C) wealth; aggregate demand curve
(D) income; long-run aggregate supply curve
(E) foreign exchange; aggregate demand curve

217. Which of the following statements accurately describes why aggregate
demand curves slope downward?
  I. When income levels rise, all else equal, consumers increase spending
     at all price levels.
  II. When interest rates fall, all else equal, firms increase investment
      spending at any price level.
  III. When the price level falls, all else equal, the value of saved assets rises
       and consumers increase spending.

  (A) I only
  (B) II only
  (C) III only
  (D) I and II only
  (E) II and III only

218. A rising price level causes consumers to reduce money savings in banks.
This begins a chain reaction that eventually reduces investment spending
by firms. This explanation for why aggregate demand is downward sloping
is referred to as the _____ effect.

  (A) wealth
  (B) interest rate
  (C) crowding out
  (D) substitution
  (E) foreign exchange

219. Economists explain the downward-sloping aggregate demand curve with
the interest rate effect. The idea is that lower price levels induce more
savings, lower interest rates, and

  (A) lower levels of consumption spending
  (B) lower levels of government spending
  (C) higher levels of import spending
  (D) higher levels of investment spending
  (E) lower levels of export spending

220. Aggregate demand curves slope downward because, all else equal,

  (A) higher levels of government spending increase real output at all price
      levels
  (B) weaker consumer confidence reduces real output at all price levels
  (C) more export spending increases real output at all price levels
  (D) lower net export spending decreases real output at all price levels
  (E) higher price levels reduce savings, increase interest rates, and reduce
      investment spending

221. When the aggregate price level falls in the US economy, net exports tend to rise and aggregate spending rises with it. The inverse relationship between price level and net exports is referred to as the

(A) wealth effect
(B) interest rate effect
(C) crowding out effect
(D) substitution effect
(E) foreign exchange effect

222. Suppose that a higher price level in the United States causes interest rates on US Treasury bonds to rise. The Mexican government invests more pesos in US Treasury bonds, appreciating the dollar and depreciating the peso. This chain of events eventually leads to lower _____ in the United States and is known as the _____.

(A) net exports; foreign exchange effect
(B) net exports; interest rate effect
(C) investment; borrowing out effect
(D) consumption; substitution effect
(E) consumption; wealth effect

223. All else equal, a lower price level in Canada causes the Canadian dollar to _____ against other currencies and a(n) _____ in Canadian gross domestic product (GDP).

(A) depreciate; decrease
(B) depreciate; increase
(C) appreciate; increase
(D) stay unchanged; increase
(E) appreciate; decrease

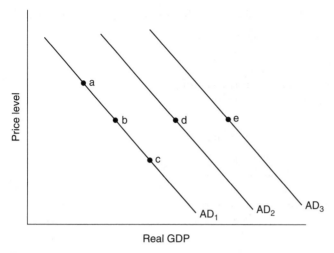

Figure 7.1

224. In Figure 7.1 the movement from point b to point d is described as

   (A) an upward movement along the aggregate demand curve
   (B) a decrease in aggregate demand
   (C) an increase in aggregate demand
   (D) a decrease in real gross domestic product (GDP)
   (E) a downward movement along the aggregate demand curve

225. In Figure 7.1 a movement from point a to point b would be caused by

   (A) a decrease in government spending
   (B) an increase in net exports
   (C) a decrease in the price level
   (D) a reduction in personal income taxes
   (E) an increase in interest rates

226. In Figure 7.1, what would cause a movement from point e to point b?

   (A) A decrease in the price level
   (B) An increase in export spending
   (C) An increase in investment spending
   (D) A reduction in consumption spending
   (E) An increase in the price level

227. In Figure 7.1, what would cause a movement from point b to point d?

(A) A decrease in the price level
(B) An increase in import spending
(C) An increase in government spending
(D) A reduction in consumption spending
(E) An increase in the price level

228. In Figure 7.1 a movement from point c to point b would be caused by

(A) a decrease in government spending
(B) an increase in net exports
(C) a decrease in the price level
(D) a reduction in personal income taxes
(E) an increase in the price level

229. Suppose that consumers are more optimistic about the job market and future incomes. All else held constant, this will

(A) shift the aggregate demand curve to the right
(B) have no impact on aggregate demand
(C) cause a movement downward along the aggregate demand curve
(D) cause a movement upward along the aggregate demand curve
(E) shift the aggregate demand curve to the left

230. Which of the following will shift the aggregate demand curve to the left?

(A) Investment spending rises.
(B) Import spending falls.
(C) Consumer spending rises.
(D) Export spending falls.
(E) Government spending rises.

231. Which of the following would cause a nation's real gross domestic product (GDP) to increase at any price level?

(A) Interest rates are rising.
(B) The stock market gets stronger, increasing the value of wealth.
(C) Government spending falls.
(D) Net exports fall.
(E) The nation's currency appreciates.

232. Suppose that firms in the country of Melaniestan are producing products that have seen increased international popularity. This should cause

(A) investment spending to decrease, shifting aggregate demand in Melaniestan to the left

(B) investment spending to increase, shifting aggregate demand in Melaniestan to the left

(C) net export spending to increase, shifting aggregate demand in Melaniestan to the right

(D) government spending to decrease, shifting aggregate demand in Melaniestan to the right

(E) net export spending to decrease, shifting aggregate demand in Melaniestan to the left

233. When the labor market in the United States is strong, unemployment is low, and incomes are rising, we expect to see

(A) no change in the aggregate demand (AD) curve

(B) a downward movement along the AD curve

(C) an upward movement along the AD curve

(D) a decrease in the AD curve

(E) an increase in the AD curve

234. Suppose that market forces in the financial sector cause interest rates to rise. All else equal, this would cause

(A) no change in the aggregate demand (AD) curve

(B) a downward movement along the AD curve

(C) an upward movement along the AD curve

(D) a decrease in the AD curve

(E) an increase in the AD curve

235. Suppose the government lowers income taxes for households. How does this affect the aggregate demand (AD) curve?

(A) By increasing disposable income, consumption spending rises and AD shifts to the right.

(B) By increasing disposable income, investment spending rises and AD shifts to the right.

(C) By decreasing disposable income, consumption spending rises and AD shifts to the right.

(D) By decreasing disposable income, consumption spending falls and AD shifts to the right.

(E) By increasing disposable income, consumption spending rises and AD shifts to the left.

236. Suppose the government eliminated some social programs like food stamps for the poor and social security payments. All else equal, this reduction in _____ would _____ disposable income and _____ aggregate demand.

(A) transfer payments; reduce; increase
(B) transfer payments; reduce; decrease
(C) tax payments; reduce; decrease
(D) tax payments; increase; decrease
(E) transfer payments; increase; increase

237. The government of Dodgetopia passes a large public works bill that increases government spending on road and rail construction, and the expansion of several air and sea ports. This kind of government spending is intended to

(A) decrease aggregate demand and real GDP
(B) increase aggregate demand and decrease real GDP
(C) increase aggregate demand and real GDP
(D) increase aggregate demand and the unemployment rate
(E) decrease aggregate demand and the unemployment rate

238. The central bank of Dodgetopia decides that the nation would be better served if interest rates were increased. This decision is intended to

(A) decrease aggregate demand and real gross domestic product (GDP)
(B) increase aggregate demand and decrease real GDP
(C) increase aggregate demand and real GDP
(D) increase aggregate demand and the unemployment rate
(E) decrease aggregate demand and the unemployment rate

239. The central bank of Dodgetopia decides that interest rates in the nation are above the target levels, and the bank acts to lower them. How will this decision affect aggregate demand in the country?

(A) Investment spending increases, net exports decrease, and aggregate demand rises.
(B) Investment spending increases, consumption spending increases, and aggregate demand falls.
(C) Investment spending decreases, net exports decrease, and aggregate demand falls.
(D) Consumption spending increases, net exports decrease, and aggregate demand rises.
(E) Investment spending increases, net exports increase, and aggregate demand rises.

240. If a central bank decides that total spending in the economy is too high, they should act to _____ interest rates so that _____.

(A) increase; investment, interest-sensitive consumption, and net exports all rise

(B) increase; investment, interest-sensitive consumption, and net exports all fall

(C) decrease; investment rises, but interest-sensitive consumption and net exports both fall

(D) decrease; investment, interest-sensitive consumption, and net exports all rise

(E) decrease; investment, interest-sensitive consumption, and net exports all fall

CHAPTER 8

Aggregate Supply

241. The short-run aggregate supply curve is _____, while the long-run aggregate supply curve is _____.

(A) upward sloping; vertical
(B) upward sloping; downward sloping
(C) downward sloping; vertical
(D) vertical; upward sloping
(E) upward sloping; horizontal

242. Which of the following is true of the long-run aggregate supply (LRAS) curve?

(A) The LRAS curve is upward sloping because at any level of real gross domestic product (GDP) the price level is constant.
(B) The LRAS curve is upward sloping because higher levels of real GDP are associated with higher price levels.
(C) The LRAS curve is vertical because higher levels of real GDP are associated with higher price levels.
(D) The LRAS is vertical because at any price level the level of real GDP is constant.
(E) The LRAS curve is vertical because higher levels of real GDP are associated with a constant price level.

243. Given a short-run aggregate supply curve, an increase in the price level will cause

(A) a downward movement along the curve
(B) an outward shift of the curve
(C) an upward movement along the curve
(D) the curve to become vertical
(E) an inward shift of the curve

244. Suppose the short-run aggregate supply curve shifts to the right. This means that

    (A) at any price level less real gross domestic product (GDP) will be supplied

    (B) at any level of real GDP a higher price level will exist

    (C) higher price levels will be associated with higher levels of real GDP on the new curve only

    (D) lower price levels will be associated with lower levels of real GDP

    (E) at any price level more real GDP will be supplied

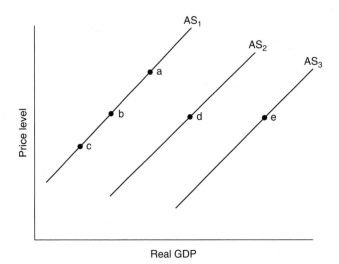

Figure 8.1

245. In Figure 8.1 the movement from point d to point e is described as

    (A) an upward movement along the aggregate supply curve

    (B) a decrease in aggregate supply

    (C) an increase in aggregate supply

    (D) a decrease in real gross domestic product (GDP)

    (E) a downward movement along the aggregate supply curve

246. In Figure 8.1 a movement from point a to point b would be caused by

    (A) a decrease in production technology

    (B) an increase in net exports

    (C) a decrease in the price level

    (D) a reduction in corporate income taxes

    (E) an increase in interest rates

247. In Figure 8.1, the movement from point e to point b is described as

(A) an upward movement along the aggregate supply curve
(B) a decrease in aggregate supply
(C) an increase in aggregate supply
(D) a decrease in real gross domestic product (GDP)
(E) a downward movement along the aggregate supply curve

248. The short-run aggregate supply curve is _____ because it is believed that _____ do not change quickly in the short run.

(A) upward sloping; real output levels
(B) upward sloping; wages
(C) vertical; wages and prices
(D) upward sloping; interest rates
(E) vertical; interest rates

249. Some economists theorize that when the price level increases, firms will increase production because wages do not rise as quickly as output prices. The implication of this theory, known as _____ theory, is an upward-sloping short-run aggregate supply curve.

(A) sticky wage
(B) misperceptions
(C) sticky output
(D) sticky interest rates
(E) crowding out

250. One explanation for an upward-sloping SRAS curve is that individual producers mistakenly perceive an increase in the aggregate price level as an increase in the individual goods those producers make. This explanation is known as the _____ theory.

(A) sticky wage
(B) crowding out
(C) sticky output
(D) misperceptions
(E) rational expectations

251. Which of the following theories are used to explain the upward-sloping short-run aggregate supply curve?
  I. Rational expectations theory
 II. Sticky wage theory
III. Misperceptions theory
(A) I only
(B) II only
(C) III only
(D) I and II only
(E) II and III only

252. Suppose that energy prices increase across the economy. How will this affect the short-run aggregate supply (SRAS) curve and the long-run aggregate supply (LRAS) curve?

	SRAS	LRAS
(A)	Decreases	No change
(B)	Decreases	Decreases
(C)	No change	No change
(D)	Increases	Decreases
(E)	Decreases	Increases

253. Suppose that the prices of key manufacturing commodities (i.e., steel, copper, aluminum) decrease across the economy. How will this affect the short-run aggregate supply curve (SRAS) and the long-run aggregate supply (LRAS) curve?

	SRAS	LRAS
(A)	Decreases	Increases
(B)	Increases	Decreases
(C)	No change	No change
(D)	Increases	No change
(E)	Increases	Increases

254. Texomabourg is a small island nation. Suppose that producers in Texomabourg experience a permanent increase in labor productivity. How will this affect the short-run aggregate supply (SRAS) curve and the long-run aggregate supply (LRAS) curve?

	SRAS	LRAS
(A)	Decreases	Increases
(B)	Increases	Decreases
(C)	No change	No change
(D)	Increases	No change
(E)	Increases	Increases

255. Texomabourg is a small island nation. Suppose that producers in Texomabourg experience a devastating earthquake, tsunami, drought, and plague of locusts that decrease productivity for many years. How will this affect the short-run aggregate supply (SRAS) curve and the long-run aggregate supply (LRAS) curve?

	SRAS	LRAS
(A)	No change	Decreases
(B)	Increases	Decreases
(C)	Decreases	Decreases
(D)	Decreases	No change
(E)	Increases	Increases

256. Suppose that nominal wages decrease across the economy. How will this affect the short-run aggregate supply (SRAS) curve and the long-run aggregate supply (LRAS) curve?

	SRAS	LRAS
(A)	Decreases	Increases
(B)	Increases	No change
(C)	No change	No change
(D)	Increases	Increases
(E)	Increases	Decreases

257. Suppose that nominal wages increase across the economy. How will this affect the short-run aggregate supply (SRAS) curve and the long-run aggregate (LRAS) supply curve?

	SRAS	**LRAS**
(A)	Decreases	No change
(B)	Decreases	Decreases
(C)	No change	No change
(D)	Increases	No change
(E)	Decreases	Increases

258. We are told that the nation's potential output has increased. In a graph this means that

(A) aggregate demand has increased
(B) short-run aggregate supply has decreased
(C) long-run aggregate supply has increased
(D) short-run aggregate supply has increased
(E) long-run aggregate supply has decreased

259. Which of the following would cause a nation's potential real gross domestic product (GDP) to increase?

(A) A decrease in energy prices
(B) A decrease in personal income taxes
(C) A decrease in nominal wages
(D) A tax credit given to firms that invest in new technology
(E) An increase in commodity prices

260. Which of the following would cause a nation's potential real gross domestic product (GDP) to decrease?

(A) A decrease in energy prices
(B) An increase in personal income taxes
(C) A decrease in high school graduation rates
(D) An increase in nominal wages
(E) An increase in labor productivity

261. If a nation's level of potential real gross domestic product (GDP) has decreased, it must be the case that
(A) aggregate demand has decreased
(B) short-run aggregate supply has decreased
(C) long-run aggregate supply has increased
(D) short-run aggregate supply has increased
(E) long-run aggregate supply has decreased

262. One of the main differences between the Keynesian and classical view of aggregate supply is
(A) Keynesian economists believe that output can be increased with a significant decrease in the price level, and classical economists believe that output cannot increase and efforts to do so will only increase the price level
(B) Keynesian economists believe that output can be increased without a significant increase in the price level, and classical economists believe that output cannot increase and efforts to do so will only increase the price level
(C) Keynesian economists believe that output can be increased with a significant increase in the price level, and classical economists believe that output cannot increase and efforts to do so will only increase the price level
(D) Keynesian economists believe that output can be increased without a significant increase in the price level, and classical economists believe that output cannot increase and efforts to do so will only decrease the price level
(E) classical economists believe that output can be increased without a significant increase in the price level, and Keynesian economists believe that output cannot increase and efforts to do so will only increase the price level

263. The classical aggregate supply curve is viewed as _____, while the Keynesian aggregate supply curve is viewed as _____.
(A) always vertical; horizontal at low levels of output but upward sloping as output increases toward full employment
(B) always vertical; always horizontal
(C) always horizontal; horizontal at low levels of output, but upward sloping as output increases toward full employment
(D) always horizontal; always vertical
(E) always vertical; always upward sloping as output increases toward full employment

264. Which of the following statements is typical of a classical view of aggregate supply?

   I. Any attempts at increasing real GDP will only succeed at raising the price level.

   II. The economy will always revert to potential real GDP at the vertical aggregate supply curve.

   III. At low levels of output aggregate supply is nearly horizontal.

   (A) I only
   (B) II only
   (C) III only
   (D) I and II only
   (E) I, II, and III

265. The aggregate supply curve is often drawn with three ranges as real gross domestic product (GDP) increases. These are

   (A) the Keynesian, the Laffer, and the classical ranges
   (B) the Keynesian, the Monetarist, and the classical ranges
   (C) the Keynesian, the intermediate, and the classical ranges
   (D) the Keynesian, the Randian, and the classical ranges
   (E) the Friedman, the intermediate, and the Smithian ranges

CHAPTER 9

Macroeconomic Equilibrium

266. Which of the following best represents the actual output produced within an economy?

(A) The full employment output

(B) The point at which the aggregate demand curve intersects the long-run aggregate supply curve

(C) The point at which the short-run aggregate supply curve intersects the long-run aggregate supply curve

(D) The point at which the short-run aggregate supply curve intersects the aggregate demand curve

(E) The point at which the aggregate demand curve is vertical

267. If the short-run aggregate supply curve increases, the price level will _____ and the amount of output will _____ in the short run.

(A) increase; increase

(B) decrease; increase

(C) decrease; remain unchanged

(D) remain unchanged; increase

(E) decrease; decrease

268. All else equal, if there is an increase in the nominal wage rate, the price level will _____ and the amount of aggregate output will _____ in the short run.

(A) increase; decrease

(B) increase; increase

(C) increase; remain unchanged

(D) remain unchanged; increase

(E) decrease; decrease

269. Fredonia has experienced an increase in the exports that they sell to their neighbor Threading. In the short run, the real gross domestic product (GDP) of Fredonia will _____ and the price level of Fredonia will _____.

    (A) increase; decrease
    (B) decrease; decrease
    (C) increase; increase
    (D) increase; remain unchanged
    (E) decrease; increase

270. Texomabourg has experienced a decline in real income of households. Therefore, the _____ curve will _____, and aggregate output will _____.

    (A) aggregate demand; decrease; decrease
    (B) short-run aggregate supply; increase; decrease
    (C) aggregate demand; increase; decrease
    (D) long-run aggregate supply; increase; increase
    (E) long-run aggregate supply; increase; increase

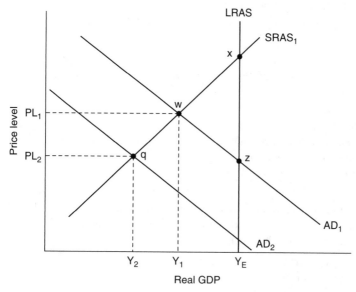

Figure 9.1

271. Refer to Figure 9.1. Which of the points represents a short-run macroeconomic equilibrium?

(A) Only x
(B) Only w
(C) Only q
(D) w and q
(E) w, q, and x

272. Refer to Figure 9.1. Which output represents an actual, rather than potential, level of output that occurs in this economy during either of the two time periods?

 I. Y_1
 II. Y_2
 III. Y_E

(A) I only
(B) II only
(C) III only
(D) I and II only
(E) I, II, and III

273. The economy exhibited in Figure 9.1 has experienced a decline in investment levels. Because of this, aggregate output has _____ and the price level _____.

(A) increased; decreased
(B) decreased; decreased
(C) increased; increased
(D) increased; remains unchanged
(E) decreased; increased

274. Refer to Figure 9.1. Which of the following represents the output gap in the second time period?

(A) $Y_E + Y_2$
(B) $Y_2 - Y_1$
(C) $Y_E - Y_2$
(D) $Y_E - Y_1$
(E) $Y_1 - Y_E$

275. Refer to Figure 9.1. The shift from AD_1 to AD_2 is called a
(A) positive demand shock
(B) negative demand shock
(C) negative supply shock
(D) negative quantity shock
(E) negative price level shock

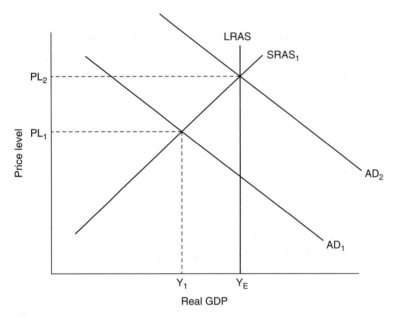

Figure 9.2

276. Refer to Figure 9.2. Which of the following is true of the shift shown?
  I. Inflation results due to the increase in aggregate demand (AD).
  II. The economy has experienced economic growth.
  III. The economy has an unemployment rate below the natural rate of unemployment.
(A) I only
(B) II only
(C) III only
(D) I, II, and III
(E) I and II only

277. Refer to Figure 9.2. What existed before the shift shown?

(A) Inflationary output gap
(B) Expansionary output gap
(C) Full employment
(D) Recessionary output gap
(E) Excess employment

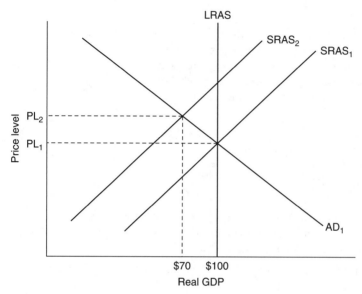

Figure 9.3

278. Refer to Figure 9.3. As a result in the shift from $SRAS_1$ to $SRAS_2$, aggregate output _____, the price level _____, and the natural rate of unemployment _____.

(A) increased; decreased; increased
(B) decreased; increased; did not change
(C) increased; increased; did not change
(D) decreased; decreased; decreased
(E) did not change; increased; decreased

279. Refer to Figure 9.3. What is the value of the output gap that occurs as a result of the shift from $SRAS_1$ to $SRAS_2$?

    (A) $100

    (B) $70

    (C) $30

    (D) −$30

    (E) $7

280. Refer to Figure 9.3. Which of the following was true of the economy before the shift in short-run aggregate supply shown?

    I. The economy was in short-run equilibrium.

    II. The economy was in long-run equilibrium.

    III. The unemployment rate was greater than 0.

    (A) I only

    (B) II only

    (C) III only

    (D) I and II only

    (E) I, II, and III

281. Refer to Figure 9.3. Suppose the government attempted to return the economy to full employment by increasing government spending. Which of the following would likely occur?

    (A) Output could return to full employment levels, and deflation would occur.

    (B) Output could return to full employment levels, and inflation would occur.

    (C) Output would decrease, and inflation would occur.

    (D) Output could return to full employment levels with no impact on inflation.

    (E) Output would be unchanged, and deflation would occur.

282. Refer to Figure 9.3. What is the term for what has occurred in Figure 9.3?

    (A) Stagflation

    (B) Immolation

    (C) Demand push inflation

    (D) Negative demand shock

    (E) Positive supply shock

283. When an economy experiences a supply shock,

(A) output and the price level move in the same direction, but unemployment moves in the opposite direction

(B) output and unemployment move in the same direction, but the price level moves in the opposite direction

(C) the price level and unemployment move in the same direction, but output moves in the opposite direction

(D) output, unemployment, and the price level all move in the same direction

(E) output and unemployment move in the same direction, but the price level is unaffected

284. Which of the following could cause inflation in the short run?

(A) An increase in the price of an energy source such as natural gas

(B) A decrease in consumer incomes

(C) A decrease in the wage rate

(D) An increase in the amount of imports

(E) A decrease in the amount of exports

285. A positive demand shock will cause the price level to _____ in the short run, and a negative supply shock will cause the price level to _____ in the short run.

(A) increase; increase

(B) decrease; decrease

(C) increase; decrease

(D) decrease; increase

(E) decrease; remain unchanged

286. If an economy is initially in long-run macroeconomic equilibrium and then experiences a positive demand shock, then in the short run, unemployment will _____ and in the long run, unemployment will _____.

(A) remain unchanged; increase

(B) remain unchanged; decrease

(C) decrease; return to the natural rate

(D) increase; return to the natural rate

(E) decrease; decrease

287. If an economy is initially in long-run macroeconomic equilibrium and then experiences a negative demand shock, then in the short run, what will happen to output, unemployment, and the price level?

	Output	Unemployment	Price Level
(A)	Will be lower than the output before the shock	Will return to the natural rate of unemployment	Will be lower than the initial price level before the shock
(B)	Will return to the full employment level of output	Will be higher than the initial unemployment rate before the shock	Will be higher than the price level before the shock
(C)	Will return to the full employment level of output	Will return to the natural rate of unemployment	Will be lower than the initial price level before the shock
(D)	Will be lower than the initial output before the shock	Will be higher than the output before the shock	Will be lower than the initial price level before the shock
(E)	Will be higher than the output before the shock	Will return to the natural rate of unemployment	Will return to the natural price level

288. If an economy is initially in long-run macroeconomic equilibrium and then experiences a negative demand shock, then in the long run, what will happen to output, unemployment, and the price level?

	Output	Unemployment	Price Level
(A)	Will be higher than the output before the shock	Will return to the natural rate of unemployment	Will be lower than the initial price level before the shock
(B)	Will return to the full employment level of output	Will be higher than the initial unemployment rate before the shock	Will be higher than the price level before the shock
(C)	Will return to the full employment level of output	Will return to the natural rate of unemployment	Will be lower than the initial price level before the shock
(D)	Will be lower than the initial output before the shock	Will be higher than the output before the shock	Will be lower than the initial price level before the shock
(E)	Will be higher than the output before the shock	Will return to the natural rate of unemployment	Will return to the natural price level

289. If an economy is in long-run macroeconomic equilibrium and experiences a negative supply shock, then in the long run, what will happen to output, unemployment, and the price level if prices are able to fully adjust?

	Output	Unemployment	Price Level
(A)	Will be higher than the output before the shock	Will return to the natural rate of unemployment	Will be lower than the initial price level before the shock
(B)	Will return to the full employment level of output	Will return to the natural rate of unemployment	Will return to the price level before the shock
(C)	Will return to the full employment level of output	Will return to the natural rate of unemployment	Will be lower than the initial price level before the shock
(D)	Will be lower than the initial output before the shock	Will be lower than the output before the shock	Will be lower than the initial price level before the shock
(E)	Will be higher than the output before the shock	Will be lower than the output before the shock	Will return to the natural price level

290. Which of the following variables will change in the long run in response to a demand shock if prices are able to fully adjust?
   I. Unemployment
   II. Output
   III. Price level

(A) I only
(B) II only
(C) III only
(D) I and II only
(E) I, II, and III

291. A positive demand shock will cause, in the short run,
   I. economic growth
   II. inflation
   III. increased employment

(A) I only
(B) II only
(C) III only
(D) II and III only
(E) I, II, and III

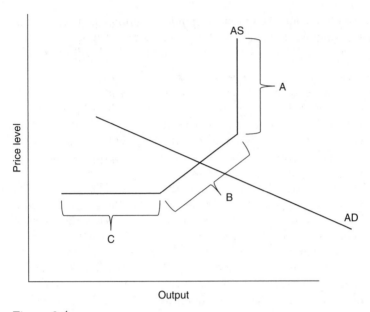

Figure 9.4

292. Refer to Figure 9.4. In which of the ranges of aggregate supply will inflation occur if aggregate demand increases?

(A) A only
(B) B only
(C) C only
(D) B and C
(E) A and B

293. Refer to Figure 9.4. The portion of the aggregate supply curve labeled A is called the

(A) Keynesian range
(B) classical range
(C) intermediate range
(D) inflammatory range
(E) free-enterprise range

294. Refer to Figure 9.4. In which of the regions of aggregate supply are prices said to be "sticky"?

(A) A only
(B) B only
(C) C only
(D) A and B only
(E) C and B only

295. The economy is currently operating at the natural rate of unemployment. If wages and prices are fully flexible, how would an increase in aggregate demand affect gross domestic product (GDP) and price level in the short run, and GDP and price level in the long run?

	Price Level in the Short Run	GDP in the Short Run	Price Level in the Long Run	GDP in the Long Run
(A)	Decreases	Unchanged	Decreases	Unchanged
(B)	Increases	Unchanged	Decreases	Increases
(C)	Increases	Increases	Decreases	Unchanged
(D)	Increases	Increases	Increases	Unchanged
(E)	Increases	Increases	Unchanged	Unchanged

296. Which of the following would be most like an increase in the long-run aggregate supply curve?

   I. A shift out of a curved production possibilities frontier
  II. A shift out of a linear production possibilities frontier
 III. A movement along a production possibilities frontier

(A) I only
(B) II and III only
(C) I and II only
(D) II only
(E) I, II, and III

297. The current price level is $120, current gross domestic product (GDP) is $200, and the full employment level of GDP is $240. Currently there is a(n) _____ of _____.

(A) inflationary gap; $80
(B) inflationary gap; $40
(C) recessionary gap; $40
(D) recessionary gap; $80
(E) recessionary gap; $120

CHAPTER 10

Money and Financial Institutions

298. In general, money can be considered anything that

   (A) is in the form of paper currency
   (B) is in the form of gold, silver, or other precious metals
   (C) can perform all functions of money
   (D) never loses any value over long periods of time
   (E) is decreed legal tender by a government

299. Liquidity is best defined as

   (A) the ability to convert a financial asset into profits
   (B) the ability to convert a financial asset into goods and services
   (C) the ability to minimize risk
   (D) the ability to maintain value
   (E) the ability to raise capital

300. A _____ is a financial instrument that is a promise to repay principal on a given date and a fixed amount of interest each year for its duration, and has the advantage that it is relatively easy to sell compared to _____.

   (A) bond; loans
   (B) mutual fund; loans
   (C) bond; financial intermediaries
   (D) loan; bonds
   (E) loan; mutual funds

301. The primary goal of a financial system is to _____ risk, _____ liquidity, and _____ transaction costs.

(A) increase; increase; increase
(B) decrease; decrease; decrease
(C) increase; decrease; increase
(D) increase; decrease; decrease
(E) decrease; increase; decrease

302. One type of financial intermediary is an institution that uses the liquid assets of many depositors to finance the illiquid needs, such as loans, of borrowers. This kind of financial intermediary is a

(A) bank
(B) mortgage backed security
(C) mutual fund
(D) stock market
(E) life insurance company

303. Which of the following is both a financial asset and the least liquid?

(A) Cash
(B) Bonds
(C) Bank deposits
(D) Life insurance company
(E) Loans

304. Eric is able to take a paycheck from his employer and use it to buy flowers for Melanie. This illustrates the _____ role of money.

(A) store of value
(B) commodity
(C) medium of exchange
(D) unit of account
(E) fiat

305. Margaret is able to take her paycheck from her employer and put it her savings account until she decides how to spend it. This illustrates the _____ role of money.

(A) store of value
(B) commodity
(C) medium of exchange
(D) unit of account
(E) fiat

306. In the nation of Maxistan, people are paid wages in the form of bars of chocolate which they can either eat or use to trade. Therefore, in Maxistan chocolate is considered
   I. an asset
  II. fiat money
 III. commodity money

(A) I only
(B) II only
(C) III only
(D) I and III only
(E) I and II only

307. In 2008, Zimbabwe experienced extreme hyperinflation, which ultimately caused the collapse of its currency. This is an example of money failing first at which function of money?

(A) Store of value
(B) Commodity
(C) Medium of exchange
(D) Unit of account
(E) Fiat

308. Gary offers you 6 pounds of cheese if you mow his lawn, but Patrick offers you 4 hours at his sauna if you mow his lawn. You cannot figure out which is a better deal. Which role of money would be useful in this situation?

(A) Store of value
(B) Commodity
(C) Medium of exchange
(D) Unit of account
(E) Fiat

309. A _____ is a claim that entitles its holder to future income, whereas a _____ is a claim on a tangible item.

(A) mortgage backed security; financial asset
(B) financial asset; physical asset
(C) physical asset; financial asset
(D) financial asset; money
(E) money; financial asset

310. The best description of a financial system is that it is a means by which
(A) buyers of goods and sellers of goods are matched
(B) buyers of services and sellers of goods are matched
(C) buyers of savings and governments are matched
(D) banks loan money
(E) borrowers and savers are matched

311. Which of the following would not be considered a financial asset?
(A) Money
(B) Stocks
(C) Bonds
(D) Loans
(E) Mortgage-backed securities

312. In the nation of Ile, one may go to any bank and exchange the paper currency of Ile for silver. The currency of Ile is therefore a
(A) fiat money
(B) commodity-backed money
(C) near money
(D) far money
(E) commodity money

313. A checkable deposit is considered money because
   I. the government requires that people consider it money
   II. it can serve all three functions of money
   III. it is commodity money
(A) I only
(B) II only
(C) III only
(D) I and III only
(E) II and III only

314. Jack has a checking account and a savings account. He can withdraw money from his checking account without limitations, but his bank allows him to withdraw funds only three times per month from his savings account. Which of the following statements is true?

(A) The money in Jack's savings account is less liquid than the money in his checking account.

(B) The money in Jack's savings account is not considered money.

(C) The money in Jack's checking account is not considered money, because it fails as a store of value.

(D) The money in Jack's checking account is not considered money, because his checking account is not a financial asset.

(E) Neither the money in Jack's savings account nor that in his checking account is considered money, because he cannot hold it physically until he withdraws it.

315. Which of the following is not counted as part of the official money supply in the United States?

(A) M1

(B) M2

(C) Small time deposits

(D) Large time deposits

(E) Cash

316. As the category of a monetary aggregate increases, for instance going from M1 to M2 to M3, the definition of money in each one is progressively

(A) more liquid

(B) less liquid

(C) more profitable

(D) less profitable

(E) more commodity based

317. Which of the following equations represents the present value of $Y loaned at an interest rate of i for t years?

(A) $PV(\$Y) = \$Y \times (1+ i)$

(B) $PV(\$Y) = \$Y \times (1+ i)^t$

(C) $PV(\$Y) = \$Y \times i^t$

(D) $PV(\$Y) = \$Y/(1 + i)^t$

(E) $PV(\$Y) = \$Y/(i)^t$

318. The interest rate in Ile is 10%. What is the present value of $500 that will be paid in 1 year?

(A) $500.00
(B) $510.10
(C) $550.00
(D) $490.00
(E) $454.55

319. The interest rate in Maxistan is 20%. Eli lends Eric $1,000. The amount that Eli receives in 1 year as a result of lending him the money is

(A) $1,002
(B) $1,020
(C) $1,200
(D) $2,100
(E) $1,000

320. Jane wants to lend $100 and would like to receive $130 one year from now. What interest rate would she need to lend at to receive this?

(A) 13%
(B) 30%
(C) 3%
(D) 31%
(E) 0.03%

321. During which decade was the Federal Reserve created?

(A) 1910s
(B) 1920s
(C) 1930s
(D) 1940s
(E) 1970s

322. Which of the following is a function of the Federal Reserve System?

(A) Providing financial services to individuals and businesses
(B) Printing currency
(C) Maintaining the stability of the financial system
(D) Overseeing the operations of the US Treasury department
(E) Insuring individual checking deposits up to $250,000

323. Within the Federal Reserve System, the Board of Governors is responsible for _____, and the 12 Regional Federal Reserve banks are responsible for _____.

(A) overseeing the entire Federal Reserve System; providing banking and supervisory services

(B) overseeing the entire Federal Reserve System; printing currency

(C) providing banking and supervisory services; overseeing the entire Federal Reserve System

(D) printing currency; overseeing the entire Federal Reserve System

(E) providing banking and supervisory services; overseeing the Board of Governors

324. The primary role of the Federal Open Market Committee is to

(A) oversee bank regulation

(B) print currency

(C) respond to the requests of the President of the United States

(D) conduct monetary policy

(E) respond to the requests of the legislative branch of government

325. Which of the following is not a policy tool that the Federal Reserve Bank has used?

(A) Changing tax rates

(B) Purchasing securities

(C) Changing the reserve requirement

(D) Changing the discount rate

(E) Conducting open market operations

326. Which of the following best describes a bank run?

(A) A massive drop in the stock market

(B) A massive increase in unemployment

(C) A massive number of people depositing money into banks

(D) A massive number of people withdrawing money from banks

(E) A massive number of people running through banks

327. A _____ is a bank regulation designed to reduce the risk of bank runs that dictate how much of its deposits it must keep on hand.

(A) required reserve ratio

(B) discount rate of reserves

(C) discount rate

(D) required discount ratio

(E) Regulation Q

328. Which of the following would not be counted in M1 or M2?

(A) Checking accounts
(B) Savings accounts
(C) Traveler's checks
(D) Reserves held in bank vaults
(E) Coins in circulation

329. Which of the following comprises the largest proportion of M1?

(A) Checking accounts
(B) Savings accounts
(C) Currency in circulation
(D) Traveler's checks
(E) Coins in circulation

330. What are "near moneys" counted in?

   I. M1
  II. The monetary base
 III. M2

(A) I only
(B) II only
(C) III only
(D) I and II only
(E) I, II, and III

331. Which of the following is the best explanation for why members of the Board of Governors of the Federal Reserve System serve 14-year terms?

(A) Because it takes 4 years to learn the job, and the governors should serve 10 years after that point
(B) Because this is the same length as the election cycle
(C) Because this is the same amount of time that fiscal policy is conducted over
(D) Because it is the same length of appointment as Supreme Court judges
(E) Because it helps insulate members from short-term political concerns

332. Which of the following entities are part of the Federal Open Market Committee?
- I. The Federal Reserve Bank of New York
- II. All of the regional bank presidents
- III. All of the Board of Governors

(A) I only
(B) II only
(C) III only
(D) I and III only
(E) I, II, and III

333. The purpose of _____ in the United States was to separate banks into two categories, commercial banks and investment banks.

(A) Regulation Q
(B) the Glass-Steagall Act
(C) the Sherman Antitrust Act
(D) the Dodd-Frank Act
(E) the Federal Reserve Act

334. Which of the following would be considered fiat money?

(A) Gold
(B) Silver
(C) Metal coins
(D) Cigarettes in prisoner of war camps
(E) Salt

335. Which monetary aggregates are included in each other?

(A) None are included in each other: they are entirely independent of each other.
(B) M1 is included in M2.
(C) M2 is included in M1.
(D) M1 is included in M2, and M2 is included in M1.
(E) M2 and M1 are the same measures.

336. The present value of $X in 1 year is $400 when the interest rate is 10%. What is $X?

(A) $440
(B) $360
(C) $364
(D) $490
(E) $410

337. The Federal Reserve lends $400,000 to a commercial bank. Which of the following statements is true?

(A) The commercial bank will pay the market interest rate.
(B) The commercial bank will pay no interest.
(C) The commercial bank will pay the federal funds rate.
(D) The commercial bank will pay the Treasury bill (T-bill) rate.
(E) The commercial bank will pay the discount rate.

CHAPTER 11

Monetary Policy

338. Monetary policy is the use of _____ to affect macroeconomic variables.

(A) taxes
(B) government spending
(C) real estate
(D) the money supply
(E) the labor market

339. The institution that is primarily responsible for conducting monetary policy in the United States is

(A) Congress
(B) the Senate
(C) the Department of the Treasury
(D) the Congressional Budget Office
(E) the Federal Reserve

340. A T-account is a balance sheet that compares the _____ and _____ of commercial banks.

(A) profits; losses
(B) assets; liabilities
(C) deposits; income
(D) income; losses
(E) liabilities; profits

341. First Bank of Fredonia has $100,000 in checkable deposits and $100,000 in cash in its vaults. The required reserve ratio in Fredonia is 20%. What is the maximum amount of money that First Bank of Fredonia can lend?

(A) $80,000
(B) $20,000
(C) $0
(D) $100,000
(E) $120,000

Refer to Table 11.1 for questions 342 and 343.

Table 11.1

Assets	Liabilities
$50,000 Reserves	+$200,000 Checkable deposits
$150,000 Loans	

342. Refer to Table 11.1. If Bank of Fredonia has no excess reserves, what is the reserve ratio of Fredonia based on Table 11.1?

(A) 15%
(B) 50%
(C) 100%
(D) 20%
(E) 25%

343. Refer to Table 11.1. Suppose the required reserve ratio in Fredonia is 10%. How much in excess reserves does the First Bank of Fredonia have on hand?

(A) $10,000
(B) $20,000
(C) $30,000
(D) $40,000
(E) $50,000

344. The term *multiple expansion of deposits* refers to the fact that

(A) when there is government spending, the final impact of that spending on aggregate demand may be greater than the dollar amount of the government spending

(B) when there is government spending, the final impact of government spending may be offset by the effect of deficit spending on the market for loanable funds

(C) an increase in the amount of excess reserves that a bank is holding will lead to an increase in the money supply larger than the amount of the excess reserves

(D) deposit accounts accrue interest on an ongoing basis, and interest is compounded

(E) loans accrue interest on an ongoing basis, and interest is compounded

345. At what point in the process of the multiple expansion of deposits is money created?

(A) When a bank receives a deposit

(B) When a bank determines it has excess reserves

(C) When a bank lends money out

(D) When a loan recipient uses that loan to purchase goods or services

(E) When a loan recipient deposits the loan in another bank

346. The required reserve ratio in Fredonia is 20%. What is the money multiplier in Fredonia?

(A) 20

(B) 2

(C) 8

(D) 5

(E) 0

347. Jacksonia has a required reserve ratio of 10%. Amandania has a required reserve ratio of 20%. Which of the following statements is definitely true?

(A) Jacksonia has a higher dollar amount of reserves on hand than Amandania.

(B) Amandania has a higher dollar amount of reserves on hand than Jacksonia.

(C) Jacksonia has fewer excess reserves than Amandania.

(D) Amandania has a larger money multiplier than Jacksonia.

(E) Jacksonia has a larger money multiplier than Amandania.

348. The Central Bank of Maxistan wants to increase the money supply by $100,000. The required reserve ratio in Maxistan is 25%. How much of an injection of money is required?

(A) Less than $25,000
(B) At least $25,000
(C) Exactly $25,000
(D) At least $100,000
(E) More than $50,000

349. If the required reserve ratio is 40% and the Federal Reserve injects $100,000 into bank reserves, what is the most likely result?

(A) The money supply will increase by exactly $250,000.
(B) The money supply will increase by $40,000.
(C) The money supply will increase by more than $250,000.
(D) The money supply will increase by $400,000.
(E) The money supply will increase by less than $250,000.

350. Which of the following would cause an increase in the demand for money?

(A) An increase in the interest rate
(B) Making ATM machines and debit cards illegal
(C) A decrease in the interest rate
(D) A decrease in the aggregate price level
(E) A decrease in real GDP

351. Which of the following would cause an increase in the money supply?
  I. An increase in the discount rate
  II. A decrease in the reserve ratio
  III. The Federal Reserve buying bonds

(A) I only
(B) II only
(C) III only
(D) II and III only
(E) I and III only

352. Which of the following would, all else equal, cause a decrease in the interest rate?

(A) The reserve ratio is increased.
(B) The Federal Reserve sells bonds.
(C) Real GDP increases.
(D) The price level increases.
(E) The Federal Reserve buys bonds.

353. What would cause a sudden stop in the multiple expansion of deposits process?

    I. People stop depositing money in banks.
   II. Banks stop making loans.
  III. The reserve requirement is increased.

(A) I only
(B) II only
(C) III only
(D) I and II only
(E) I, II, and III

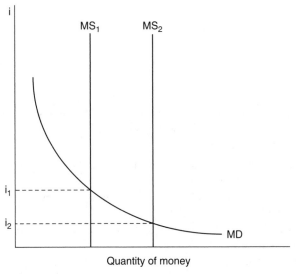

Figure 11.1

354. Refer to Figure 11.1, on the previous page. As a result of the change in the money supply shown, what is now true about the quantity of money demanded at the initial equilibrium interest rate and how interest rates will respond?

At the Initial Equilibrium Interest Rate	The Interest Rate Will Respond By
(A) The quantity of money supplied exceeds the quantity of money demanded.	Decreasing
(B) The quantity of money demanded exceeds the quantity of money demanded.	Decreasing
(C) The quantity of money supplied exceeds the quantity of money demanded.	Increasing
(D) The quantity of money demanded exceeds the quantity of money supplied.	Increasing
(E) The quantity of money supplied exceeds the quantity of money demanded.	Not changing

355. How does the Federal Open Market Committee usually increase the money supply?
(A) By raising the required reserve ratio
(B) By lowering the required reserve ratio
(C) By buying bonds
(D) By selling bonds
(E) By increasing the discount rate

356. Suppose the Federal Reserve announces that it will "lower the interest rate by 50 basis points." Which of the following best describes the chain of events that will occur and the result?
(A) The Federal Reserve will buy bonds, which increases the money supply, to lower the interest rate by 50%.
(B) The Federal Reserve will buy bonds, which increases the money supply, to lower the interest rate by 0.5%.
(C) The Federal Reserve will buy bonds, which increases the money supply, to lower the interest rate by 5%.
(D) The Federal Reserve will sell bonds, which increases the money supply, to lower the interest rate by 50%.
(E) The Federal Reserve will sell bonds, which decreases the money supply, to lower the interest rate by 0.5%.

357. Which part of aggregate demand is monetary policy primarily intended to target?

(A) Consumption

(B) Investment

(C) Government spending

(D) Exports

(E) Imports

358. Suppose the Federal Reserve is concerned about rising inflation and notes that the unemployment rate is very low. What will it be likely to do, and why?

(A) Sell bonds, which will decrease the interest rate and increase aggregate demand

(B) Sell bonds, which will increase the interest rate and increase aggregate demand

(C) Buy bonds, which will increase the interest rate and increase aggregate demand

(D) Sell bonds, which will increase the interest rate and decrease aggregate demand

(E) Buy bonds, which will decrease the interest rate and increase aggregate demand

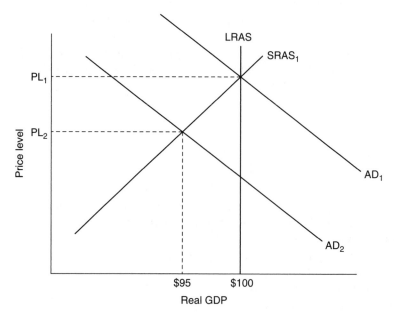

Figure 11.2

359. Refer to Figure 11.2, on the previous page. Suppose that aggregate demand has recently shifted from AD_1 to AD_2. What action will the Federal Open Market Committee take if it wants to use monetary policy to correct the situation shown?

(A) Set money market interest rates lower.
(B) Sell bonds.
(C) Buy bonds.
(D) Set money market interest rates higher.
(E) Increase the demand for money.

360. Refer to Figure 11.2. Suppose that aggregate demand has recently shifted from AD_1 to AD_2. Which of the following describes the chain of events involved to correct the level of output shown with monetary policy?

(A) Sell bonds → money supply increases → interest rates decrease → investment increases → aggregate demand increases
(B) Buy bonds → money supply increases → interest rates decrease → investment increases → aggregate demand increases
(C) Sell bonds → money supply decreases → interest rates decrease → investment increases → aggregate demand increases
(D) Buy bonds → money supply increases → interest rates decrease → investment increases → aggregate demand decreases
(E) Sell bonds → money supply increases → interest rates decrease → investment decreases → aggregate demand increases

361. Refer to Figure 11.2. According to the Taylor rule, if inflation is 10%, what interest rate should the Federal Open Market Committee target to correct what is seen in Figure 11.2?

(A) 18.5%
(B) 10.5%
(C) 13.5%
(D) 10%
(E) 5%

362. _____ states that monetary policy should not be discretionary, but rather should follow a formula that sets interest rates based on unemployment and output.

(A) Regulation Q
(B) The Glass-Steagall Act
(C) The Dodd-Frank Act
(D) The Sherman Anti-Trust Act
(E) The Taylor rule

363. A liquidity trap refers to a situation where

(A) the interest rate in the money market cannot be lowered any more, because the demand for money is too high

(B) the interest rate in the money market cannot be lowered any more, because it is already at or near zero percent

(C) the interest rate in the money market is too high because all of the money supply is being restricted by the Federal Reserve

(D) banks choose to keep inadequate reserves

(E) the Federal Reserve refuses to take any action

364. Which of the following is one of the reasons that the demand for money is downward sloping?

(A) There is an opportunity cost of holding money, the interest rate, and as the interest rate increases, people will respond by holding less money.

(B) People prefer to keep none of their assets in the form of cash.

(C) When new innovations like ATMs are introduced, the demand for money increases.

(D) The amount of money in the economy at any given time is fixed.

(E) The Federal Reserve can buy bonds to lower the interest rate.

365. When the interest rate increases, people want to hold less money because the _____ has _____.

(A) transactions motive; increased

(B) transactions motive; decreased

(C) opportunity cost of holding money; decreased

(D) opportunity cost of holding money; increased

(E) purpose of money; disappeared

366. The Federal Open Market committee has sold bonds. Which of the following statements is most likely true?

(A) The Federal Reserve is concerned that the unemployment rate is too high.

(B) The Federal Reserve is concerned that aggregate output is too low.

(C) The Federal Reserve is concerned that people are spending too little.

(D) The Federal Reserve is concerned that inflation is too high.

(E) The Federal Reserve is concerned about the outcome of the next election.

367. Which of the following equations describes the quantity theory of money?

(A) Federal funds rate = 1 + (1.5 × inflation) + (0.5 × output gap)

(B) MV = PY

(C) PV = MY

(D) Federal funds rate = 1 + (1.5 × output gap) + (0.5 × inflation)

(E) MR(Q) = MC(Q)

368. The nation of Ergo is a tiny country that has only one product: oranges. Oranges currently sell at a price of $2 each, and there is $600 in the money supply in Ergo. If there are a total of 1,200 oranges that are bought and sold in this economy, how many times does each of the dollars in Ergo's money supply change hands?

(A) 1,200

(B) 2

(C) 3

(D) 4

(E) 600

369. According to the classical version of the quantity theory of money, _____ and _____ are _____, which means an increase in the money supply will only _____.

(A) M; V; constant; lower the price level

(B) M; Y; constant; raise the price level

(C) V; Y; variable; decrease the price level

(D) V; Y; variable; increase the price level

(E) V; Y; constant; raise the price level

370. Suppose there is an increase in the demand for money. If the Federal Reserve wants to keep interest at the same rate, what will it need to do?

(A) Lower the demand for money

(B) Lower the supply of money by buying bonds

(C) Increase the demand for money by buying bonds

(D) Increase the supply of money by buying bonds

(E) Nothing—the Federal Reserve can do nothing to counter this.

371. Suppose there is a financial innovation that allows people to carry less cash, like a debit card. If the Federal Reserve wants to increase interest rates at the same time, what must it do?

(A) Decrease the money supply by a greater amount than the decrease in the demand for money

(B) Decrease the money supply by the same amount as the decrease in the demand for money

(C) Decrease the money supply by a lesser amount than the decrease in the demand for money

(D) Increase the money supply by a greater amount than the decrease in the demand for money

(E) Decrease the money supply by the same amount as the decrease in the demand for money

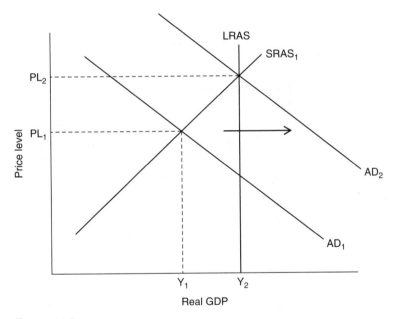

Figure 11.3

372. Refer to Figure 11.3, on the previous page. Which of the following could have caused the shift indicated?
  I. The Federal Reserve selling bonds
  II. The Federal Reserve lowering the reserve requirement
  III. The Federal Reserve buying bonds

(A) I only
(B) II only
(C) III only
(D) I and III only
(E) II and III only

373. Refer to Figure 11.3. Which of the mandates that the Federal Reserve operates under was the main motivation for the action that caused the shift in the graph?

(A) The mandate to have stable prices
(B) The mandate to maintain full employment
(C) The mandate to keep interest rates low
(D) The mandate to keep inflation at 0%
(E) The mandate to keep the unemployment rate at 0%

374. The Bank of Mitchell is fully loaned out and has no excess reserves. One of its depositors withdraws the entire balance of her checking account. Which of the following is not an option for the bank to keep its required reserves?
  I. Lower their required reserve ratio
  II. Borrow from another bank
  III. Borrow from the Federal Reserve

(A) I only
(B) II only
(C) III only
(D) II and III only
(E) I, II, and III

375. The nation of Cam has had an increase in the amount of exports to other nations. If the Central Bank of Cam wanted to use monetary policy to counteract the effect this has, what would the Central Bank do if it used open market operations similar to the Federal Reserve?

(A) Sell bonds
(B) Increase the rate of interest set by the Central Bank
(C) Decrease the rate of interest set by the Central Bank
(D) Buy bonds
(E) Increase government spending

376. In Lilistan the required reserve ratio is 20%. If the central bank of Lilistan buys $100 million in bonds from banks in open market operations, what will be the impact on excess reserves and what will be the maximum impact on the money supply?

	Excess Reserves Will	**Maximum Impact on Money Supply**
(A)	Increase by $100 million	Increase by $400 million
(B)	Increase by $100 million	Increase by $500 million
(C)	Increase by $20 million	Increase by $400 million
(D)	Increase by $100 million	Decrease by $500 million
(E)	Decrease by $80 million	Decrease by $100 million

377. Suppose the central bank of Lilistan buys $100 million in open market operations. What does this tell us about the current level of output and unemployment?

	Current Level of Output Is	**Current Level of Unemployment Is**
(A)	Lower than full employment output	Lower than the natural rate of unemployment
(B)	Higher than the full employment output	Lower than the natural rate of unemployment
(C)	Lower than full employment output	Higher than the natural rate of unemployment
(D)	Higher than the natural rate of unemployment	Higher than the natural rate of unemployment
(E)	Equal to the full employment output	Higher than the natural rate of unemployment

CHAPTER **12**

Fiscal Policy

378. In the nation of Xela, if people get \$1 in new income, they tend to spend \$0.75 and save \$0.25. Therefore, the _____ is _____.

   (A) multiplier; 25
   (B) marginal propensity to consume; 0.25
   (C) marginal propensity to save; 0.75
   (D) marginal propensity to consume; 0.75
   (E) multiplier; 0.75

379. Which of the following represents the formula for the government spending multiplier?
   I. $1/(1 - MPC)$
   II. $1/MPS$
   III. $\Delta GDP/\Delta G$

   (A) I only
   (B) II only
   (C) III only
   (D) I and II only
   (E) I, II, and III

380. In the nation of Ile the marginal propensity to consume is 0.8. If there is no crowding out effect, what will be the impact on gross domestic product (GDP) of a \$20 million increase in government spending?

   (A) \$20 million increase
   (B) \$2 million increase
   (C) \$80 million increase
   (D) \$100 million increase
   (E) \$160 million increase

381. In the nation of Ile the marginal propensity to consume is 0.8. If Ile increases its taxes by $20 million, what will be the impact on gross domestic product (GDP) as a result of these taxes?

(A) GDP will increase by 0.8%.
(B) GDP will increase by $80 million.
(C) GDP will decrease by $80 million.
(D) GDP will decrease by 0.8%.
(E) An increase in taxes has no effect on GDP.

382. In the nation of Ile the marginal propensity to consume is 0.8. To pay for $20 million in new government spending, the government of Ile collects $20 million in new taxes. What is the final effect of this spending on gross domestic product (GDP)?

(A) $2 million decrease
(B) $180 million increase
(C) $80 million increase
(D) $100 million increase
(E) $20 million increase

383. The government of Xela is considering a number of policy options. Which of the following options would decrease gross domestic product (GDP) by the largest amount?

(A) The government increases spending with no change in the taxes collected.
(B) The government increases spending, which it pays for with an equal amount of new taxes collected.
(C) The government decreases spending and matches this with a decrease in taxes of an equal amount.
(D) The government decreases spending and does not change the amount of taxes collected.
(E) The government decreases spending while increasing the amount of taxes collected.

384. Which of the following are fiscal policy options?
   I. Changing tax rates
   II. Changing government spending
   III. Changing the money supply

   (A) I only
   (B) II only
   (C) III only
   (D) I and II only
   (E) I, II, and III

385. A _____ is a situation in which a government spends more than it collects in tax revenues in a given time period.

   (A) budget deficit
   (B) fiscal scenario
   (C) liquidity trap
   (D) deflation
   (E) national debt

386. Over the past 20 years, the government of Maxistan has routinely collected $2 million less in tax revenues than it has spent. Over this 20-year time frame, this has led Maxistan to accumulate

   (A) a budget deficit
   (B) a national debt
   (C) a fiscal policy
   (D) a monetary policy
   (E) a large number of unemployed

387. Contractionary fiscal policy refers to

   (A) using a decrease in the money supply to lower inflation
   (B) using higher tax rates to lower inflation
   (C) using more government spending to lower unemployment
   (D) using an increase in the money supply to lower unemployment
   (E) using a decrease in the money supply to increase inflation

388. Expansionary fiscal policy is intended to

   (A) increase inflation and decrease employment
   (B) decrease inflation and increase unemployment
   (C) increase gross domestic product (GDP) and decrease unemployment
   (D) decrease unemployment and decrease output
   (E) decrease unemployment and keep output unchanged

389. Jacksonia is experiencing a rate of unemployment that is higher than the natural rate of unemployment. Which of the following statements is true?

(A) The government may decrease government spending, which would increase output and decrease unemployment.

(B) The government may increase taxes, which would increase output and decrease unemployment.

(C) The government may increase government spending, which would increase output and decrease unemployment.

(D) The government may decrease taxes, which would decrease output and decrease unemployment.

(E) The government may decrease taxes, which would decrease output and increase unemployment.

390. An example of an automatic stabilizer is

(A) a discretionary decrease in taxes when unemployment is high

(B) a nondiscretionary increase in taxes when unemployment is high

(C) a nondiscretionary decrease in government spending when unemployment is high

(D) a nondiscretionary decrease in government spending when unemployment is low

(E) a discretionary decrease in government spending when unemployment is low

391. A progressive tax rate acts as _____ when the gross domestic product (GDP) is high and _____ when GDP is low.

(A) expansionary monetary policy; contractionary fiscal policy

(B) contractionary fiscal policy; expansionary fiscal policy

(C) contractionary fiscal policy; expansionary monetary policy

(D) contractionary fiscal policy; contractionary fiscal policy

(E) expansionary fiscal policy; contractionary monetary policy

392. In the market for loanable funds, the supply of loanable funds comes from _____ and the demand for loanable funds comes from _____ .

(A) the government; private citizens

(B) private citizens; the government

(C) borrowers; savers

(D) savers; borrowers

(E) the government; savers

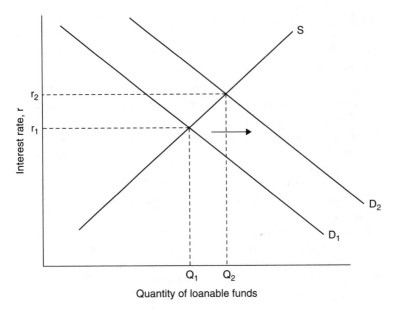

Figure 12.1

393. Refer to Figure 12.1. As a result of the change shown, what would happen if the interest rate was fixed?

(A) Borrowers would want to borrow more money than was available to lend.

(B) Lenders would want to borrow more money than borrowers wanted to lend.

(C) The quantity of loanable funds would increase.

(D) The quantity of loanable funds would decrease.

(E) Borrowers would want to borrow less money than lenders were willing to supply.

394. Refer to Figure 12.1. Which of the following could have caused the change shown?

(A) A decrease in government deficits

(B) An increase in private savings

(C) A large capital outflow from this economy to another country

(D) An increase in government borrowing

(E) A decrease in perceived business opportunities

395. The inhabitants of Maxistan notice that interest rates in their financial markets are lower than interest rates available to them in the neighboring nation of Ile. What effect will the actions of the savers of Maxistan have on the market for loanable funds in both countries?

(A) The demand for loanable funds in Maxistan will increase, the supply of loanable funds in Ile will decrease, and the interest rates in both countries will increase.

(B) The demand for loanable funds in Maxistan will increase, the supply of loanable funds in Ile will decrease, and the interest rates in both countries will increase.

(C) The supply of loanable funds in Maxistan will increase, the supply of loanable funds in Ile will decrease, and the interest rates in both countries will increase.

(D) The supply of loanable funds in Maxistan will increase, the supply of loanable funds in Ile will decrease, the interest rates in Maxistan will increase, and the interest rates in Ile will decrease.

(E) The supply of loanable funds in Maxistan will decrease, the supply of loanable funds in Ile will increase, and the interest rates in Maxistan will increase and the interest rate in Ile will decrease.

396. According to the crowding out effect

(A) deficit government spending decreases the interest rate, making investment more attractive

(B) deficit government spending increases the interest rate, making investment less attractive

(C) deficit government spending decreases the interest rate, making investment less attractive

(D) balanced budget government spending increases the interest rate, making investment less attractive

(E) balanced budget government spending decreases the interest rate, making investment more attractive

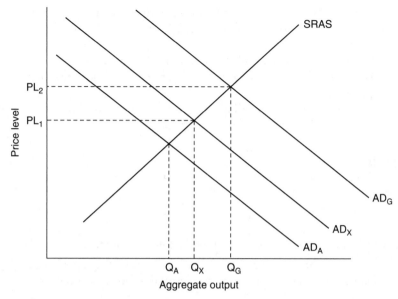

Figure 12.2

397. Refer to Figure 12.2. If an economy was initially producing a gross domestic product (GDP) of Q_A and engages in deficit spending, what happens in the economy?

(A) Aggregate demand initially decreases from AD_G to AD_A, and then increases to AD_X as a result of the crowding out effect.

(B) Aggregate demand initially increases from AD_A to AD_G, and then decreases to AD_X as a result of the crowding out effect.

(C) Aggregate demand initially increases from AD_X to AD_G, and then increases to AD_X as a result of the crowding out effect.

(D) Aggregate demand initially increases from AD_G to AD_X, and then increases to AD_G as a result of the crowding out effect.

(E) Aggregate demand initially decreases from AD_A to AD_X, and then decreases back to AD_A as a result of the crowding out effect.

398. Refer to Figure 12.2. Which of the following is an explanation as to why, after increasing from AD_A to AD_G, aggregate demand could shift back down to AD_X?

   I. As a result of deficit spending, net exports decreased.
   II. As a result of an increase in the supply of loanable funds, investment spending decreased.
   III. As a result of deficit spending, the demand for loanable funds increased.

   (A) I only
   (B) II only
   (C) III only
   (D) II and III only
   (E) I and III only

399. According to the Fisher effect, which of the following is true?

   (A) An increase in expected future inflation will cause the supply of loanable funds to decrease and the demand for loanable funds to decrease.
   (B) An increase in expected future inflation will cause the supply of loanable funds to decrease and the demand for loanable funds to increase.
   (C) An increase in expected future inflation will cause the supply of loanable funds to increase and the demand for loanable funds to increase.
   (D) An increase in expected future inflation will cause the supply of loanable funds to increase and the demand for loanable funds to decrease.
   (E) A decrease in expected future inflation will cause the supply of loanable funds to decrease and the demand for loanable funds to increase.

400. When the federal government borrows money to finance deficit spending, the increased interest rate will _____ through an effect known as the _____.

   (A) decrease private investment; crowding out effect
   (B) increase private investment; multiplier effect
   (C) increase the money supply; money multiplier effect
   (D) decrease tax rates; tax multiplier effect
   (E) increase the money supply; money neutrality

401. When economies are in recessions, they tend to experience _____,
and when they are in expansions, they are more likely to run
_____. For this reason, it may be useful to separate out the effects
of discretionary fiscal policy using the _____.
- (A) deficits; surpluses; cyclically balanced budget
- (B) surpluses; deficits; cyclically balanced budget
- (C) deficits; debts; cyclically balanced budget
- (D) inflation; deflation; monetarily balanced budget
- (E) disinflation; deflation; monetarily balanced budget

402. Keynesian theory says that discretionary fiscal policy should _____
to fight recessions, classical macroeconomics says that discretionary policy
should _____ to fight recessions, and the modern consensus is
that discretionary fiscal policy should _____.
- (A) never be used; always be used; be used only in special circumstances
- (B) always be used; be used only in special circumstances; never be used
- (C) never be used; never be used; be used only in special circumstances
- (D) always be used; never be used; only be used in special circumstances
- (E) always be used; always be used; never be used

403. Which combination of fiscal policy and monetary policy might have
contradictory effects on inflation?

	Fiscal Policy	**Monetary Policy**
(A)	Decrease taxes	Increase the money supply
(B)	Decrease government spending	Increase the money supply
(C)	Decrease government spending	Decrease the money supply
(D)	Increase the money supply	Decrease government spending
(E)	Increase the money supply	Increase taxes

404. Which of the following actions would undermine attempts by the Federal Reserve to control inflation?
    I. If the government increased taxes
    II. If the government decreased government spending
    III. If the government used a surplus to pay down debt
    (A) I only
    (B) II only
    (C) III only
    (D) I and II only
    (E) I, II, and III

405. Which of the following would decrease the size of the tax multiplier?
    (A) A higher proportional tax
    (B) A lower proportional tax
    (C) The more people save from each additional dollar of income
    (D) The less people save from each additional dollar of income
    (E) The less people spend from each additional dollar of income

406. Which of the following fiscal policies would decrease interest rates?
    (A) The government increases government spending and increases its borrowing.
    (B) The government collects more in tax revenue than it spends and uses it to pay down national debt.
    (C) The government increases government spending but does not increase taxes.
    (D) The government decreases government spending and decreases taxes by the same amount.
    (E) The government places strict limits on saving.

407. Most economists believe that discretionary expansionary fiscal policy _____ the rate of unemployment in the _____.
    (A) has no effect on; short run
    (B) increases; long run
    (C) has no effect on; long run
    (D) increases; short run
    (E) has no effect on; short run or long run

408. The gross domestic output of Teragram is $400 million, but the full employment output of Teragram is $500 million. If the marginal propensity to save is 0.2, what is the effect of a $20 million increase in government spending?

(A) Gross domestic product (GDP) will increase by $20 million if the increase in government spending is paid for by raising $20 million in tax revenue, and as a result interest rates will increase.

(B) GDP will increase by $20 million if the increase in government spending is paid for by borrowing, and as a result interest rate will increase.

(C) GDP will increase by $80 million if the increase in government spending is paid for by raising $20 million in tax revenue, and interest rates will remain unchanged.

(D) GDP will initially increase by $100 million if the increase in government spending is not paid for by raising tax revenues, and as a result interest rates will rise, lowering private investment and decreasing GDP.

(E) GDP will initially increase by $100 million if the increase in government spending is not paid for by raising tax revenues, and as a result interest rates will rise, attracting more investment and further increasing GDP.

409. After the nation of Ile increased government spending by $100 million dollars, the gross domestic product (GDP) of Ile increased by $150. If the marginal propensity to consume in Ile is 0.5, which of the following is possible?

I. Ile ran a deficit to increase spending by $100 million and financed this deficit through borrowing, and the crowding out effect in Ile is larger than the multiplier effect.

II. Ile ran a deficit to increase spending by $100 million, increased taxes by $50 million, and borrowed $50 million.

III. Ile ran a deficit to increase spending by borrowing the full amount, and the crowding out effect is smaller than the multiplier effect.

(A) I only
(B) II only
(C) III only
(D) I and II only
(E) II and III only

410. Which of the following is an advantage that discretionary monetary policy has over discretionary fiscal policy?

(A) Discretionary monetary policy suffers from serious lags.
(B) Discretionary monetary policy could be subject to a liquidity trap
(C) National fiscal policy may be offset by state and local policies.
(D) Discretionary monetary policy takes a long time to implement.
(E) Fiscal policy affects only the government spending component of GDP, while monetary policy affects only the investment component.

Use Table 12.1 for questions 411–413.

Table 12.1

Increase in National Income	Additional Consumption Spending
$100	$75
$200	$150
$300	$225
$400	$300

411. The marginal propensity to consume in the nation described by Table 12.1 is equal to

(A) 1
(B) 0.75
(C) 3
(D) 0.67
(E) 0.25

412. Refer to the data in Table 12.1. Which of the following policies would, all else equal, increase gross domestic product (GDP) in this nation by $2,400?

(A) Increase government spending by $600
(B) Increase government spending by $400
(C) Decrease taxes by $1,200
(D) Increase government spending by $600 and increase taxes by $600
(E) Decrease taxes by $600

413. Refer to Table 12.1. Suppose that the economy is currently experiencing an inflationary gap of $1,800. How could the economy return to full employment?

(A) Increase government spending by $450 with no change in taxes
(B) Decrease government spending by $1,800 and increase taxes by $1,800
(C) Increase taxes by $450 with no change in government spending
(D) Decrease government spending by $450 and decrease taxes by $450
(E) Increase taxes by $600 with no change in government spending

414. It takes several months for government economists to gather enough data to declare that a recession is underway. By this time, discretionary fiscal policy may be ineffective. This problem is referred to as

(A) a developmental lag
(B) an implementation lag
(C) crowding out
(D) a recognition lag
(E) a legislative lag

CHAPTER 13

The Relationship Between Inflation and Unemployment

415. Which of the following is the best description of the short-run Phillips curve?

(A) At high rates of interest people demand less money, and at low rates of interest people demand more money.

(B) As prices and expectations adjust, inflation has no impact on the level of unemployment.

(C) In the short run, high rates of unemployment are associated with low levels of inflation.

(D) As the price of Phillips screwdrivers increases, people will buy less screwdrivers.

(E) The flow of money through an economy can be replicated using water.

416. What would be the short-run effect on the Phillips curve model of a decrease in investment spending?

(A) A movement up (or leftward) along the short-run Phillips curve

(B) A decrease (or leftward) shift of the short-run Phillips curve

(C) An increase (or rightward) shift of the short-run Phillips curve

(D) A movement down (or rightward) along the short-run Phillips curve

(E) A movement up along the long-run Phillips curve

417. Which of the following describes the long-run Phillips curve?
   (A) An upward sloping curve that intersects the unemployment rate axis at 0% unemployment
   (B) A vertical curve that is vertical at the natural rate of unemployment
   (C) A horizontal curve that is horizontal at the natural rate of inflation
   (D) A downward sloping curve that is slightly to the right of the short-run Phillips curve
   (E) A downward sloping curve that is slightly to the left of the short-run Phillips curve

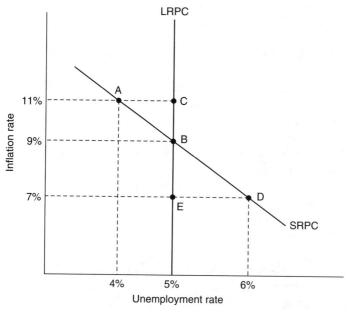

Figure 13.1

418. Refer to Figure 13.1. Which of the following points represents an economy in recession as a result of a decrease in aggregate demand?
   (A) A
   (B) B
   (C) C
   (D) D
   (E) E

419. Refer to Figure 13.1. According to this graph, what is the NAIRU and what is the natural rate of unemployment?

(A) NAIRU = 5%, natural rate of unemployment = 5%
(B) NAIRU = 5%, natural rate of unemployment = 7%
(C) NAIRU = 5%, natural rate of unemployment = 4%
(D) NAIRU = 11%, natural rate of unemployment = 6%
(E) NAIRU = 9%, natural rate of unemployment = 5%

420. Refer to Figure 13.1. If the economy was initially at full employment output and then experienced a 1% decrease in unemployment, what would happen to the price level?

(A) The price level would be unchanged.
(B) The price level would increase by 2%.
(C) The price level would increase by 1%.
(D) The price level would decrease by 1%.
(E) The price level would decrease by 2%.

421. Which of the following could cause the short-run Phillips curve to shift to the right?

(A) A decrease in the price of oil
(B) An increase in the price of oil
(C) An increase in the cost of investment
(D) An increase in consumption spending
(E) An increase in net exports

422. If people expect that inflation is going to be 5% this year, they will try to get an increase in wages of 5% in anticipation of the higher prices. Seeking higher wages in fact will cause the inflation. This is the concept that underlies

(A) great expectations
(B) adaptive expectations
(C) mutual expectations
(D) production expectations
(E) rational expectations

423. Stagflation would cause which change?

(A) A leftward shift of the long-run Phillips curve
(B) A rightward shift of the long-run Phillips curve
(C) A leftward shift of the short-run Phillips curve
(D) A rightward shift of the short-run Phillips curve
(E) A leftward rotation of the short-run Phillips curve

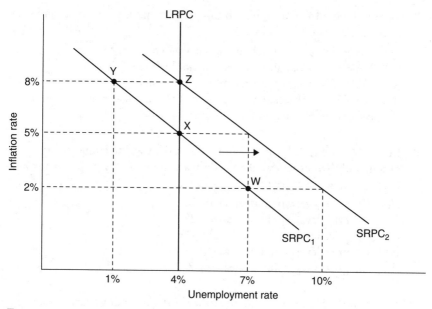

Figure 13.2

424. Refer to Figure 13.2. What could have caused the shift indicated?

(A) A decrease in expectations of inflation
(B) A decrease in the price of energy
(C) A positive supply shock
(D) An increase in the price of factors of production
(E) An increase in investment spending

425. Refer to Figure 13.2. What would cause the move from point X to point Y?

(A) Short-run aggregate supply unexpectedly increased.
(B) Short-run aggregate supply unexpectedly decreased.
(C) Aggregate demand suddenly increased.
(D) Aggregate demand suddenly decreased.
(E) Long-run aggregate supply unexpectedly decreased.

426. Refer to Figure 13.2. What could cause the move from point Y to point Z?
   I. Expectations of inflation adjust to higher levels of inflation.
   II. Workers start demanding higher wages as their real wages decrease.
   III. Consumption spending decreases.

   (A) I only
   (B) II only
   (C) III only
   (D) I and II only
   (E) I, II, and III

427. Refer to Figure 13.2. Suppose a government tried to keep the unemployment rate below the non-accelerating inflation rate of unemployment (NAIRU). What would be the effect on the natural rate of unemployment in the long run?

   (A) There would be no effect.
   (B) Unemployment would increase to 7%.
   (C) Unemployment would decrease to 1%.
   (D) Unemployment would increase to 10%.
   (E) Unemployment would decrease to 0%.

428. Refer to Figure 13.2. Suppose a government tried to keep inflation below 8% after the shift in the short-run Phillips curve (SRPC). What would the resulting effect on the price level be called?

   (A) Inflation
   (B) Hyperinflation
   (C) Disinflation
   (D) Deflation
   (E) No effect

429. Refer to Figure 13.2. What would the unemployment rate need to be for inflation to remain at 5% after the shift in the short-run Phillips curve (SRPC) in the short run?

   (A) 1%
   (B) 4%
   (C) 5%
   (D) 8%
   (E) 7%

430. Describe what would happen in the Phillips curve model if a country suddenly experienced an economic expansion due to an increase in net exports.

(A) The unemployment rate will increase along with an accompanying increase in inflation as the economy moves down along the long-run Phillips curve.

(B) The unemployment rate will increase along with an accompanying increase in inflation as the economy moves down along the short-run Phillips curve.

(C) The unemployment rate will decrease along with an accompanying increase in inflation as the economy moves down along the long-run Phillips curve.

(D) The unemployment rate will decrease along with an accompanying increase in inflation as the economy moves up along the short-run Phillips curve.

(E) The unemployment rate will decrease along with an accompanying decrease in inflation as the economy moves down along the long-run Phillips curve.

431. An economy is currently experiencing inflation of 6%, and the NAIRU in this economy is known to be 10%. The current rate of unemployment in the economy is equal to the natural rate of unemployment. If people had anticipated inflation of 6%, which will occur?

(A) There will be no change in either the rate of inflation or the rate of unemployment.

(B) There will be a new anticipation of higher inflation in the future, and as a result, there will be a ratcheting up of the long-run Phillips curve.

(C) There will be a new anticipation of higher inflation in the future, and as a result, there will be a ratcheting up of the short-run Phillips curve.

(D) There will be a new anticipation of lower inflation in the future, and as a result, there will be a shifting down of the long-run Phillips curve.

(E) There will be a new anticipation of lower inflation in the future, and as a result, there will be a shifting up of the long-run Phillips curve.

432. Which of the following statements, according to the Phillips curve model, is true?

(A) It is possible to have policies that keep unemployment at rates lower than the natural rate of unemployment, but this will lead to deflation.

(B) It is possible to have policies that keep unemployment at rates lower than the natural rate of unemployment; this will lead to deflation in the short run but not the long run.

(C) It is possible to have policies that keep unemployment at rates lower than the natural rate of unemployment, but this will lead to disinflation.

(D) It is possible to have policies that keep unemployment at rates lower than the natural rate of unemployment, but this will lead to decreases in the natural rate of unemployment.

(E) It is possible to have policies that keep unemployment at rates lower than the natural rate of unemployment, but this will lead to constantly increasing rates of inflation.

CHAPTER 14

Growth and Productivity

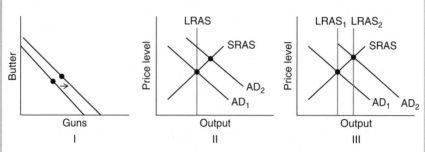

Figure 14.1

433. Refer to Figure 14.1. Which of the following demonstrates economic growth?

(A) I only

(B) II only

(C) III only

(D) I and III only

(E) I, II, and III

434. Refer to Figure 14.1. Which of the following demonstrates an increase in output?

(A) I only

(B) II only

(C) III only

(D) II and III only

(E) I, II, and III

435. An economy has a gross domestic product (GDP) of $100 million and is growing at the rate of 5% per year. In how many years will the GDP of this economy be $200 million?

(A) 20 years
(B) 7 years
(C) 14 years
(D) 100 years
(E) 25 years

436. The economy of Ile went from $375 billion to $750 billion in 10 years. Therefore, the annual rate of growth in Ile is

(A) 20%
(B) 10%
(C) 7%
(D) 70%
(E) 2%

437. All else equal, which of the following would not lead to economic growth?

(A) An increase in consumption
(B) An increase in the number of workers
(C) An increase in the skills of workers
(D) An improvement in technology
(E) An increase in the stock of machinery

438. A nation is not producing enough capital to replace the capital that is depreciating. What will be the likely effect of this?

(A) The production possibilities curve will increase.
(B) The long-run aggregate supply curve will increase.
(C) The short-run aggregate supply curve will increase.
(D) The long-run aggregate supply curve will decrease.
(E) Aggregate demand will increase.

439. An increase in technology will allow a nation to produce more

(A) even if it does not have more land, labor, or capital
(B) only if it has more of all of the factors of production
(C) only if it has more capital
(D) only if it has more land
(E) only if it has more labor

440. Which of the following has been identified as being a more significant source of growth than the other options over the past 100 years?

(A) An increase in the stock of physical capital
(B) An increase in the stock of human capital
(C) An increase in the energy resources
(D) An increase in the water resources available
(E) An increase in the number of factories

441. Which of the following would lead to a decrease in the long-run aggregate supply of a country?

(A) A decline in literacy rates
(B) An increase in immigration
(C) Discovery of a new source of energy
(D) A decrease in taxes on investment
(E) An increase in technology

442. Which of the following policies would be likely to lead to economic growth?

(A) A tax on higher education
(B) A tax on nondurable consumption goods
(C) A tax on capital expenditures
(D) A tax on basic health care
(E) An additional tax on the income of immigrants

443. Which of the following effects would be the most likely to decrease growth?

  I. The crowding out effect
  II. The government spending multiplier
  III. The tax multiplier

(A) I only
(B) II only
(C) III only
(D) I and III only
(E) II and III only

444. Maxistan has experienced economic growth. As a result of this growth, which of the following statements is most likely to be true?

(A) Maxistan has experienced a decline in immigration.
(B) Maxistan has fewer factories operating and producing less pollution.
(C) Maxistan will have to produce a higher amount of output to fully use its resources.
(D) Maxistan has implemented policies restricting land use.
(E) Maxistan has eliminated free primary education.

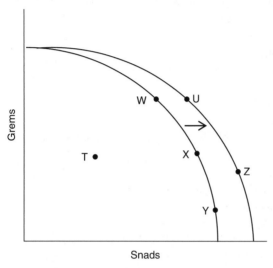

Figure 14.2

445. Refer to Figure 14.2. Suppose this economy is initially at point X. Which of the following points would be consistent with this economy experiencing economic growth?

(A) U only
(B) Z only
(C) Y and Z only
(D) W, X, and U only
(E) U and Z only

446. Refer to Figure 14.2. Which of the following is most likely to cause the shift shown?

    (A) An improvement in the technology to produce Snads

    (B) An improvement in the technology to produce Grems

    (C) An increase in the energy resources of the country

    (D) An increase in the capital used to produce all goods

    (E) An increase in the labor that can be used to produce any good

447. Refer to Figure 14.2. Which of the following movements would not represent economic growth?

    (A) From W to U

    (B) From T to W

    (C) From W to Z

    (D) From Y to U

    (E) From X to U

448. Which of the following gives the best indication of economic growth in a nation?

    (A) The rate of inflation

    (B) The rate of increase of nominal gross domestic product (GDP)

    (C) The rate of increase of real GDP

    (D) The rate of increase of real GDP per capita

    (E) The rate of unemployment

449. Which of the following is generally believed to be the primary source of growth that has been experienced worldwide?

    (A) An increase in technology

    (B) An increase in capital stock

    (C) An increase in the stock of money

    (D) An increase in the stock of human capital

    (E) An increase in arable land mass

450. If there is no corresponding increase in technology, which of the following will happen as the capital stock of a country increases, all else equal?

    I. Production per worker will increase.

    II. Economic growth will increase.

    III. The rate of economic growth will decrease.

    (A) I only

    (B) II only

    (C) III only

    (D) I and II only

    (E) I, II, and III

451. Maxistan is currently experiencing an average growth rate of 15% per year, while Ile is experiencing an average growth rate of 5% per year. Assuming their population is growing at the same rate, which of the following would not be a possible explanation for the difference in growth rates?

(A) Maxistan currently has a very low stock of capital, while Ile has a large capital stock.

(B) The capital stock of Ile is depreciating at a faster rate than the capital stock of Maxistan.

(C) Maxistan has less secure property rights than Ile.

(D) Maxistan is making improvements to its primary education system, while Ile already has an established primary education system.

(E) Maxistan has a larger increase in total factor productivity than Ile.

452. The government of Maxistan predicts that its population will double in size in 16 years. What rate of growth of real gross domestic product (GDP) will it need to maintain the same standard of living?

(A) The doubling time will depend on the initial GDP of Maxistan.

(B) 10.5%

(C) 5.5%

(D) 4.4%

(E) 8%

453. In 2009 the real gross domestic product (GDP) per capita of Ile was $200 million, and in 2010 the real GDP of Ile was $210 million. In 2009 the real GDP per capita of Maxistan was $20 million, and in 2010 the real GDP of Maxistan was $25 million. Which of the following statements is true?

   I. Ile is growing at a faster rate than Maxistan.
  II. Maxistan will double in size in less time than Ile.
 III. Ile had a larger increase in GDP than Maxistan.

(A) I only

(B) III only

(C) I and II only

(D) II and III only

(E) I, II, and III

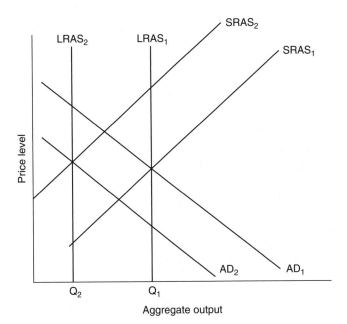

Figure 14.3

454. Refer to Figure 14.3. What could have caused the change shown?

(A) An increase in immigration
(B) Tax policies to promote investment in capital
(C) A plague that kills a large number of the population
(D) A country beginning to subsidize education
(E) A nation removing regulations on pollution

455. Refer to Figure 14.3. Which of the following would be a policy that could likely restore long-run aggregate supply to its initial level?

(A) Prohibit foreign workers from entering
(B) Create strong antipollution regulations
(C) Eliminate spending on public health
(D) Create institutions of higher learning
(E) Encourage more consumption spending by households

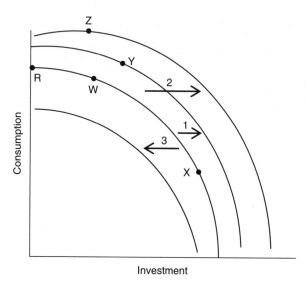

Figure 14.4

456. Figure 14.4 shows three possible shifts in the production possibilities frontier of a country. Which allocation would be the most likely explanation for shift number 3?

(A) R
(B) W
(C) X
(D) Y
(E) Shift number 3 is not possible.

457. Figure 14.4 shows three possible shifts in the production possibilities frontier of a country. Suppose this country would prefer shift number 2. What allocation should they choose?

(A) R
(B) W
(C) X
(D) Y
(E) Z

458. Refer to Figure 14.4. Which of the following is plausible reason that a country would choose allocation W instead of allocation X?

    I. Consumption bundle X may provide a standard of living below subsistence level.

    II. Consumption bundle X may cause political instability.

    III. The population is shrinking.

    (A) I only
    (B) II only
    (C) III only
    (D) I and II only
    (E) I, II, and III

459. The term *human capital* refers to

    (A) the machinery used per worker
    (B) the effective amount of labor that exists
    (C) the population of a nation
    (D) the total amount of population plus machinery
    (E) the total amount of population plus machinery plus natural resources

460. All else equal, nation X with _____ will have _____ growth rates than nation Z.

    (A) higher investment taxes; faster
    (B) higher literacy rates; slower
    (C) greater environmental pollution; faster
    (D) better technology; slower
    (E) better transportation and communication infrastructure; faster

CHAPTER 15

Balance of Payments and Foreign Exchange

461. A country's official record of the payments between themselves and other countries is known as that country's

(A) trade account
(B) monetary account
(C) balance of payments account
(D) currency account
(E) tariff account

462. A nation has a trade surplus in goods and services if

(A) the value of exports to other nations exceeds the value of imports from other nations
(B) the number of goods exported to other nations exceeds the number of goods imported from other nations
(C) the value of exports to other nations is less than the value of imports from other nations
(D) the number of goods exported to other nations is less than the number of goods imported from other nations
(E) the value of exports to other nations is equal to the value of imports from other nations

463. When a nation is said to have a negative trade balance, it means that the nation has

(A) a budget deficit
(B) a trade deficit
(C) exported more goods and services than they have imported
(D) exported the same quantity of goods and services as they have imported
(E) a trade surplus

464. Which of the following transactions would be recorded as a positive entry into Canada's current account?

(A) A Canadian resident buys a coat made in Honduras.
(B) A bank in New York City buys real estate in Toronto.
(C) A Canadian publisher pays an author in London for her book of short stories.
(D) A Canadian firm sells a coat to a consumer in Europe.
(E) The Canadian government sells bonds to a bank in Japan.

465. Jerry sells his Texas beef to a restaurant in Mexico. In the US balance of payments, in which account is this transaction recorded, and is it an addition or a subtraction?

	US Balance of Payment?	Addition or Subtraction?
(A)	Current account	Subtraction
(B)	Domestic account	Subtraction
(C)	Financial account	Addition
(D)	Financial account	Subtraction
(E)	Current account	Addition

466. Sherman sells his chain of Texas Beefhouse restaurants to a corporation in Mexico. In the US balance of payments, in which account is this transaction recorded, and is it an addition or a subtraction?

	US Balance of Payment?	Addition or Subtraction?
(A)	Current account	Subtraction
(B)	Factor income account	Subtraction
(C)	Financial account	Addition
(D)	Financial account	Subtraction
(E)	Current account	Addition

467. Which of the following transactions would be recorded as a negative entry into Japan's financial account?

(A) A Canadian resident buys a car made in Japan.
(B) A bank in New York City buys real estate in Tokyo.
(C) A Japanese filmmaker pays a writer in the United States for her screenplay.
(D) A Canadian firm sells a book to a consumer in Japan.
(E) The Canadian government sells bonds to a bank in Japan.

468. Suppose that the interest rate in the United States market for loanable funds is 5% and the interest rate in Britain's market for loanable funds is 7%. What do we expect to happen to the flow of financial capital?

(A) Financial capital will flow out of Britain and into the United States, raising interest rates in Britain and lowering interest rates in the United States.

(B) Financial capital will flow out of Britain and into the United States, raising interest rates in the United States and lowering interest rates in Britain.

(C) Financial capital will flow out of the United States and into Britain, raising interest rates in Britain and lowering interest rates in the United States.

(D) Financial capital will flow out of the United States and into Britain, lowering interest rates in Britain and raising interest rates in the United States.

(E) Financial capital will flow out of Britain and into the United States, raising interest rates in Britain and raising interest rates in the United States.

469. Suppose that the interest rate in the US market for loanable funds is 6% and the interest rate in Japan's market for loanable funds is 4%. What do we expect to happen to the flow of financial capital in US financial markets, Japanese financial markets, and the interest rate in each market?

	Flow of Financial Capital in the United States	Effect on Interest Rates in the United States	Flow of Financial Capital in Japan	Effect on Interest Rates in Japan
(A)	Outflow	Decrease	Inflow	Decrease
(B)	Outflow	Decrease	Inflow	Increase
(C)	Inflow	Increase	Inflow	Decrease
(D)	Inflow	Decrease	Outflow	Increase
(E)	Outflow	Increase	Inflow	Increase

470. Which of the following would cause an increase in the demand for US dollars?

(A) Interest rates in the United States are low relative to other countries.

(B) The United States raises tariffs on imported products.

(C) Trading partners raise tariffs on US-made products.

(D) The inflation rate in the United States is low relative to other countries.

(E) Products made in the United States become less popular and trendy.

471. If the demand for Japanese products becomes more popular and fashionable outside of Japan, this causes _____ in the _____ curve for the Japanese yen.

(A) a decrease; demand
(B) a decrease; supply
(C) an increase; demand
(D) no impact on; demand
(E) an increase; supply

472. Suppose that reduced government borrowing on behalf of the Icelandic government decreases interest rates on bonds issued by Iceland. All else equal, how will this affect the Icelandic currency, the króna?

(A) The demand decreases.
(B) The supply decreases.
(C) The supply increases.
(D) The supply decreases and demand decreases.
(E) The demand increases.

473. The next soccer World Cup is being held in Brazil, and thousands of tourists will travel to Brazil to see the soccer matches. How will this huge event affect the Brazilian currency, the Brazilian real?

(A) The demand increases and supply decreases.
(B) The demand increases.
(C) The supply increases.
(D) The demand decreases.
(E) The supply decreases.

474. When an American tourist travels to Europe, she must exchange her dollars for euros. This causes _____ in the supply of dollars and _____ in the demand for euros.

(A) an increase; an increase
(B) a decrease; a decrease
(C) no change; an increase
(D) an increase; a decrease
(E) a decrease; an increase

475. When a Japanese firm buys American-made clothing, which of the following occurs in the market for the Japanese yen?

(A) The demand increases.
(B) The supply decreases.
(C) The supply increases.
(D) Both the supply and demand increase.
(E) The demand decreases.

476. Suppose that a recession in Europe reduces European travel and tourism to the United States. All else equal, how will this affect the market for the euro?

(A) The demand increases.
(B) The supply decreases.
(C) The supply increases.
(D) The demand decreases.
(E) Both the supply and demand decrease.

477. When the Chinese government purchases bonds issued by the United States government, all else equal, how will this affect the market for the US dollar and the market for the Chinese yuan?

	Market for the Dollar	**Market for the Yuan**
(A)	No change	Supply increases
(B)	Demand increases	No change
(C)	Demand increases	Demand decreases
(D)	Demand increases	Supply increases
(E)	Demand decreases	Supply decreases

478. If a foreign exchange student from France exchanges his 50 euros for 30 US dollars, the exchange rate would be described as

(A) 1 euro = $3
(B) $1 = 0.60 euro
(C) 1 euro = $0.30
(D) $1 = 1.20 euro
(E) 1 euro = $0.60

479. Suppose the official exchange rate between the euro and the US dollar is that $1 can be exchanged for 0.50 euro. If an American is traveling in Germany and sees a hotel room for 75 euro, how many US dollars will this cost him?

(A) $37.50
(B) $75
(C) $50
(D) $150
(E) $125

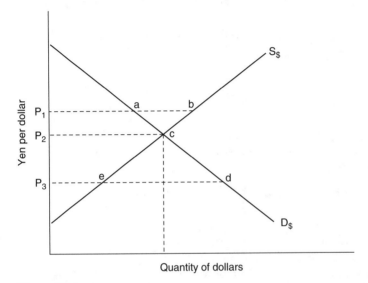

Figure 15.1

480. Figure 15.1 shows the foreign exchange market between the Japanese yen and the US dollar. The price P_2 represents

(A) how many yen it takes to buy $1
(B) how many dollars it takes to buy 1 yen
(C) the dollar price of a yen
(D) the quantity of yen you would receive in exchange for $1
(E) the nominal interest rate between the yen and the dollar

481. Figure 15.1 shows the foreign exchange market between the Japanese yen and the US dollar. If the exchange market for the dollar was currently at P_3

(A) a surplus of dollars exists and the price of a dollar must fall
(B) a shortage of dollars exists and the price of a dollar must fall
(C) a shortage of dollars exists and the price of a dollar must rise
(D) a surplus of dollars exists and the price of a dollar must rise
(E) the market for dollars is in equilibrium

482. Figure 15.1 shows the foreign exchange market between the Japanese yen and the US dollar. If the market moves from point c to point a, we can say that

(A) the dollar has depreciated and the yen has depreciated
(B) the dollar has appreciated and the yen has depreciated
(C) the dollar has appreciated and the yen has appreciated
(D) the dollar has depreciated and the yen has appreciated
(E) the dollar has appreciated and the yen has not changed in value

483. Figure 15.1 shows the foreign exchange market between the Japanese yen and the US dollar. If the market moves from point c to point e, we can say that

(A) the dollar has depreciated and the yen has depreciated
(B) the dollar has appreciated and the yen has depreciated
(C) the dollar has appreciated and the yen has appreciated
(D) the dollar has depreciated and the yen has appreciated
(E) the dollar has appreciated and the yen has not changed in value

484. Suppose that European products become more popular and fashionable to consumers in Canada. How will this affect the value of the European euro and the Canadian dollar?

(A) There will be no impact on either currency.
(B) The euro will appreciate, but there will be no impact on the dollar.
(C) The euro will appreciate, and the dollar will depreciate.
(D) The dollar will depreciate, but there will be no impact on the euro.
(E) The euro will depreciate, and the dollar will appreciate.

485. Suppose that a recession in the United States reduces imports from Mexico. How will this affect the value of the US dollar and the Mexican peso?

(A) The dollar will depreciate, but there will be no impact on the peso.

(B) The peso will appreciate, but there will be no impact on the dollar.

(C) The peso will appreciate, and the dollar will depreciate.

(D) There will be no impact on either currency.

(E) The peso will depreciate, and the dollar will appreciate.

486. The exchange rate between the US dollar and the Mexican peso is currently $1 = 10 pesos. On June 1, a travel agent tells his American client Stan that he can pay 1,200 pesos for a hotel room in Mexico City. On July 1 Stan arrives in Mexico City but discovers that the exchange rate has changed and now $1 = 12 pesos. What has happened to the dollar price that Stan pays for the hotel room?

(A) The price has fallen from $120 to $100.

(B) The price has risen from $100 to $120.

(C) The price has not changed.

(D) The price has fallen from $1,200 to $1,000.

(E) The price has risen from $10 to $12.

487. Suppose that fear of political instability in Russia has decreased the number of European tourists that travel to Russia. How will this affect the value of the Russian ruble and the European euro?

(A) The euro will depreciate, and the ruble will appreciate.

(B) The euro will appreciate, and the ruble will depreciate.

(C) The euro will appreciate, but there will be no impact on the ruble.

(D) The ruble will depreciate, but there will be no impact on the euro.

(E) There will be no impact on either currency.

488. If net exports in the United States begin to decrease, all else equal we should expect to see

(A) less foreign currency flowing into the United States with no impact on the value of the US dollar

(B) less foreign currency flowing into the United States, appreciating the value of the US dollar

(C) less foreign currency flowing into the United States, depreciating the value of the US dollar

(D) more foreign currency flowing into the United States, appreciating the value of the US dollar

(E) more foreign currency flowing into the United States, depreciating the value of the US dollar

489. Which of the following statements accurately describes the relationship between the value of the dollar and net exports in the United States?

    I. When the value of the dollar is low in currency markets, foreign consumers will increase imports from the United States, increasing net exports in the US economy.

    II. When the value of the dollar is high in currency markets, American consumers will increase imports into the United States, decreasing net exports in the US economy.

    III. If the United States has a growing trade deficit in goods and services, we expect that the value of the US dollar will be falling in currency markets.

(A) I only
(B) II only
(C) III only
(D) I and II only
(E) I, II, and III

490. Suppose we observe that Canadian banks and financial institutions are receiving a growing number of deposits of foreign currency from foreign investors. All else equal, this should

(A) depreciate the Canadian dollar relative to foreign currencies
(B) decrease the positive balance on the financial account in Canada
(C) decrease the quantity of foreign currencies held in Canadian banks
(D) appreciate the Canadian dollar relative to foreign currencies
(E) increase the positive balance on the current account in Canada

491. You hear on the news that the trade deficit the United States has with Mexico is widening. This news means that, all else equal

(A) the US dollar is depreciating against the Mexican peso
(B) there is no change in the value of the US dollar relative to the Mexican peso
(C) the US dollar is appreciating against the Mexican peso
(D) the US dollar and Mexican peso are both appreciating
(E) the US dollar and Mexican peso are both depreciating

492. The central bank of Portlandia has increased the money supply to fight a recession. How will this affect the flow of financial capital into Portlandia, and how will it affect the value of Portlandia's currency on the foreign exchange market?

	Inflow of Financial Capital	**Value of Currency**
(A)	No change	No change
(B)	Decrease	Depreciation
(C)	Increase	Appreciation
(D)	Decrease	Appreciation
(E)	Increase	Depreciation

493. The central bank of Portlandia has decreased the money supply to fight inflation. How will this affect the flow of financial capital into Portlandia, and how will it affect the value of Portlandia's currency on the foreign exchange market?

	Inflow of Financial Capital	**Value of Currency**
(A)	No change	No change
(B)	Decrease	Depreciation
(C)	Increase	Appreciation
(D)	Decrease	Appreciation
(E)	Increase	Depreciation

494. If the government budget deficit gets larger and is financed with extensive amounts of borrowing, how will this affect the value of the domestic currency and the size of domestic net exports?

	Value of Domestic Currency	**Domestic Net Exports**
(A)	Depreciation	Increase
(B)	Depreciation	Decrease
(C)	Appreciation	No change
(D)	Appreciation	Decrease
(E)	No change	Increase

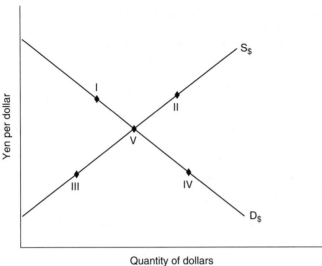

Figure 15.2

495. Figure 15.2 shows the market for the US dollar, priced in yen per dollar.
If the Federal Reserve were to purchase billions of dollars in US Treasuries
in an open market operation, at what point on the graph would the
exchange rate be?

(A) Point V
(B) Point I
(C) Point III
(D) Point IV
(E) Point II

496. Figure 15.2 shows the market for the US dollar, priced in yen per dollar.
If the Federal Reserve were to sell billions of dollars in US Treasuries in an
open market operation, at what point on the graph would the exchange
rate be?

(A) Point V
(B) Point I
(C) Point III
(D) Point IV
(E) Point II

497. Suppose that Argentina is experiencing hyperinflation of 100% per year and Brazil, a neighboring trade partner, is experiencing inflation of 5% per year. How will this affect the flow of goods and services between the two nations and the exchange rate between the Argentine peso and Brazilian real?

(A) Net exports in Brazil will rise, and the real will appreciate against the peso.

(B) Net exports in Argentina will rise, and the peso will depreciate against the real.

(C) There will be no effect on the exchange rate between the real and peso, but Argentina's net exports will fall.

(D) Net exports in Brazil will fall, and the real will depreciate against the peso.

(E) Net exports in Argentina will fall, and the peso will appreciate against the real.

498. A country that pursues a contractionary monetary policy will most likely experience

(A) an increase in the level of investment spending

(B) an increase in the demand for its currency in foreign exchange markets

(C) a decrease in domestic interest rates

(D) an increase in the supply of its currency in foreign exchange markets

(E) a depreciation of the currency in foreign exchange markets

499. All else equal, if the US dollar appreciates against the Indian rupee,

(A) goods made in the United States will look less expensive to Indian consumers

(B) goods made in India will look more expensive to American consumers

(C) physical capital investments in the United States will look less attractive to Indian firms

(D) goods made in India will look less expensive to American consumers

(E) physical capital investments in India will look less attractive to American firms

500. The _____ market is where currencies from different nations are traded.

(A) bond
(B) real estate
(C) foreign exchange
(D) stock
(E) investment

ANSWERS

Chapter 1: Basic Economic Concepts

1. (D) Economics is the study of how individuals, households, firms, and entire societies choose to allocate scarce resources. Societies face unlimited wants, but because resources are scarce, decisions must be made on how to best allocate them. Resources might be allocated in markets, by using prices, or by a central planning agency in the government. Therefore, all choices besides choice D represent aspects of the study of economics, but not the definition of the field itself. Selecting a choice other than D, therefore, implies that this aspect, and none of the others, are economic concepts.

2. (E) The United States has a system that is largely market based, but a significant portion of the economy is public. Therefore, while the United States in general has a free enterprise system, the economic system is, overall, a mix of public and private. For instance, while most healthcare decisions are made in the free market, we also have government-run programs such as Medicare in which allocation decisions are made.

3. (C) Normative analysis, sometimes called normative economics, is prescriptive. It says what should happen and is a recommendation for what should happen. In the same way that social norms dictate how people should behave, normative analysis describes, from the describer's point of view, the way things should be. Examples of normative statements might include "we should promote lower taxes" or "we should promote higher taxes." On the other hand, positive analysis, sometimes called positive economics, is descriptive. It says how things are or how the economy actually works rather than how it should work. An example of a positive economic statement would be something like "An increase in income will result in more goods being purchased," or "An increase in the price of a good will lead to higher profits for a firm."

4. (B) The characteristics of a free market economy are that prices allocate resources in a market setting with minimal government intervention and established property rights. In a centrally planned system, resources are allocated by a central planning authority (usually a government), which decides both what and how much is produced, as well as who enjoys the production and how much of the production each entity in the economy is entitled to have. Prices in a centrally planned economy, because they are set, will contain much less information about the cost of a good to produce and the value of a good to buyers.

5. (A) Microeconomics is a combination of *micro*, meaning "small," and *economics*. Therefore, microeconomics is "small" decision making about how to allocate scarce resources. So microeconomics focuses on economic decision making of households, firms, and individuals. The other options reflect questions that may arise in the study of macroeconomics, which focuses on problems and questions that face an economy as a whole.

6. (A) Macroeconomics is a combination of *macro*, meaning "large," and *economics*. There-fore, macroeconomics is "large" decision making, not on how individuals choose to allocate scarce resources, but on how these resources are allocated for an economy as a whole. All of the other choices reflect problems that a microeconomist would consider. Macroeconomics tends to be concerned with issues such as unemployment in a society, rather than at an indi-vidual level. Other macroeconomics issues include aggregate production in an economy (as opposed to production of a firm or a single industry) and an increase in the general price level (as opposed to an increase in a single price).

7. (B) In economics, the term *scarcity* refers to the fact that all of the economic resources (land, labor, capital, and entrepreneurial ability) are limited. Scarcity is an important concept because if it were not for scarcity, economics would not be a particularly important field of study. If society was faced with unlimited wants, but also had unlimited resources, we could satisfy the unlimited wants without having to make trade-offs.

8. (C) A normative statement is prescriptive, describing what should be done, as opposed to a positive statement, which describes the way things are. It is often said that a positive state-ment describes a fact rather than an opinion. A positive statement can also include a testable hypothesis such as "If gas prices continue to rise, we may see higher unemployment." When evaluating whether a statement is normative or positive, look for the presence of a value judg-ment (explicit or implied) of whether something is "good" or "bad." When people say that "taxes should be lowered" they are telling you that, in their judgment, taxes are currently too high. This is almost always a giveaway that the statement is normative.

9. (E) In going from a centrally planned economy to a market-based economy, Kittyania is moving from a centralized rationing system to a decentralized rationing system that will rely on prices. Scarcity still exists, so some sort of rationing function is still necessary to allocate scarce resources. In moving to a market economy, Kittyania will need to shift to freedom of individuals to acquire resources to produce goods and services and to choose which of their resources to sell to others. The nation will also need to embrace the private ownership of those resources, an economy driven by self-interest, competition, and prices for goods that are determined by markets, with no (or minimal) government intervention.

10. (D) Labor is one of the four factors of production, that is, the four resources that are combined to create goods and services in an economy. Labor refers not just to the actual quantity of labor, but also to the skills (such as literacy) that workers possess. Despite the fact that these skills are sometimes called human capital, they are counted in labor, not capital.

11. (B) The four resources are land (usually abbreviated lowercase l), labor (L, which includes not only the physical units of labor but the skills that workers possess), physical capital (K, such as equipment, factories, and tools), and entrepreneurial ability (which has various abbreviations). Contrary to the assumptions of many students, money is not an economic resource. Money is merely a tool that is used to facilitate the exchange of resources, goods, and services.

12. (B) Included under the category of capital are the things that are produced that are used to produce other goods, such as bowls, ovens, oven mitts, and so on. Natural resources include things such as actual land, energy, the production of the land (primary products such as agriculture such as wheat), and minerals. The work of the person mixing the dough would be considered labor, since it is the work of a person.

13. (A) Opportunity cost of an action is the sum of the explicit (or out-of-pocket) costs of that action and also the value of the next best alternative. Implicit opportunity costs are different from explicit costs such as tuition or books. If she goes to art school, she will not be able to work at all, or at a minimum she will not be able to work as much as when she is not in school. Therefore, the income that she will lose when she goes to school would be considered an opportunity cost. Additionally, while borrowing money may have a cost, any limitation on the dollar amount she can borrow is not in itself a cost (although it is a constraint).

14. (D) Opportunity cost of an action is the value of all that must be given up to take that action. If there are no direct out-of-pocket costs, we still must consider the cost of the single next-best alternative. For instance, suppose you have the choice of working as a babysitter at $8 per hour, restaurant cashier at $9 per hour, landscaper at $10 per hour, or dog walker at $11 per hour. The opportunity cost of being a dog walker is $10, because the next-best alternative is being a landscaper.

15. (A) Since all projects have the same cost, the opportunity cost is the cost of the next best alternative, and the next best alternative to building roads, which earns $120,000,000, is building a university, which earns $110,000,000. Note that it would not be correct to add up all of the next best alternatives, because it is not possible to do both of them. It would also be incorrect to subtract the value of the next best alternative, which in this case would yield $10,000,000 opportunity cost.

16. (E) The economy is producing at an efficient level when it produces at point B, meaning that it is currently using all of its resources to produce this combination of cars and hamburgers. It cannot make more of one good without reducing the amount of the other good that it produces. In order to produce more hamburgers, as the move from point B to point C reflects, the economy must give up producing some cars (which this movement also reflects).

17. (C) Point D is on a production possibilities frontier (PPF) that has rotated outward. Notice that even after this rotation of the PPF, if this country devotes all of its resources to producing cars, the amount of cars it can make doesn't change, but if it devotes all of its resources to producing hamburgers, it can now produce more hamburgers. Therefore, this rotation must have occurred because it now has more economic resources, or better technology, used in the production of hamburgers.

18. (B) Productive efficiency is producing at a point that is on the production possibilities frontier (PPF), meaning that all resources are being put to their best productive use. Allocative efficiency is when the combination of production that is occurring is the amount that an economy would best like. On any given production possibilities curve, only one point is allocatively efficient. Without more information about the nation's preferences for cars and hamburgers, we cannot tell if any of these points are allocatively efficient. However, since B, C, and D are all on the same PPF, we can tell that for an economy that has that PPF, all three of these points would be productively efficient.

19. (D) Allocative efficiency is when a particular combination of goods maximizes welfare, whereas productive efficiency is when a combination of goods produced does not leave resources idle. In other words, productive efficiency implies that there is no waste, but it doesn't necessarily mean that a combination of goods that is productively efficient is the combination that would maximize the well-being of an economy. To be allocatively efficient, the combination must be where the marginal cost equals the marginal benefit. Since there are only two goods, if the economy is allocatively efficient in the production of hamburgers, it is also allocatively efficient in the production of cars.

20. (B) Economic growth is an increase in the possibility of making more goods and services. In other words, an economy must have more of one of the four resources (land, labor, capital, or entrepreneurial ability). Graphically, this is represented on a production possibilities frontier (PPF) as a shift out of the PPF, which only occurs from point G to point B in the options listed. While it might be tempting to say that moving from point F to G is economic growth, it is not. An economy producing at point F may have exactly the same resources as an economy producing at point G (or even points B, C or D). The economy that is producing at point F is simply not using those resources efficiently.

21. (A) Comparative advantage is having the lower opportunity cost of producing a good. So to solve this, we need to find out what the opportunity cost for each good is for each producer. For Crabtown, they can use all of their resources to produce 15 boats (B) or 10 hush puppies (H), so mathematically resources = 15B or resources = 10H, which we can rearrange to get 15B = 10H. Solving for B gets B = ⅔H and solving for H gets 1½B = H, so a boat equals ⅔ of a hush puppy and a hush puppy equals 1½ boats. For Lobstertown, 15B = 5H, so B = ⅓H and 3B = H. Since Lobstertown gives up fewer hush puppies for each boat, Lobstertown has comparative advantage in producing boats. Crabtown gives up fewer boats to produce hush puppies, so Crabtown has comparative advantage in producing hush puppies.

22. (D) Absolute advantage is the ability to produce more goods given the same resources. In this case, the only resource we know of is a single day. In a single day Crabtown can produce 10 hush puppies if they devote all of their resources to producing hush puppies, but Lobstertown can only produce 5 hush puppies if it does the same. Therefore, Crabtown has absolute advantage in producing hush puppies. Similarly, if Lobstertown devotes all of its resources to making boats, it can produce 15 boats; but if Crabtown does the same, it can produce only 12.

23. (B) If Rachel uses all of her resources to produce coffee, she can produce 16 cups. Since Anitha can produce only a maximum of 10 cups of coffee, Rachel has absolute advantage in coffee production. For every additional bagel that Anitha produces, she must give up ¼ cup of coffee. For every additional bagel that Rachel produces, she must give up ½ cup of coffee. This tells us that Anitha has the comparative advantage in bagel production.

24. (D) Any level of production that lies on Rachel's production possibility frontier (PPF) would be an efficient level of production. The first choice, 16 cups of coffee and 0 bagels clearly lies on her PPF. According to Figure 1.2, Rachel's production possibilities could be described as 16C = 32B. Solving for C and B, we get C = 2B and ½C = B, so every time she makes a bagel, she gives up ½ cup coffee. If she moved from making 16 cups of coffee to 13, she would give up 3 cups of coffee and get 6 bagels (3 × C = 3 × 2B, so 3C = 6B), so the second choice is also efficient. However, if she gave up one more cup of coffee, she would not gain 6 more bagels (she would only gain 2), so the third choice is unattainable.

25. (B) To find Rachel's opportunity cost of making bagels, we can use the information given in Figure 1.2. If she devoted all of her resources to making coffee, she will make 16 cups of coffee, so $16C$ = resources. If she devoted all of her resources to making bagels, she would make 32 bagels, so $32B$ = resources. Putting this together, we get $16C = 32B$. We then solve for B to get her opportunity cost of making bagels, which yields $\frac{1}{2}C = B$. Therefore, her opportunity cost of a bagel is ½ cup coffee.

26. (D) For Rachel and Anitha to be willing to trade, the trading price must lie between both of their opportunity costs. For Rachel, $16C = 32B$, so $C = 2B$ and $\frac{1}{2}C = B$. For Anitha, $10C = 40B$, so $C = 4B$ and $\frac{1}{4}C = B$. Therefore, any trading price for a bagel would have to be between ½ and ¼ cup coffee.

27. (D) If Anitha splits her time between making coffee and bagels, then she can produce 5 cups of coffee and 20 bagels. If Rachel splits her time, then she can produce 8 cups of coffee and 16 bagels. Rachel has the comparative advantage in producing coffee (her opportunity cost is $C = 2B$), and Anitha has the comparative advantage in producing bagels (his opportunity cost is $C = 4B$). If they each specialized, Rachel would have 16 cups of coffee and Anitha 40 bagels before trade. A trade price of $\frac{5}{16}$ cup coffee for a bagel would be between ½ and ¼ cup coffee, and both would be willing to trade. Rachel could sell 5 cups of coffee and get 16 bagels for that, leaving her with 11 cups of coffee and 16 bagels. Anitha would then have 5 cups of coffee, which she sold 16 bagels to get, leaving her with 5 cups of coffee and 24 bagels. Both are better off as a result of specializing and trading.

28. (A) This question is asking you to find the opportunity cost of coffee for Anitha. In a single day, she can produce either 10 cups of coffee or 40 bagels, so $10C = 40B$. Solving for coffee yields $C = 4B$. Therefore, every time she gives up a cup of coffee, she gives up making 4 bagels.

29. (E) If Anitha is consuming 10 cups of coffee, there is no way that she could also produce 4 bagels according to the production possibilities in Figure 1.2. If she became better at producing only bagels, then the only way she could still consume 10 cups of coffee is if she spent all of her time producing coffee, so I is not a correct choice. However, if she improved at producing both goods, her production possibilities frontier could shift out and she could consume that amount. Alternatively, the other way to consume at a point beyond her production possibilities is to specialize and trade with Rachel.

30. (E) If Oscar was being efficient, then he could not produce more of a good without giving up some of the other good. So if he was efficient on Monday and made 3 loaves of bread and 18 cupcakes, he would not be able to somehow make 4 loaves of bread and 18 cupcakes using the same resources. However, on Tuesday, Oscar could make 18 cupcakes and was still able to make an additional loaf of bread. Therefore, his production possibilities frontier has either shifted (due to more resources) or rotated out.

31. (A) Here we are given two points on a linear production possibilities frontier. We can use this to determine that every time Max goes to 2 meetings, he gives up editing 5 papers. So if he is going to 6 meetings and can edit 5 papers, a movement to 7 meetings implies that he will be able to edit 0 papers. After that point there is nothing more to give up, so II is incorrect. Similarly, if he goes from 4 meetings to 3 meetings, he will be able to edit 12.5 papers, so III would be inefficient. Max's opportunity cost indicates when he goes to 2 meetings, he gives up editing 5 papers. So if Patti will exchange 6 papers for 2 meetings, he would be better off.

32. (A) Elmo has comparative advantage in producing quiches because his opportunity cost of a quiche is only ⅓ of a pasta bake, as opposed to the ½ pasta bake that Zoe gives up every time she bakes a quiche. Zoe has comparative advantage in producing pasta bakes because she gives up only 2 quiches for each pasta bake, but Elmo gives up 5 quiches for each pasta bake he makes. When two agents specialize and trade, they will be willing to trade if the trading price lies between the opportunity costs for the two traders. If Zoe produces 5 pasta bakes and trades 2 of those pasta bakes, she will in return get 8 quiches, leaving her with 3 pasta bakes and 8 quiches. This combination of goods is outside of her production possibilities with trade (it might help to draw her PPF). Likewise, if Elmo produces 15 quiches and trades 8 of those for 2 pasta bakes, he is left with 2 pasta bakes and 7 quiches, which is also outside of his original production possibilities.

33. (D) Jane and Clark won't agree to trade unless the trading price makes them at least better off than they would be without trading. Suppose Clark currently uses ⅓ of his land to produce cotton and the rest to produce lumber, which yields him 40 bales of cotton and 53⅓ tons of lumber, and Jane splits her land between cotton and lumber, which gives her 50 bales of cotton and 25 tons of lumber. If they specialize in what they have comparative advantage in, Jane produces 100 bales of cotton and Clark produces 80 tons lumber. At a trading price of ⅝ of a ton of lumber for each bale of cotton, Jane can trade 50 of those bales for 31¼ tons of lumber (50 × ⅝ = 31¼), so she now has 50 bales of cotton and 31¼ tons of lumber, leaving her better off. Clark now has 50 bales of cotton and 48¾ tons of lumber. Therefore, since the trading price was between the opportunity costs for the two traders, both are left better off and would be willing to specialize and trade.

Chapter 2: Supply and Demand

34. (B) A larger population results in more consumers buying a good. The number of consumers in the market is a demand determinant, or factor that will shift demand curves to the right or left. Simply having more bodies will increase the demand for goods like cookies. On the other hand, a decrease in the price of cookies will increase the quantity demanded of cookies (a movement along the demand curve), but would not increase demand (a shift of the entire demand curve). If glasses of milk are a complement to cookies, and if the price of milk increases, the demand for cookies will decrease. If the price of crackers, a substitute for cookies, goes down, then the demand for cookies will decrease.

35. (D) If the price of hotel rooms, a complement for air travel, decreases, then the demand for airplane tickets would increase. If a product, like air travel, is deemed to be unsafe, consumers will have a weaker preference for the product, thus shifting the demand for it to the left. The price of jet fuel, an input into the production of air travel, would affect supply. If the price of an airplane ticket increases, the *quantity demanded* would decrease, rather than demand.

36. (A) A change in the price of regular milk will affect the demand for chocolate milk because regular milk is a substitute good for chocolate milk. A lower price of regular milk would increase the quantity of regular milk demanded. But it would shift the demand for chocolate milk to the left because at any given price of chocolate milk, it is now relatively more expensive than regular milk. A determinant of demand is a factor that will fundamentally affect (shift) the demand curve. A change in the price results in a movement along the fixed demand curve, not a shift of the curve. This is a distinction that, if you're not careful, can often result in points being lost on an exam. Choices C, D, and E are all determinants of supply; they would shift the supply of chocolate milk, but not affect the demand for it.

37. (E) If we are told that fewer cartons of cigarettes are being purchased, regardless of what the price of cigarettes is, it is an indicator that the demand has decreased (or graphically, shifted to the left). If you draw a graph where a demand curve has shifted to the left, you can see that at every possible quantity, the price that consumers are willing and able to pay has decreased. A weaker taste or preference for these products, due to the successful educational efforts, would result in such a shift of demand. The cost of producing cigarettes and number of firms involved in selling cigarettes all are factors that would affect the supply curve, rather than the demand curve.

38. (B) A rightward shift in a demand curve indicates that consumers are willing or able to buy more of a good at any given price. In other words, the demand for good X has increased. A change in the technology used to produce good X, or the price of a production input, would cause a shift in the supply of good X rather than a shift in demand. A change in the price of good X would cause only a movement along the fixed demand curve, but a stronger preference of consumers would increase (or shift rightward) demand for the product. The determinants of demand are consumer income, the price of complements and substitutes, tastes and preferences, consumer expectations about price, and the number of consumers.

39. (C) A normal good is a good for which the demand will increase if incomes increase. This is the opposite of an inferior good, which is a good for which the demand will decrease if incomes increase. If pie is a normal good, then demand for it will increase with higher incomes and decrease with lower incomes. Demand for all normal goods moves in the same direction as income. A change in the price of sugar, an input to the production of pies, would change the supply of pies.

40. (D) Like demand curves, supply curves are also affected by external variables (the supply determinants) that shift the curve to the right or left. These supply determinants are costs of production, expectations, technology, the price that producers can get for other goods they can produce, and number of sellers. The supply of any good will increase if one of these determinants, such as the price of factors of production, decreases. When it becomes less costly to build a house, the supply of houses will shift to the right. This is because for any given quantity of houses, it will cost the producer less to make that quantity, and therefore, the producer would be willing to accept a lower price for that quantity.

41. (B) Production technology will affect (or shift) the supply curve. If producers acquire better technology, they can produce more of Z with the same amount of inputs. This translates into a supply curve that lies further to the right; more output is produced at any price. If there are fewer suppliers of good Z, the supply curve will shift to the left. Thus at any given price, the market supply will be lower when a supplier exits this market.

42. (E) Consumer income, tastes and preferences, the number of consumers, and consumer income expectations are all demand determinants but do not affect the supply curve, because supply and demand are independent of each other. The number of suppliers is a determinant of supply. If there are more producers of a good, this means that at any price, more units of that good will be supplied to the market.

43. (D) If producers can get a higher price, they will respond to the higher price by producing a higher quantity. Because recliners are selling at higher prices, the supplier will increase quantity of recliners supplied along the supply curve for recliners. This is the law of supply in action: responding to a higher price of a good by increasing the quantity supplied of that good. However, this new production plan would require a decrease in the supply of couches as firms reallocate resources away from the production of couches and toward a greater number of recliners. The price of an alternative product, the recliners, is a determinant in the supply of couches.

44. (C) If producers expect *future* car prices to be higher, they will reduce *current* supply of cars while they wait for those higher prices to occur. This would decrease supply (or shift the supply curve to the left). Better production technology shifts supply curves to the right. This is because better technology would allow the same quantity of production at a cheaper price (or looking at it slightly differently, a higher quantity of production at the same price), which would make a supplier willing to accept a lower price for any given quantity.

45. (A) There are two ways to look at a leftward shift in the supply curve for good W. If we hold quantity constant, such a shift means that at this constant quantity, suppliers must receive a higher price to bring this quantity to the market. Equivalently, if we hold price constant, a leftward shift means that at this constant price, suppliers will reduce the quantity that they supply to the market. Both interpretations are accurate and they are often used interchangeably by economists.

46. (E) Equilibrium occurs at the only price where the quantity demanded equals the quantity supplied. At this price all units that are produced by sellers are purchased by buyers. The term *equilibrium* refers to a state of balance, just as in physics it refers to the balance between opposing forces. Note that it is *not* where "supply equals demand." To say that "supply equals demand" is saying that these two opposing forces are the same. Graphically, that would mean the two curves were the same curve! Rather, equilibrium refers to a price that makes the *quantity supplied* equal to the *quantity demanded*.

47. (B) At prices below the equilibrium price, quantity demanded will exceed quantity supplied. For instance, if the market price were $3, then buyers would want to buy 4,000 pounds, but sellers would be willing to sell only 1,600 pounds at that price. When there are fewer units supplied than consumers wish to buy, a shortage (or excess demand) exists and it is equal to the difference between the quantity demanded and the quantity supplied.

48. (D) When given equations for supply and demand, we can solve for the equilibrium price and quantity by remembering what it means for a market to be in equilibrium: there is only one price where the quantity demanded is equal to the quantity supplied. This means that the price paid by buyers is equal to the price received by suppliers. Knowing this, we simply set these two equations equal to each other and solve for Q ($Q_d = Q_s$): $50 - Q = 10 + Q$ or $40 = 2Q$ and $Q = 20$. To find price, plug $Q = 20$ into either equation: $P = 50 - 20 = \$30$.

49. (A) When supply and demand are combined in a graph, the equilibrium point is found at the intersection of the supply curve and the demand curve. The quantity point on the demand curve that corresponds to a price of P_2 is Q_3. The quantity point on the supply curve that corresponds to a price of P_2 is Q_3. Thus at the price of P_2, quantity demanded is equal to quantity supplied at quantity Q_3.

50. (C) The price P_1 is above the equilibrium price of P_2 that brings the quantity supplied and quantity demanded into balance. This high price creates a surplus because the quantity demanded is less than the quantity supplied at that price: quantity demanded at P_1 is Q_1 and quantity supplied at P_1 is Q_5. The size of the surplus is equal to $Q_5 - Q_1$. When a surplus exists, there is pressure on the price to fall, as suppliers must clear this surplus.

51. (E) There is only one price in a market that is considered equilibrium: the price where quantity demanded equals quantity supplied ($Q_d = Q_s$). This is seen in a graph as the intersection of the supply curve and the demand curve. At this intersection not only are the quantities equal, but it is also true that the buyer's price is the same as the supplier's price.

52. (B) When a market is out of equilibrium, there is either a shortage of the good ($Q_d > Q_s$) or a surplus of the good ($Q_d < Q_s$). A shortage exists when the price is lower than equilibrium, and a surplus exists when the price is above equilibrium. Such a situation is not equilibrium, because the price will be fluctuating in response to the shortage (a rising price) or the surplus (a falling price). If the price is fluctuating, the market has still not reached equilibrium. Only when the quantity demanded equals the quantity supplied will there be no pressure on the price to change.

53. (A) If we start at a point where a market is in equilibrium, a decrease in demand will create a temporary surplus of cheese. This is because the new quantity demanded is less than the original quantity supplied at the original price. As the market adjusts to a new equilibrium, the price falls to eliminate the surplus and less cheese is exchanged in the market. Therefore, when demand curves decrease, price and quantity both decrease.

54. (D) If we start at a point where a market is in equilibrium, an increase in demand will create a temporary shortage of gasoline. This is because the new quantity demanded exceeds the original quantity supplied at the original price. This is due to the fact that when demand increases, people are willing to buy more of a good at any given price. As the market adjusts to a new equilibrium, the price rises to eliminate the shortage and more gasoline is exchanged in the market. Therefore, when demand curves increase, price and quantity both increase.

55. (B) If you know that both the price and quantity have increased in the tea market, it is most likely that the demand for tea has increased. An increase in demand places an upward pressure on both price and quantity. On the other hand, a change in supply will yield opposite effects on price and quantity (one will increase and one will decrease). If both supply and demand were changing at the same time, we would be able to tell whether either price or quantity had increased, but the effect on at least one of price or quantity would be ambiguous. When in doubt, draw a quick graph in the margin of your test book to see the impact of an increase in demand.

56. (C) Whenever you see a situation in which you can tell the effect on both price and quantity, you know for certain that only supply has changed or only demand has changed. Recall that whenever you see price and quantity moving in the same direction, be that both price and quantity are rising or both price and quantity are falling, you know that demand has to be changing. Price and quantity move in different directions when supply changes. In this case you know that both the price and quantity of lumber have decreased in the market for lumber. This is a clear sign that the demand for lumber has decreased.

57. (A) Knowing that the price of butter has fallen while the quantity has increased is a clear sign that supply has increased. First of all, if we know both a new price and quantity with no ambiguity, then we know for certain that only one curve has shifted. The change in quantity is always in the same direction as the change in supply, while the price moves in the opposite direction.

58. (D) We know that the price of carpet has increased and the quantity has decreased, so a new price and quantity are both known and the new price and quantity moved in different directions. A decrease in supply would cause these changes. Again, a quick sketch of the carpet market would confirm that decreased supply is the correct answer and the other choices are incorrect.

59. (B) Quantity always moves in the same direction as the change in supply, and because of this fact you can quickly focus on the choices that state the quantity of wine is going to increase. Because an increase in supply causes a surplus, and because a surplus is eliminated by falling prices, look for the choice that also includes a decreased price of wine.

60. (E) A rightward shift in the supply of houses creates a surplus of houses in the market. This occurs because at the original price of houses, the new quantity supplied exceeds the original quantity demanded. With a surplus of houses, home builders must lower the price to find willing buyers. Thus an increase in the supply of houses will produce more homes sold at lower prices.

61. (B) When both curves are shifting in a market, it is helpful to analyze each shift one at a time. A decrease in demand will decrease both the price and quantity of rental housing. An increase in supply will increase the quantity but will decrease the price. Therefore, we know for sure that price is going to decrease, but there are competing effects on the quantity of rental housing. The only thing we can say about the new quantity is that it is either uncertain or it would depend upon which effect (downward from demand versus upward from supply) is strongest. Since we cannot tell from the statement which effect is stronger, we must state that the effect on quantity is uncertain.

62. (C) When the demand for sugar increases, it will increase both the price and quantity of sugar. When the supply decreases, it will cause a smaller quantity but a higher price of sugar. Therefore, we know that the price of sugar will be higher, but there is an uncertain change in the new quantity of sugar. Because the two market forces, supply and demand, are exerting opposite and opposing forces on quantity, we cannot determine which side of the market will exert more force.

63. (A) When the demand for a good increases, both price and quantity will increase. When the supply of a good increases, the price will decrease and the quantity will increase. We can say for sure that the quantity is going to rise. The new price will increase if the demand shift is greater than the supply shift. The new price will decrease if the supply shift is stronger than the demand shift.

64. (D) Price floors are legal minimum prices that are set above the equilibrium price because the government has concluded that the equilibrium price is "too low." Sellers cannot sell the good at a price below the controlled price. For a price floor to be effective, it must therefore be set above equilibrium. When a legal minimum price is set above the equilibrium price, such a price is sometimes called a "binding price floor." If it is set below equilibrium, it would be ineffective because market forces would drive the price upward to equilibrium, which is sometimes called a "nonbinding price floor."

65. (E) Price ceilings are legal maximum prices that are set below the equilibrium price because the government has concluded that the equilibrium price is "too high." Sellers cannot sell the good at a price above the controlled price. For a price floor to be effective, it must therefore be set below equilibrium. If it is set above equilibrium, it would be ineffective because market forces would drive the price downward to equilibrium.

66. (C) This question requires several steps to find the correct answer. First, you must know that a price ceiling lies below equilibrium, so an effective price ceiling in this market would be d. Second, you must know that quantity demanded at this price (which would be h) exceeds quantity supplied at the controlled price (f), and this defines a shortage equal to the difference (h − f).

67. (B) This question requires you to understand several things about a price floor. First, you must know that an effective price floor lies above equilibrium, so in this market an effective price floor would be b. Second, you must know that quantity demanded at this price floor (in this case, e) is less than quantity supplied at the controlled price (in this case, r) and this defines a surplus. Finally, the size of the surplus is measured in units of output, and the difference between these defines a surplus equal to the difference (r − e).

68. (A) When a quota is imposed at a quantity below equilibrium, it drives a wedge between the maximum price buyers are willing to pay and the minimum price suppliers will accept. This difference is referred to as the quota rent, so called because it acts like a "bonus" to the price of the supplier. At the quantity of e units, buyers would pay $j for those units. However, suppliers only incur a marginal cost of $p, so this difference, or rent, goes to those suppliers who are allowed to produce.

69. (C) Price controls, like floors and ceilings, are restrictions on the price a supplier can charge for a good or service. A quantity control, or quota, restricts market output because the equilibrium is judged to be too great. Quotas can be seen in the market for fish or lumber if the harvest of those renewable resources is unsustainably high.

70. (D) A market quota restricts output below the equilibrium level. At a restricted output level, an artificial shortage is created and prices rise because consumers are willing to pay higher prices for goods that are in short supply. This is not efficient, as there are units of output for which a consumer's willingness to pay exceeds a supplier's marginal cost. This creates deadweight loss, as those transactions are not going to take place.

71. (B) A binding price floor is a price set above the equilibrium price. Because the price rises, sellers increase output supplied and consumers reduce the quantity of output demanded. The resulting excess supply of units in the market will not be eliminated by competitive pressures, the market equilibrium quantity will not be exchanged, and therefore deadweight loss exists. If we follow the logical reasoning, the higher the price floor, the further the actual level of output lies from the equilibrium output, and the larger the resulting deadweight loss.

72. (E) This question precisely describes what is happening in market equilibrium. The demand curve represents the consumer's maximum willingness to pay. The supply curve represents the producer's marginal cost or the minimum price the producer would accept. Units are bought and sold so long as the price is somewhere in between willingness to pay and marginal cost. When this happens, total surplus continues to rise. When the diminishing willingness to pay intersects in the increasing marginal cost, no more beneficial transactions can be made, total surplus is maximized, and allocative efficiency is achieved.

73. (E) The first statement is correct because price controls, be they floors or ceilings, reduce the number of transactions away from the equilibrium quantity. In both cases, not enough of the product is exchanged and the willingness to pay exceeds the marginal cost. The second statement is incorrect because if the market had been allowed to be in equilibrium, the price would have attracted the perfect amount of resources (labor, capital, land, and entrepreneurial ability) to produce the efficient quantity of output. The third statement is correct because quotas, like price controls, reduce the number of transactions below the efficient equilibrium quantity. Deadweight loss emerges whether the policy controls price or quantity.

Chapter 3: General Macroeconomic Issues

74. (C) The economy rises and falls over time as a result of many factors like economic policy, international events, and political decisions. Economists describe these fluctuations as the business cycle. When the economy is weakening, it is said that we are in a contraction or recession; the end of a contraction is called the trough of the cycle. When the economy is strengthening, we are going through an expansion; the end of an expansion is called the peak of the cycle. One full business cycle is measured from peak to peak or trough to trough.

75. (A) Prior to the Great Depression, it was commonly accepted that the economic business cycle was impervious to policy decisions. No matter what a government might choose to do, the natural expansion and contraction of the economy would keep moving forward over time. The pain of the Great Depression convinced many economists that there was certainly a role for a more activist approach to smoothing out the swings of the business cycle. John Maynard Keynes is one of the most well-known economists to take this position, and his prescriptive policies have come to be known as Keynesian economics.

76. (C) The business cycle is typically described in four stages: contraction, trough, expansion, and peak. If the level of economic activity is rising, the economy is improving, and we are in the expansion stage. When expansion ends at the peak, the economy is about to take a downturn into contraction. If this contraction is severe, it is a recession, and if it is prolonged, it is a depression. At the end of the contraction is the trough, and we are about to turn back into the expansion stage.

77. (B) The unemployment rate is inversely related to the strength of the economy. When the economy is strong, or in the expansion stage of the business cycle, jobs are plentiful and the unemployment rate falls. The unemployment rate, even when we are at the peak of the business cycle, will never be equal to zero, because there will always be people who are moving back and forth between jobs looking for better opportunities.

78. (D) As the economy moves through the business cycle, the unemployment rate moves in the opposite direction. When the economy is weakening, or going through the contraction stage, employers are reducing their hiring of labor, and the unemployment rate goes up. At the bottom of the business cycle, the trough, the unemployment rate is usually the highest.

79. (D) As the economy moves through the business cycle, household purchasing is moving in the same direction. When the economy is beginning to get stronger and moving into the expansion phase, households begin to increase their purchasing of goods and services. Firms begin seeing an increase in sales and a decline in inventories. This consumption begins to increase prices throughout the economy, so we begin to see more inflation as the economy is in expansion. At the peak of the business cycle, inflation should be at its highest point and is about to slow down as economic activity falls into the contraction phase.

80. (A) As the economy is moving through the business cycle, the inflation rate is moving in the same direction. When the economy is weakening, or going through the contraction stage, households are buying fewer goods and services, firms are finding inventories rising, and prices begin to fall. At the bottom of the business cycle, the trough, the state of economic activity is at its lowest and the inflation rate is usually lowest.

81. (B) National output, or GDP, is the broadest measure of economic activity. When the economy is expanding, GDP will be rising and rising at a faster rate. On the other hand, when the economy is contracting, GDP will be slowing down and perhaps even declining. At the bottom of the business cycle, the trough, economic activity is its weakest.

82. (C) Gross domestic product (GDP) is the measure of a nation's level of economic activity, and therefore, GDP rises and falls with the business cycle. During a recession, or contraction, households and firms reduce their spending and GDP falls. However, during a strong expansion, households and firms boost their spending, employers increase the quantity of labor hired, and GDP rises.

83. (A) Economic growth is a long-run phenomenon that describes more than just the short-term ups and downs of the business cycle. Consider the output of a restaurant. In the short run, the restaurant will see changes in daily output (number of meals served); some days they are extremely busy with lots of customers, and some days they are rather slow. In the day-to-day business of the restaurant, a busy day would not signify economic growth. However, if the restaurant was so busy that ownership needed to build a second restaurant to handle the many customers, the restaurant has now fundamentally increased its ability to produce output; this is growth.

84. (E) Points b and e both represent points in a contractionary phase of the short-term business cycle. Both points are also, however, on the long-term growth line (Line Z) for this economy. Even though both points describe a weakening economy in the short term, point e tells us that even in the midst of that recession the economy is still producing more output than a similar recession in the past. There has, therefore, been economic growth between point b and point e.

85. (B) The up-and-down movements represented by Curve Y are the short-term fluctuations in economic output of the nation's business cycle. However, we can see that Curve Y fluctuates around the long-term upward trend of Line Z. Line Z tells us that no matter the current stage of the business cycle, over time the nation is producing more economic output. This is the nature of growth.

86. (B) A recession is a prolonged contraction of economic output, so it is depicted as a downturn in the business cycle measured in length of time from a previous peak of economic activity to a trough. Once the economy begins to recover and the business cycle turns upward, the recession is officially over. While there is no strict definition, a recession is typically defined as at least two quarters (6 months) of declining output. The National Bureau of Economic Research (NBER) has determined that the average length of a recession since the end of World War II is 11 months.

87. (D) One full length of a business cycle is the time that it takes for a nation's economy to move from a peak to a peak or a trough to a trough. Therefore, one full business cycle includes all four stages: peak, contraction, trough, and expansion. The National Bureau of Economic Research (NBER) has determined that the average length of a business cycle from peak to peak since World War II is 66 months.

88. (C) An expansion in the business cycle is defined as the period between a trough and a peak in economic activity. The expansion describes a nation that was in a recession and is now beginning to employ idle resources and increase output. This is not the same as economic growth, which is more of a long-term picture of a nation's capacity for producing goods and services.

89. (E) All of these statements are correct. Economic growth is a long-term upward trend in a nation's productive capacity, while the business cycle represents the short-term recessions and recoveries of the macroeconomy. At any given point in time, the economy is somewhere in the short-term business cycle, which may be above or below the long-term path of growth.

Chapter 4: National Income Accounts

90. (C) A useful way to model the flow of money and goods throughout an economy is the circular-flow model, also known as the circular-flow diagram. In its simplest form, households spend money on goods and services produced by firms. That money is received by firms as revenue, and firms use that revenue to hire factors of production (labor, capital, land) from households. The hiring of factors means that money flows back to households as wage and interest income. The idea is very intuitive: any dollar spent by one person (or firm) is a dollar earned by another person (or firm).

91. (B) In the simplest version of the circular-flow diagram, households spend their money on goods and services in the product markets. These products are sold by firms who receive the household spending as revenue. To produce these goods and services, the firms need to hire labor, capital, and land in the factor markets. The households own these factors, so they end up selling the factors to the firms and receive wages, interest, and rent payments in return.

92. (D) A closed economy refers to an economy that has no foreign sector, so there are no imports and exports. Without a government presence, the only economic actors are the households and the firms. Households own the factors of production and sell those factors to the firms in the factor markets. The most common example is the labor market where households offer their labor supply to employers in exchange for money wages. The households take those wages and buy the goods and services produced by the firms and sold in the product markets.

93. (C) A monetary leakage from a nation's circular flow of spending is any kind of spending that leaves the economy. When the households of Portlandyburg purchase goods produced in other nations, those imported products come into the Portlandyburg economy but the money leaks out. The other choices given are examples of money that stays within the Portlandyburg economy and simply changes hands as transactions are made.

94. (E) A private closed economy is an economy without a government sector and that does not engage in foreign exchange. In the circular-flow diagram with no government and no foreign sector, a household has only two ways in which to use the income earned from the factor markets: consumption or savings. If the household decides to save money, those funds go into the banks of the financial markets. In this closed economy, money saved can only reenter the economy when the banks lend it to firms for investment projects; thus all funds that are saved end up being invested.

95. (A) One way to tabulate the amount of money that is being circulated throughout the economy is to add up all sources of income for the factors of production. In the factor markets, the labor resource earns wages, capital earns interest, land earns rent, and entrepreneurial ability earns profit. The sum of all sources of factor income in a nation is called national income.

96. (C) There are two common ways to compute the total value of economic activity in a nation, and the circular-flow diagram helps demonstrate this. The expenditure approach adds up all of the dollars that are spent on all goods and services. However, dollars that are spent in product markets must end up as income for factors in the factor markets. The income approach is therefore to sum up all of the income that is earned by the land, capital, labor, and entrepreneurial factors of production.

97. (B) The income approach tabulates all of the income paid to the factors of production in the nation's factor markets. Capital is paid interest income, land is paid a rental rate, and labor is paid wages. The leftover profit is paid to the entrepreneurial ability supplied to the factor markets.

98. (D) We refer to the factor income earned by labor in the labor markets as wages, or wages and salaries. These are the payments that firms make to households in exchange for supplying their labor. Firms also employ capital and land, and we call those payments interest and rent, respectively. If a firm also earns a profit, we allocate that source of income to the entrepreneurial talents employed by the owners of the firm.

99. (E) When the circular-flow model includes the government (the public sector), the government influences how much income households actually have to spend on goods and services. Households earn gross labor income from the labor markets and pay taxes to the government. However, some households receive transfer payments back from the government because they qualify for certain benefits (like veteran's benefits or food stamps). Once taxes are subtracted and transfers are added, the household is left with disposable income that they can save or spend.

100. (A) In the circular-flow diagram, all dollars earned by some factor of production are spent by some sector of the economy. There are four groups who can spend money on goods and services within the nation: domestic consumers, firms, the government, and foreign consumers. If we add up the value of all of this spending within the economy, we have computed the value of the goods and services that were produced within the economy.

101. (C) This equation quite simply tells us that the value of all things produced is equal to the value of the spending on those things that were produced. Domestic spending can come from consumers (C), firms (I), and the government (G). However, we must also consider the flow of dollars to and from other nations. When a foreign citizen buys a product made domestically, the domestic economy adds it as an export (X). However, when a domestic consumer buys a product made in another country, we must subtract that spending from the domestic economy as an import (M). When we subtract import spending from export spending, we are adding the final component of net exports (X − M). Note that occasionally (X − M) is shortened to NX, which stands for net exports (or the difference between exports and imports).

102. (B) When we compute the total value of the products made in the economy, it is important to note that we are adding up the value of the final goods, not the intermediate goods. An intermediate good is a product that requires further modifications before it reaches its final consumptive purpose. For example, suppose that a frozen cheese pizza is composed of three items: a crust, some sauce, and some cheese. The pizza company buys a crust for $2, some sauce for $0.50, and some cheese for $1 and produces a final product, the frozen cheese pizza, which it sells for $6 at the store. The pizza is worth only $6 as a contribution to a nation's GDP. If we added up all of the intermediate products, we would mistakenly believe that the pizza was worth $9.50 ($9.50 = $2 + $0.50 + $1 + $6). This form of double counting is avoided if we focus only on the final $6 value of the pizza.

103. (D) We know that total GDP is $10,000 and that GDP is the sum of consumption (C), investment (I), government spending (G), and net exports (X − M). If we use the information given, we can solve for the missing component of net exports. GDP = $10,000 = $7,000 + $1,500 + $2,500 + (X − M) = $11,000 + (X − M). It must be the case that net exports are −$1,000. Note that net exports can be negative: this occurs when imports exceed exports.

104. (E) There are two ways of solving this problem that give the same result: the expenditures approach and the income approach. The expenditures approach is to add up the spending: GDP = C + I + G + (X − M), and this is equal to $82. The income approach is to add up factor income: NI = wages + interest + rent + profit, and this is also equal to $82. Resist the temptation to add up all of the numbers, as you would be counting each dollar twice; once when it was spent and once when it was earned.

105. (E) An intermediate good is something that requires further processing or modification for it to serve its final purpose. The coal is not the final product because it must be transformed (burned) to generate the electricity and that electricity is the final product. Gasoline is also burned, but it is burned to drive you around town. As a final product, the gasoline has reached its final purpose.

106. (A) New construction, whether it is residential (like a house) or commercial (like a stadium), is considered investment spending. Investment spending also includes a firm's purchase of physical capital equipment like trucks, forklifts, computers, or photocopiers. Last, investment spending includes the value of any unsold product inventories that were produced in one year but not sold until the next.

107. (B) Ellie's enrollment at the university is consumption spending, as she is purchasing a service in those college courses. The state's purchase of police cars and the US Air Force's construction of a base are both examples of government spending (G). The farmer's construction of a barn is part of investment spending (I), and the Canadian purchase of Oklahoma-raised cattle is export spending (X).

108. (C) In the accounting of GDP, we want to sum up the value of all things produced. But what if it is produced and not yet sold? In this case, the value of the product (cans of chili) are counted as unsold inventory and added to 2011 investment spending. It may seem like an unusual way of handling things, but we know that the chili was produced, so it should count as part of national production. We also know that it was not consumed (yet), so it cannot rightly be counted as consumption spending.

109. (D) If a product, like a laptop computer, is bought by a private citizen (you), it is considered consumption spending. If it is bought by a local, state, or federal government (the US Department of Agriculture), it is considered government spending. In many cases, households and the government buy many similar things. However, in other cases, as with military weapons and weather satellites, the goods purchased by the government are quite different from those bought by private citizens.

110. (A) The tables were produced in the United States so they must be included in US GDP. Had they been purchased by a domestic furniture store and sold to domestic customers, they would be counted as consumption spending (C). Since they were purchased by Canadian consumers, they are counted as export spending (X). The tables were not produced in Canada, so the value of that consumption is subtracted from Canadian GDP as import spending (M).

111. (B) Gross domestic product (GDP) is the value of all goods and services produced in a nation. However, some items produced in a nation are actually not consumed in that nation; they are exported to other nations. Likewise, not all goods consumed in a nation were actually produced within that nation; they were imported from other countries. If we are trying to tabulate all of the production in a nation, we can add up all of the spending in a nation, but we must subtract any spending on goods that were imported from other nations.

112. (E) The American consumer who buys a truck produced in South Korea has purchased an imported product. The value of his spending on the imported truck is subtracted from US GDP because it was not produced in the United States. However, because it was produced in South Korea, it is added in that nation's GDP as an export.

113. (C) To get a more accurate picture of whether the value of a nation's output is really growing, we must take into account the impact that rising prices will have on nominal GDP. Since nominal GDP reflects both units of output produced and the price at which those units were sold, to compute real GDP we adjust for the impact of price inflation by using prices from a reference or base year. In this way, by holding prices constant we can see whether (in real terms) the value of a nation's output has indeed risen.

114. (D) Between years 1 and 2, nominal GDP increased by 5%. We compute this percentage change as $100 \times (\$2,100 - \$2,000)/\$2,000 = 5\%$. Real GDP is nominal GDP adjusted for inflation, so if inflation increased by exactly 5%, then real GDP stayed constant. If inflation had risen by more than 5%, real GDP would have fallen. If inflation had risen by less than 5% or even decreased, real GDP would have risen.

115. (A) Gross domestic product (GDP) is the combined function of a nation's output in a year and the price of that output. The value comes from the prices that prevailed in that year, so nominal GDP is the value of 2007 output measured in 2007 prices. To compute nominal GDP, we tabulate: $\$2 \times (10 \text{ peaches}) + \$0.50 \times (24 \text{ herbs}) = \$20 + \$12 = \$32$.

116. (B) Because prices can change from year to year, the computation of real GDP requires that we account for changes in the price level, rather than changes of output. One way of doing this is to use the prices that prevailed at a fixed point in time: the base year. Since 2006 is labeled as the base year, all real GDP computations must use 2006 prices. To compute real GDP in 2007, we tabulate: $\$1 \times (10 \text{ peaches}) + \$0.50 \times (24 \text{ herbs}) = \$10 + \$12 = \$22$.

117. (C) Because 2006 is the base year, nominal GDP and real GDP are the same in 2006. To see how much real GDP has changed between 2006 and 2008, we first need to compute real GDP in both years. Real GDP in 2006 = $\$1 \times (10 \text{ peaches}) + \$0.50 \times (20 \text{ herbs})$ = $20. Real GDP in 2008 requires using 2006 prices and 2008 output. Thus real GDP in 2008 = $\$1 \times (5 \text{ peaches}) + \$0.50 \times (30 \text{ herbs}) = \$20$. Since real GDP in both years is equal to $20, there was 0% growth.

118. (A) This is the actual definition of nominal GDP. In fact, another description of nominal GDP is "current year" GDP because it reflects current year output valued in that same current year's prices. When comparing nominal GDP from one year to the next, we must adjust nominal GDP for any price inflation (or deflation) that might have occurred, because rising prices will make it appear that the economy is growing when in fact it may just be a result of inflation and not greater output levels.

119. (E) It is typical for a nation's real GDP to gradually increase over the long run, but during the short-run business cycle, the growth of real GDP can be fast at times and slower at other times. Negative growth (or declining real GDP) is usually observed when the economy is in the contraction stage. During this point of the business cycle, spending and investment are low, unemployment runs higher than normal, and national output slows.

120. (C) Since real GDP is growing at a faster and faster rate from year 1 to year 3, the economy is expanding. Typically the business cycle shows that economic activity, like real GDP, grows more quickly during an expansion. At the peak of an expansion, the economy begins to slow down and may even enter a recession.

121. (C) All three of these situations describe individuals who are contributing productive goods and services to the economy. However, despite how productive and useful these tasks might be, the official calculations of gross domestic product fail to include any of them. When people mow their own lawn or iron their own clothes, the value of their service is not included in GDP. When a babysitter is paid cash (under the table), the service is also not counted.

122. (D) The calculation of a nation's gross domestic product does not include the value of volunteerism, despite the benefits that the community receives from those services. The accounting of GDP also fails to include the value of household production. If a parent like Sue decides to care for her own children, rather than hiring a nanny, that production is not counted. If Linda cleans out her own gutters, rather than hiring a professional, that production is not counted. The only person who is counted is Kathy, the part-time paid soccer coach. If Kathy had been volunteering her time, she would not be counted, even though she would still be providing the same productive service.

123. (B) The car had been produced in 1968 at a value of $5,000, and this was the car's contribution to GDP in 1968. Despite the fact that the "classic" car is now worth $40,000, it was not produced in 2008—it was simply resold. A secondhand car (or anything for that matter) only counts once in GDP: in the year in which it was produced. The only exception to this rule of thumb is if the item has been enhanced over the years. For example, if the original car had been given a brand-new paint job in 2008, the value of the paint job would count toward 2008 GDP. The idea of GDP is that it captures current production, and the car represents production that occurred in 1968.

124. (A) The value of the lawyer's service is $150 per hour for 4 hours, or $600. The cost of the cell phone and the office space are the costs of inputs that go into the production of legal services. It is incorrect to say that these inputs are not counted; they are. They are counted in the final cost of the lawyer's services.

125. (E) When a new romance novel is bought at the bookstore, the nation's GDP goes up. However, when a used book or used golf clubs are resold to someone else, the GDP does not go up. There is a logical reason for this rule. Suppose that a set of golf clubs is bought new for $400 and then sold three times in the span of 3 days. If we counted each sale as an addition to GDP, this would amount to $4 \times \$400 = \$1,600$ of GDP in only 3 days. But this is misleading because the golf clubs were produced only once, and they are worth only $400. This situation leads us to the conclusion that we should count only the value of the original production in the year in which it was produced.

126. (C) Even though *Gone with the Wind* was first produced in 1939, if a movie theater is selling tickets to it now, then those tickets will count in 2011 GDP. After all, the service of showing this movie to paying customers is happening in 2011, so the value of that service should be counted in 2011. Social Security payments are not counted in GDP. These are cash payments from the government to retirees because they are retirees. These funds are not payment for the production of some good or service that the retiree has just provided to the government.

127. (B) The government collects taxes from many people and uses the tax revenue to pay for government spending and government programs. Some of the government programs are used to provide supplemental income to certain segments of the nation, and the supplemental income payments are called transfer payments. For example, members of the military qualify for veterans' benefits once they retire. The elderly qualify for Social Security benefits once they reach the qualifying age. These transfer payments simply redistribute tax payments from some groups to recipients in other groups. They do not add to GDP, because they are not payments for goods or services currently being produced.

128. (D) Gross domestic product does not necessarily translate into a good measure of a nation's well-being. For example, GDP calculations omit the value of volunteerism and do-it-yourself work and leisure time. If you spend an hour working at your job, that counts in GDP. But if you spend that hour coaching your son's baseball team, that does not count in GDP. If you spend that hour pulling weeds in your herb garden, it doesn't count. Many people would agree that volunteerism and leisure time are important and have value. But because GDP doesn't include them, maybe it is underestimating our nation's true well-being.

129. (A) To compute GDP in Ericksburg we just need to tabulate all of the spending. Gross domestic product by this accounting method is equal to $C + I + G + (X - M)$. Using the values given in the problem, GDP = $9 + $3.5 + $3 - $1 = $14.5 billion.

Chapter 5: Inflation

130. (C) While a price index can be created for any good or service, and GDP can be adjusted for inflation in a number of different ways, the most commonly used price index to measure inflation across the economy is the consumer price index, or CPI (technically the CPI-U is what is typically reported as *the* CPI). The CPI computes the cost of purchasing a basket of items bought by a typical urban American household, and changes in the CPI then describe the rate of inflation.

131. (B) The consumer price index (CPI) is designed to capture changes in the amount of money that a typical consumer spends to maintain the same standard of living every year. In other words, the CPI is designed to capture changes in the cost of living. A common misperception is that the CPI captures changes in the prices of all goods and services produced in an economy, but the CPI is not actually intended to do this. There are actually a variety of price indexes used to capture changes in other prices, such as the producer price index. However, the CPI is the most commonly reported price index.

132. (B) Current wages (i.e., wages that are measured in current dollars) are referred to as nominal wages. To remove the effect of price inflation on those wages, we must adjust (or deflate) the nominal wages to real wages. Real wages tell us whether the actual purchasing power of the nominal wages has risen or fallen.

133. (A) The inflation rate is not just the value of a particular price index, like the consumer price index (CPI), but it is the rate at which the price index is changing. In other words, any given level of the CPI is not particularly revealing, but changes in that rate are what matter. If an aggregate price index is rising, the percentage change is the rate of price inflation. If it is falling, the percentage change is the rate of price deflation.

134. (D) The consumer price index (CPI) is designed to capture changes in the prices of goods that a typical consumer produces. However, consumers do tend to change their pattern of purchases over time. Currently, the CPI bundle of goods is based on surveys conducted in 2007–2008 (the period 1982–1984 represents the "base year" that the Bureau of Labor Statistics currently uses).

135. (C) The consumer price index (CPI) includes all items that a typical household might purchase, even if purchase of those items is sporadic or even very rare. To account for the frequency of purchases, items in the CPI are weighted to reflect how often, or rare, their purchase is. Investments such as stocks and bonds are essentially savings, rather than consumption, and are therefore not included.

136. (D) To calculate any rate of change, you subtract the old value from the new value, then divide by the old value. In other words, (new − old)/old. To calculate inflation, you essentially are finding the rate of change of the CPI. The value is then the ratio that the measure changed by. So for instance, if you find that this equals 0.05, multiply by 100 to get the percentage change; 0.05 is the same as saying 5%.

137. (C) Because of the way in which a price index is created, the price index in the base year is always equal to 100. A price index is created by calculating the price of a basket of items in a given year, dividing by the cost of that same basket in a base year, and then multiplying by 100. So if the market basket in 2007 cost $5,000, and if 2007 was chosen to be the base year, the 2007 price index = 100 × ($5,000)/($5,000) = 100.

138. (D) The rate of inflation is the percentage (or rate of) change in the price index between 2008 and 2009. To compute the percentage change, we subtract the 2008 value from the 2009 value, divide by the 2008 value, and multiply the ratio by 100. Therefore, the rate of inflation is equal to [(110 − 104)/104] × 100 = 5.8%. An easy way to remember how to do this is "100 × (new − old)/old."

139. (E) The price index increased by 4% (from 100 to 104) between those years, so the rate of price inflation was 4%. If we know that nominal wages increase by 4%, then nominal wages kept pace with inflation and purchasing power remained constant. In a real sense, consumers are able to buy the same market basket in 2008 as they did in 2007 without spending a larger share of their paychecks to do so.

140. (B) Several economic indicators give us a sense of whether prices are rising or falling across the economy. The consumer price index (CPI) is the measure of what it costs a typical urban household to purchase a market basket of goods and services. While no statistic can perfectly measure changes in overall prices, the CPI is the best one to determine whether consumers are gaining or losing purchasing power due to price changes.

141. (E) We know two things about this price index: it is equal to 210 in 2011, and it is equal to 100 in the base year. We don't need to know which year is the base year; we can determine the rate of inflation between that year and 2011 by calculating the percentage change. The inflation rate was 100 × (210 − 100)/100 = 110%.

142. (E) The CPI is an index, not a dollar measure. This means that there is no true unit of measures (such as dollars), but rather it is a scale indicating the amount of change relative to the reference year (or base year) in terms of percent. For any CPI, the difference between that CPI and the base year CPI (which is always 100) indicates the percentage change in the CPI since the base year (in this case, 22%). This can be verified by using the formula to calculate the rate of change between any two years.

143. (C) The first step in calculating a CPI is to calculate the cost of the bundle of goods in any given year. To do this, simply multiply the number of each goods bought by the price that it sold for in that year. For 2001, 5 Grubs are bought at $3 each, 10 Snars are bought for $2.50 each, 3 Jems are bought for $2.10 each, and 2 Pols are bought for $1.75 each, so (5 × $3) + (10 × $2.50) + (3 × $2.10) + (2 × $1.75) = $49.80.

144. (E) The purpose of a CPI is to find the cost of a bundle of goods in reference to some base year, and the formula to find the CPI reflects this. To find the CPI in any given year X, you divide the cost of the bundle of goods in year X by the cost of the same bundle of goods in the base year and multiply by 100, or mathematically, $CPI_X =$ (cost year X/cost base year) × 100. Here, ($49.80/$33.30) × 100 = 149.55.

145. (A) To find the rate of inflation between any two years, subtract the old CPI from the new CPI and divide by the old rate of inflation; in other words: inflation rate = 100 × $(CPI_{new} - CPI_{old})/CPI_{old}$. This gives you a percentage that reflects the increase in the price level between those two years. $CPI_{2001} = 149.55$ and $CPI_{2002} = 238.32$, so the rate of inflation between 2001 and 2002 is 100 × (238.32 − 149.55)/149.55 = 59.36%. Therefore, prices for the goods in the bundle increased 59.35% between 2001 and 2002.

146. (B) Whenever you are comparing a given year to the base year, an easy way to find the rate of inflation is to subtract the base year's CPI from the current year's CPI. Note that 149.55 − 100 = 49.55 and also 100 × (149.55 − 100)/100 = 49.55%. Be careful, however, as this can be done only when comparing the CPI in a given year to the base year. If you attempt this with any other two years, you will get an incorrect result.

147. (E) Note that one may find the rate of inflation between any two years, not merely between two consecutive years or between a given year and the base year. However, it is no longer an annual rate, but rather the total rate of inflation during the time period. Here, (400 − 345)/345 = 15.94%, indicating that prices rose 15.94% during the two-year period 2007–2009.

148. (D) Between 2006 and 2007, the rate of inflation was 10.34%. To find the real rate of growth of GDP, you subtract the rate of inflation from the nominal rate of growth: 6% − 10.34% = −4.34%, meaning that real GDP actually declined during this period. Note that this difference between nominal and real rates of growth also applies to household incomes and savings: if a household did not earn at least 10.34% in 2007 more than they did in 2006, their standard of living actually decreased. Similarly, unless they are earning at least the rate of inflation in interest, the purchasing power of their savings will go down from year to year.

149. (B) In this question, the cost of the bundle of goods each year has already been calculated, so we merely need to apply the CPI formula, $CPI_{year X} =$ (cost in year X/cost in base year) × 100, to find the CPI. In this case, ($750/$500) × 100 = 150. When calculating CPI, make sure you use the correct base year.

150. (B) To solve this, you must remember that the formula for CPI in 1983 would be CPI_{1983} = (cost of bundle in 1983/cost of bundle in base year) × 100. Since we don't know the base year, we can rewrite this so we are solving for x = cost of bundle in the base year. Therefore, $150 = (900/x) \times 150$. Solving for x, we get $x = 600$. Since the bundle of goods cost $600 in 1980, 1980 must be the base year.

151. (A) The idea of menu costs comes from the fact that when firms face higher costs for their inputs, they must raise the prices that they charge their consumers to produce the same goods. The mere act of changing a price is not itself productive, so if this happens often enough, it is an inefficiency associated with inflation. Consider your favorite local restaurant and all of the menu items that they have. If there was significant daily inflation, the restaurant would have to have someone change the menus to reflect new prices every single day, taking that person away from productive activities such as preparing food or serving customers.

152. (B) The idea of shoe leather costs comes from the fact that when people observe a higher price on something they were planning on buying, they tend to look around to see if they can find a lower price somewhere else. This act of searching is not, however, costless. In Bill's case he burns gasoline while he is looking for cheaper gasoline. The term *shoe leather costs* refers to the fact that shoes used to have leather soles, and people would wear down their shoes looking for lower prices.

153. (C) If a person borrows money at a variable rate of interest or loans money at a variable rate, the variation in the rate of interest paid (or received) tends to follow the rate of inflation. However, if someone borrows money at a fixed rate, the real value of the amount of money that they have to pay back goes down if there is unexpected inflation.

154. (A) Deflation is a decline in the overall price level. In calculating the rate of inflation between two years, deflation would be reflected in a negative rate of inflation. Deflation occurs when prices are actually going down, rather than when there is a slower increase in prices—a process known as disinflation.

155. (E) Disinflation is a decrease in the rate of inflation. Note that this means that a country is still experiencing inflation, but the rate at which the inflation is occurring is slowing down. Note that if Ile had experienced inflation anywhere between 0% and 6% inflation in 2006, they would be experiencing both inflation and disinflation in 2006. If instead Ile had experienced a −1% change in the price level in 2006, they would have been experiencing deflation.

156. (D) Menu costs refer to the time and expense associated with firms that must change prices when inflation occurs. Shoe leather costs refer to the time and expense associated with consumers who must seek out lower-priced goods when inflation occurs. While some attribute inflation itself to the printing of too much money, the expense of printing money is not a cost of the inflationary prices in the economy.

157. (A) If Barb is receiving fixed pension payments, her purchasing power will begin to fall if price inflation occurs over time. To maintain her purchasing power (or real income), her pension payments are indexed, or adjusted, for inflation. For example, if inflation is 5%, her payments will rise by 5%. In this way Barb can purchase the same basket of items without spending a larger share of her income.

158. (A) If the CPI is 225 in 2010 and 210 in 2009, then the rate of inflation between the two years is 7.14%. We can calculate the rate of increase of her salary in the same way we calculate the rate of increase in CPI: ($42,000 − $40,000)/$40,000 = 5%. Therefore, she is having to pay 7.14% more for all goods and services, but only got a 5% raise to cover this. Effectively, her real increase in earnings is 5% − 7.14% = −2.14%.

159. (E) While there are generally costs associated with inflation, deflation is widely agreed to be a "worst case scenario." The intuition behind this is clear on a number of levels. One reason is that deflation can lead to declines in production and investment, since people may hoard money (rather than save and invest money) that has now become more valuable. For instance, if you observed that the prices of goods were going down, you would likely postpone making large purchases such as automobiles until the price had declined. This can lead to a deflationary spiral, and deflationary periods are generally (although not always) associated with recessions or even depressions.

160. (D) One of the reasons that deflation is considered undesirable is that it effectively raises the interest rates on loans. Before deflation, you have to give up 5% worth of goods and services to pay the interest on the loan. However, if there is deflation, then your income is also decreasing, effectively taking away an additional 10% of purchasing power, relative to the unchanging amount that you owe, and then effectively the interest rate is 15%. Consider this: if there is deflation, even if someone were able to get a 0% loan in this situation, that person would be unlikely to take it because he or she would effectively be paying 10% interest.

161. (A) When the base year is changed, the cost of the basket of goods in each year is unaffected. However, because the denominator in the formula for calculating the CPI is different, the CPI will be different for each year. This will not, however, significantly change the rate of inflation from year to year.

162. (E) When new goods are introduced, they are not reflected in the CPI immediately, as the CPI is calculated with the same bundle of goods and services from year to year. This can lead to a bias in the CPI in correctly capturing the true cost of living. Because of this, the Bureau of Labor Statistics (which calculates the CPI in the United States) periodically adjusts the bundle of goods in the basket.

163. (D) Substitution bias occurs when households, faced with a sudden increase in the price of one of the goods in their bundle, alter their consumption habits to consume more of another good instead. For instance, if the price of beef doesn't change, and in response to a doubling of chicken prices households stop buying chicken, then households' cost of living would not have changed at all. However, the CPI would be capturing the effect of the increase in the price of chicken by assuming that households do not alter their consumption bundles.

164. (D) The actual level of prices is generally unimportant. What is important, however, is whether the rate of inflation is high and volatile. Economists generally agree that a modest rate of inflation is not of great concern, but a sudden and unexpected increase (or decrease) in the price level can have serious and significant consequences.

165. (A) Because of the costs associated with unexpected (or unanticipated) inflation, firms and households may alter their decisions when faced with unexpected inflation. For instance, firms may have priced contracts inappropriately when prices suddenly rise and may face higher than expected costs. Households may agree to labor contracts in which they earn less in real terms than they had bargained for. Further, lenders who cannot correctly anticipate inflation may be unwilling to lend money, as lenders are generally worse off when inflation occurs.

166. (B) If Sarah currently makes $30,000 and wants a net 2% increase in her standard of living, she needs to also account for the increase in the price level of 5%. We know that the real change in salary is approximately equal to the nominal change minus inflation. To solve for the nominal change, we calculate the following: nominal change − 5% = 2%, so we see that her nominal rate of pay must increase by 7%, and 7% of $30,000 is $2,100.

167. (A) The bank experienced unexpected inflation. This means that they were expecting to earn a real rate of interest of 4% (6% − 2% = 4%); they instead earned a real rate of interest of 6% − 3.5% = 2.5%. From this it is clear why banks might be hesitant to loan money during periods of high rates of unexpected inflation—they may end up earning less money than they had planned.

168. (A) Hyperinflation refers to a period when there are extremely rapid increases in the price level, sometimes even on a daily basis. There are numerous examples of hyperinflationary periods throughout history. For instance, Germany experienced a period of hyperinflation in the 1920s, and more recently Zimbabwe has experienced inflation of a magnitude so severe it ultimately abandoned its currency altogether.

Chapter 6: Unemployment

169. (E) The labor force is made up of the people who are involved in the world of work (the employed) or actively attempting to become involved (the unemployed). To be counted as a member of the labor force, one must first be at least 16 years of age and then must be either working or seeking work. A person who is not working and is not seeking work is considered out of the labor force.

170. (A) Eric is not 16 years old, so despite the fact that he is being paid to work at the family business, he would not be counted officially as an employed worker. Children under the age of 16 are considered out of the labor force, or "not of working age." Adults can also be out of the labor force, but that would be a result of their choice, not of their age.

171. (B) While in any nation there are many people who are not working, many of these people are not actually counted as unemployed. Among those not working, many are not old enough to be counted. Others who are not working but not counted as unemployed would be those who do not wish to work at this point in their lives.

172. (C) Sven is working at least 1 hour in a week, so he is counted as an employed person. While he may not like his job very much, he is not considered a discouraged worker, a term that has special meaning in economics. A discouraged worker is a person who has removed him- or herself from the labor force due to long-term unemployment. This person has stopped searching for a job due to discouragement about ever finding one that fits his or her skills.

173. (D) A person who is working at least 1 hour in a week is employed (E). A person who is not working but seeking work is unemployed (U). When we add up all of the employed persons and all of the unemployed persons, we get the labor force (LF), or LF = U + E.

174. (A) One way to gauge the attachment of a population to the labor market is to measure the labor force participation rate (LFPR)—the fraction of the working-age population that is in the labor force (or LFPR = LF/Working Age Population). The labor force (LF) is the 80 million people who are working plus the 5 million people who are not working but are seeking work, or LF = U + E = 80 million + 5 million = 85 million. This allows us to compute LFPR = 85 million/100 million = 85%.

175. (B) To find the labor force participation rate (LFPR), we need three pieces of information: the number of unemployed (U), the number of employed (E), and the working-age population. We are given that there are 85 million people employed (E = 85), but we are not given U—we are only told that 10 million are not seeking work (they are not in the labor force, or NILF). Since U + E + NILF must be equal to the working-age population, then U + 85 + 10 = 100, there must be 5 million who are unemployed and seeking work. The labor force participation rate is therefore LFPR = (85 + 5)/100 = 90%.

176. (E) Officially Frank is unemployed because he is over the age of 16, is not currently working, but is actively seeking work. To be counted as unemployed, someone must meet all three of these criteria. When asking people what they have done to actively seek work, activities such as sending résumés and having job interviews certainly qualifies as active search. If Frank had been passively reading the help-wanted ads in a newspaper, this would not qualify as active search.

177. (D) The labor force participation rate (LFPR) is the fraction (or percentage) of the working-age population that is engaged in the labor force (LF) either by working (E) or being unemployed (U). Therefore, to compute LFPR rate, we divide the size of the labor force (E + U) by the working-age population.

178. (B) There are 200 million people in this nation and 170 million are working, so 30 million are not working. Of that 30 million not working, 14 million are not seeking work, so these people are not counted in the labor force. Since there are 16 million who are unemployed and seeking work, the labor force participation rate is LFPR = (170 + 16)/200 = 93%.

179. (C) A common misconception about the unemployment rate is that it means that, in this case, 8% of the entire population is jobless. Some also believe that it means that 8% of adults (the working-age population) are jobless. It really means that 8% of only the labor force is jobless and seeking work. There are many other people who are voluntarily jobless, and they are not included in this statistic.

180. (A) In situations like Jermaine's, he is still employed by the mill and will return to work when the routine maintenance is completed. His employment would have to completely cease and he would have to seek work to be counted as unemployed. Similarly, he is not out of the labor force because he is waiting to return to work. Similar situations arise when employees take a week or two of vacation time. Such employees aren't detaching themselves from the labor force or quitting their jobs, they are merely taking a vacation.

181. (E) To find the unemployment rate, we must first find the size of the labor force, which consists of the employed (E) and unemployed (U), or LF = U + E. Everyone in the working-age population must either be counted in E, U, or not in the labor force (NILF), or 200 = E + U + NILF. There are 200 million people in the working-age population, and 170 million are employed. Of the remaining 30 million, 14 million are not seeking work so they are out of the labor force. Thus we conclude that 16 million are officially unemployed. The unemployment rate (UR) is the number of unemployed divided by the labor force, or UR = U/(E + U). Therefore, the UR = 16/(170 + 16) = 8.6%.

182. (A) There are 95 million people in the working-age population, and 5 million people are not looking for a job. This leaves 81 million people who are working and 9 million people who are unemployed but looking for work. The labor force is the sum of the employed and unemployed, and thus the unemployment rate is UR = 9/(9 + 81) = 10%.

183. (B) The LFPR is the percentage of the working-age population that is in the labor force: either employed or unemployed and looking for a job. In Costa Erica, the labor force is the 200 million employed workers and the 10 million unemployed but seeking work. When we divide the labor force by the working-age population, we get LFPR = (200 + 10)/250 = 84%.

184. (D) The unemployment rate is the percentage of the labor force that is unemployed but looking for a job. We know that there are 10 million people in Costa Erica who fall into this category, so they are the unemployed. The labor force is the sum of the 10 million unemployed plus the 200 million employed persons. The unemployment rate is therefore: UR = 10/(10 + 210) = 4.8%.

185. (C) As a nation's economy improves, some people who were previously out of the labor force may begin to look for jobs. When 10 million of Costa Erica's citizens enter the labor force, this increases the ranks of the unemployed and the labor force. Clearly the labor force participation rate should also increase. Since all of these people are unemployed, the unemployment rate is going to rise. In fact, we can show this by recomputing the unemployment rate as UR = 20/(20 + 200) = 9.1% and the labor force participation rate as LFPR = (200 + 20)/250 = 88%.

186. (E) The unemployment rate tells us the fraction (or percentage) of the labor force that is unemployed. This is sometimes a misleading statistic because to be counted as employed, a person only needs to work 1 hour each week. Many people who are working just a few hours would really rather be working a full 40 hours, yet they are considered employed. Additionally, many do not have a job and are not, for whatever reason, seeking a job. These people are not considered unemployed. In these two ways, the unemployment rate doesn't always give us a perfect measure of the health of the labor market.

187. (A) When a worker loses her job and seeks a new job, she is unemployed. However, when she becomes tired of searching and stops trying to find a new job, she drops out of the labor force. This change of classification actually creates some difficulty in estimating the true state of the labor market.

188. (D) When people have searched a long time for a job but haven't found one, they might come to the conclusion that no job exists for their skill sets. If these people drop out of the labor force, they are classified by the Bureau of Labor Statistics as discouraged workers. They are no longer in the labor force and no longer in the ranks of the unemployed, so this causes the official unemployment rate to fall. Because this official measure falls, it understates the true state of the unemployment in the economy.

189. (B) One of the most common economic indicators of a recession is a rising unemployment rate. To understand how this happens, we just need to visualize the circular-flow model. A recession is caused by weak household spending on goods and services in the product markets. As firms see their product sales decline, they need to hire fewer inputs from the factor markets. And as fewer units of labor are hired, the level of employment falls, and thus the unemployment rate rises.

190. (C) An economic expansion is the opposite of a recession. An expansion boosts household spending on goods and services in the product markets. As firms see product sales rise, they must hire more inputs from the factor markets. As more units of labor are hired, the level of employment rises, and the unemployment rate falls. In general, our macroeconomic indicators tend to move in the same direction: when GDP increases, employment tends to increase as well; and when GDP decreases, employment tends to decrease as well.

191. (C) Because Eric is actively seeking another job, he is unemployed. Alex and Max are considered employed. Even if Max has not finished his book, he is a writer employed in the production of the book. Eli and Melanie are out of the labor force for different reasons. Eli is a full-time student, and Melanie has retired. At this time, neither wants to seek a job, so they are not unemployed.

192. (D) One way to think about frictional unemployment is that it occurs when the worker (Oscar in this case) or the employer finds that there is not a good match between the job and the employee. Oscar had a job but wants one that will suit him better, so he is an example of this form of frictional unemployment.

193. (E) Cyclical unemployment occurs as a result of the economic business cycle. When the economy is expanding, jobs are easy to find and unemployment falls. On the other hand, when the economy goes into recession, employers start trimming the payroll and people like Grover lose their jobs. Car sales as a skill set has not disappeared; there has just been a decrease in demand for car salespeople at the moment. When the economy rebounds, more cars will be demanded, and more salespersons will be demanded.

194. (B) Some occupations see a rise and fall in employment at different times of the year. For example, the employment of construction workers increases in the summer and decreases in the winter. When a ski resort closes due to the end of winter, people like Ros become seasonally unemployed. This form of unemployment is expected and not terribly damaging to the greater labor market or national economy.

195. (A) When a worker quits a job to find a better one, or when an employer fires a poor worker to find a better one, this is an example of the nature of frictional unemployment. It is common for a worker and a job to be poorly matched, and this can often end in unemployment. It is not the result of a downturn in the economy, a fundamental change in the labor market, or a change in the calendar seasons, it is just the natural process of the labor market trying to operate more efficiently.

196. (C) Structural unemployment can occur in a couple of different ways, but they all boil down to a permanent decrease in the demand for a particular skill set. For example, when technology makes a certain occupation obsolete (e.g., phonograph production) or when laws create a wedge that prevents the market from reaching equilibrium (a minimum wage), workers are displaced and unemployed. Unlike cyclical unemployment, these jobs won't come back when the economy improves. And unlike seasonal unemployment, a change of seasons won't bring back these jobs.

197. (D) Changes in the business cycle are the source of cyclical unemployment. As the economy gets stronger (an expansion in the business cycle), more workers are hired and cyclical unemployment falls. As the economy worsens (a recession), fewer workers are needed and cyclical unemployment rises. This form of unemployment is largely the target of fiscal and monetary policy.

198. (A) The job at the textile mill is not coming back, so this is structural unemployment. While there is still demand for the skill set that Burgin possesses, there is not enough of that demand in Tennessee where he lives. These sorts of fundamental changes in local and national labor markets are almost impossible for government policies to alleviate. Fortunately when some jobs become structurally obsolete, others are becoming structurally demanded.

199. (B) If the market is in equilibrium, the quantity of labor demanded and supplied would be equal to Q_3. A binding minimum wage must lie above the equilibrium wage of W_2; otherwise, the market will just revert to equilibrium wage of W_2. Once the minimum wage is in place, the quantity of labor supplied increases to Q_5 along the upward-sloping labor supply curve.

200. (E) Because the binding wage must lie above W_2, employers will respond to the higher W_1 by reducing the quantity of labor demanded along the downward-sloping labor demand curve. Since the market quantity of labor hired begins at Q_3, this movement along the labor demand curve will be from Q_3 to Q_1.

201. (D) A minimum wage, by design, raises the wage in a labor market above equilibrium. The only binding minimum wage in this graph is W_1. Employers will reduce the quantity of labor demanded to Q_1, and people will increase the quantity of labor supplied to Q_5. Because more units of labor are supplied than demanded, there is a surplus of labor. This surplus of $(Q_5 - Q_1)$ represents the unemployed in this market.

202. (A) A binding minimum wage creates a surplus of labor in the market by raising the wage above equilibrium. When the market is in equilibrium, the quantity of labor demanded equals the quantity of labor supplied, so there is no unemployment. A surplus of labor represents unemployed workers, so to find the unemployment rate, we just need to divide the size of the surplus by the size of the labor force. The labor force is Q_5, the quantity of labor being supplied, but only Q_1 units of labor are employed. This allows us to determine that the unemployment rate is the surplus $(Q_5 - Q_1)$ divided by Q_5.

203. (B) An efficiency wage is a wage that exceeds equilibrium and is deliberately paid by an employer to accomplish higher levels of productivity. A higher wage should reduce absenteeism because the wage is the opportunity cost of missing work. Because the wage is higher than what the market might provide, the efficiency wage should reduce turnover, as a current worker is less likely to quit for another job. Absenteeism and turnover are costly to a firm because they lose productivity and have to retrain a new worker. So an efficiency wage can actually save the firm money.

204. (D) The economy naturally goes through the business cycle with peaks and valleys in the level of unemployment. When the economy is at full employment, cyclical unemployment is zero, but there still exists frictional and structural forms of unemployment. The point where cyclical unemployment is zero is believed to be where the level of unemployment is at its long-run natural rate. This means that even in a well-functioning labor market, we can expect the unemployment rate to be greater than 0%.

205. (E) There will always be some level of unemployment in the economy. The natural rate of unemployment is the rate that would exist if the economy was operating at full employment. No matter the level of national output (GDP), there will always be frictional and structural forms of unemployment in the economy, but the cyclical unemployment rises and falls with the strength of the economy. At full employment, cyclical unemployment is zero; so all that is left is frictional and structural unemployment.

206. (C) National output rises and falls with the business cycle. If the economy is going through a recession, cyclical unemployment will rise, and if the economy is in an expansion, cyclical unemployment will fall. Only at full employment output is the cyclical unemployment equal to zero. At this level of output, the natural rate of unemployment is the collective frictional and structural unemployment.

207. (B) A minimum wage is an artificial source of unemployment because it interferes with the market equilibrium wage and equilibrium quantity of employment. If the market is in equilibrium, there is no unemployment at all, as the quantity of labor demanded is exactly equal to the quantity supplied. The minimum wage creates a wedge between the quantity supplied and quantity demanded, thus it is a structural form of unemployment.

208. (A) A labor union is another source of structural unemployment because the union, if successful, will negotiate a wage that exceeds market equilibrium. Once this occurs, the quantity of labor demanded will be reduced below the quantity of labor supplied. A union offers the membership higher wages, better benefits, and better work conditions, but at the cost of fewer jobs once the wage is increased. Like the minimum wage, this is a form of structural unemployment.

Chapter 7: Aggregate Demand

209. (B) In the United States, consumption spending is about 70% of all spending that goes into aggregate demand. This spending consists of all goods (durable and nondurable) and services purchased by domestic households. Durable goods are items that are expected to last for at least 3 years, and nondurable goods are expected to last fewer than 3 years. For example, a car is a durable good, but the gasoline to power the car is a nondurable good. Services are intangible benefits that are also purchased by consumers. Examples of services would include a car wash, a massage, a medical checkup, or legal advice.

210. (D) Aggregate demand is the total sum of all spending in the domestic economy. Since domestic spending comes from households (C), firms (I), and government (G), we must add these three components. However, spending in the domestic economy can also come from foreign sources, so we must also add export spending (X) and subtract domestic spending on imported foreign goods (M). When we subtract imports from exports, we get net exports $(X - M)$.

211. (A) Investment spending (I) captures the spending on physical capital (like machines) and new construction done by firms. These large (and expensive) projects often require the firm to borrow the funds from the banking sector. Naturally, the banking sector charges an interest rate to lend to these firms, so firms can be quite sensitive to changes in the interest rate before investment spending is planned.

212. (C) Government spending captures virtually any good or service purchased by all levels of government (local, state, or federal). Government also engages in spending on broad programs such as public education. Government spending in the educational programs can include small items (textbooks), large items (school buses), or services (teacher salaries).

213. (E) Total spending in the US economy must also include the spending that comes from and goes to foreign countries. If there is more open trade between the United States and the European Union (EU), it is likely that consumers in Europe will buy more products made in America. These transactions will increase exports in the US economy. It is also likely that American consumers will buy more products made in Europe. These transactions will increase imports in the US economy. Since net exports is the difference between export spending and import spending, more open trade directly affects, upward or downward, net exports in both the United States and the European Union.

214. (D) If we focus on the domestic components of spending, there are three sources. Firms engage in investment spending on new equipment and construction, the government purchases both goods and services, and individuals and households engage in consumption spending of goods and services. In the United States, consumption spending is the largest component of aggregate demand.

215. (A) Households hold assets, including money, which amounts to the total wealth available for consumption. When the price level falls, the value of such wealth increases and consumers increase spending on goods and services. Economists refer to this relationship as the "wealth effect," and it partly explains why the aggregate demand curve is downward sloping.

216. (C) Households sell their labor to labor markets and earn income that is used to consume goods and services. When some of that income is saved in the bank or in the form of other assets (i.e., stocks, bonds, property), the household accumulates wealth. The value of this wealth can also influence the household's level of spending. When the price level rises (inflation), this wealth is reduced in value and this prompts less spending. The inverse relationship between the price level and spending helps explain the downward-sloping aggregate demand curve.

217. (C) The downward-sloping aggregate demand curve describes an inverse relationship between the aggregate price level and total spending (real GDP) in the economy. When total spending changes at all price levels, it means something has happened to shift the aggregate demand curve. Statements I and II are both accurate, but they describe outward shifts in the aggregate demand curve, not the negative slope of the curve.

218. (B) A rising price level makes it more expensive to consume goods and services so households will reduce their savings to buy these more expensive items. A reduction in savings causes banks to decrease the level of excess cash reserves, reducing the funds available to lend, and this causes interest rates to rise, reducing investment spending by firms. The chain of events from a higher price level to higher interest rates is called the "interest rate effect," and this partly explains why aggregate demand slopes downward.

219. (D) The interest rate effect describes the connection between price levels and investment spending. A lower price level means that households need less money for consumption of goods and services. Households respond by saving more money in the banking sector, and as more money is saved, the interest rates begin to fall, prompting more investment spending.

220. (E) This choice describes what economists call the "interest rate effect." A higher price level reduces the ability of consumers to buy goods and services with the same amount of money, so consumers must reduce their savings. As savings leave the banks, interest rates rise and investment spending falls. This relationship between higher prices and reduced spending describes a downward-sloping aggregate demand curve. The other choices describe either outward or inward shifts in the entire curve because spending has either risen or fallen at all price levels.

221. (E) The foreign exchange effect recognizes that a lower price level in a nation causes an increase in net exports in that nation's economy. If prices are lower in nation X relative to nation Y, consumers in nation Y will increase their imports from nation X. Consumers in nation X will reduce their imports from nation Y. The nation with the lower price level (nation X) sees an increase in exports and a decrease in imports, thus increasing real GDP along the aggregate demand curve.

222. (A) The higher interest rates on financial assets like US Treasuries attract investors and their currencies from other nations, like Mexico and the peso. An increase in the demand for the US dollar causes it to appreciate against the peso. This means that the dollar can buy more pesos in global currency markets. With a "stronger" dollar, Americans will import more goods from Mexico. The "weaker" peso means that American firms will export fewer goods to Mexico. The higher price level thus reduces net exports in the United States, and this is seen as an upward movement along the aggregate demand curve.

223. (B) A lower price level in Canada will lower interest rates on Canadian financial assets, like government bonds. Lower interest rates on bonds reduces foreign investment in these financial assets and decreases the demand for the Canadian dollar in currency markets. When the value of the Canadian dollar falls, it means that imports into Canada will fall and exports out of Canada will rise. This increase in net exports, due to the lower price level, is seen as an increase in real GDP along the aggregate demand curve in Canada.

224. (C) When there has been an increase in real GDP at a constant price level, it is said that there has been an increase in aggregate demand, or that there has been a rightward or outward shift in the entire aggregate demand curve. A change in the price level will not cause the curve to shift; some other external factor must have changed to increase total spending in the economy.

225. (C) A movement along a fixed aggregate demand curve is caused by a change in the price level. In this case, the price level must have fallen, so all else equal, the total spending on goods and services has increased in the nation's economy. If an external factor (not the price level) changes, the entire curve will shift inward or outward. For example, a boost of consumer confidence would increase household spending at all price levels; an outward shift would occur.

226. (D) A movement to from point e to point b is a leftward shift of the aggregate demand curve. This is telling us that, at any price level, total spending in the economy has fallen. A so-called decrease in aggregate demand is the result of a decrease in any of the four categories of spending in the nation's economy. A decrease in consumption spending would certainly cause such a leftward shift.

227. (C) A movement to from point b to point d is a rightward shift of the aggregate demand curve. This is telling us that at any price level, total spending in the economy has increased. An increase in aggregate demand happens whenever there is an increase in any of the four categories of spending in the nation's economy. An increase in government spending would cause a rightward shift.

228. (E) A movement along any aggregate demand (AD) curve is caused by a change in the price level. In this case, the price level has risen, so all else equal, the total spending on goods and services has decreased in the nation's economy. If an external factor (other than the price level) changes, the entire curve will shift inward or outward. If firms were pessimistic about the economic outlook, they may reduce investment spending across the board; this would be seen as an inward shift of the AD curve.

229. (A) Consumers are the largest component of total aggregate demand. If households are more optimistic about the economy, their job prospects, and future incomes, they will typically increase consumption spending at any price level. This boost of consumer optimism results in an increase, or rightward shift, in the aggregate demand curve.

230. (D) Aggregate demand is the sum of consumption spending (C), investment spending (I), government spending (G), and net exports (X − M). Any decrease in one of these components of spending will shift the aggregate demand curve to the left. Net exports can decrease in one of two ways: exports can fall or imports can rise.

231. (B) If we are told that real GDP has risen at any price level, this is an indication that aggregate demand has shifted to the right. Whenever consumer wealth increases, in this case due to a strong stock market, it allows households to increase their consumption of goods and services. Wealth and income are different, but they both have a direct relationship with consumption spending.

232. (C) The nation of Melaniestan is producing products that have become more popular with consumers in other countries. This should allow firms in Melaniestan to export more products to those foreign consumers. All else equal, this boost to export spending (X) will increase net exports (X − M) and shift aggregate demand (AD) to the right.

233. (E) A strong economy with low unemployment and rising incomes will cause the aggregate demand (AD) curve to shift to the right. This shift is often the indication that an economy is in the expansion stage of the business cycle as real GDP is rising, no matter the price level. When the economy is weakening, or contracting, the AD curve is drawn as shifting to the left.

234. (D) Interest rates are determined by the financial markets and have an impact on aggregate demand through the effect they have on the costs of borrowing. Most investment projects (physical capital or construction) require firms to borrow, and thus higher interest rates reduce investment spending (I). There is some big-ticket consumption spending (C), like cars and trucks, that also is sensitive to higher interest rates.

235. (A) When taxes are subtracted from household income and government transfer payments are added, what is left over is called disposable income. Households can then choose to consume or save this disposable income. When disposable income rises due to the tax cuts, consumption rises and shifts aggregate demand to the right.

236. (B) For many citizens, transfer payments from the government act to increase disposable income. Social programs like food stamps, medical care for the elderly, veterans' benefits, and others take tax revenue from some segments of society and transfer those dollars to other segments. All else equal, a reduction in transfer payments therefore reduces disposable income and causes aggregate demand to fall.

237. (C) Government spending (G) programs (or "fiscal policy"), such as infrastructure improvements, are designed to shift the aggregate demand (AD) curve to the right. Such increases in government spending have the same impact as any other increase in consumption, investment, or net exports. As the AD curve shifts to the right, real GDP also increases at any price level.

238. (A) The central bank of a nation can influence interest rates by changing the supply of money circulating through the banking sector. By affecting interest rates, this monetary policy also affects some spending components in the economy. Higher interest rates make it more costly for firms to borrow, and this reduces investment (I), shifting aggregate demand (AD) to the left and reducing real GDP.

239. (E) When a central bank uses monetary policy to reduce interest rates, investment, consumption, and net exports all increase. Investment spending (I) rises because firms can now borrow large sums of money at lower interest rates, thus making large projects more profitable. Consumption spending (C) also rises for items like cars and appliances when interest rates are low. Finally, net exports (X − M) also rise with lower interest rates because of the depreciation of the nation's currency. This depreciation increases exports out of Dodgetopia and decreases imports into the country.

240. (B) Total spending in a nation can get too high and eventually cause inflation. To curtail this, central banks can rein in some of that spending if the interest rates are increased. A higher interest rate makes it more costly for firms to borrow so investment falls. Any kind of consumer spending that is sensitive to interest rates (borrowing for a college degree) would also be reduced with this policy. Finally, a higher interest rate causes the nation's currency to appreciate against other currencies. An appreciating currency makes it cheaper to buy from other nations, so imports rise. On the other hand, it makes that nation's exports more expensive to foreigners so exports fall.

Chapter 8: Aggregate Supply

241. (A) Unlike aggregate demand, which is downward sloping in both the long run and the short run, the aggregate supply relationship between price and real GDP depends upon the time period involved. In the short run, it is believed that suppliers will respond to a higher price level by increasing output, and therefore, the short-run aggregate supply is upward sloping. In the long run, however, it is thought that the economy will naturally return to full employment output no matter the price level, because all prices can adjust in the long run. This implies that the long-run relationship between real GDP and the price level is vertical.

242. (D) The LRAS curve is consistent with the assumptions of classical economics. The long-run implication of classical economics is that the economy has a tendency to always return to the level of real GDP that is associated with the economy's full potential output. If this is the case, then a rising price level is not associated with rising real GDP in the long run, and the only way to illustrate such a relationship is with a vertical LRAS curve.

243. (C) The short-run aggregate supply (SRAS) curve is upward sloping, which describes a positive relationship between the aggregate price level and aggregate output (or real GDP). If the price level were to rise, this would simply be seen as a movement upward along a fixed SRAS curve. While there are other factors that are believed to shift the SRAS curve to the left or to the right, a change in the price level does not cause such a shift but rather a movement along the curve.

244. (E) An outward (or rightward) shift in the short-run aggregate supply (SRAS) curve describes an economy where firms are willing and able to supply more output no matter the price level. An alternative way to think of an increase in SRAS is that firms will supply the same level of output at a lower price level.

245. (C) A movement from point d to point e indicates that the short-run aggregate supply curve has increased, or shifted to the right. At the same price level, firms are willing and able to supply more units of their goods and services, so real GDP rises. Such a shift might occur due to lower factor prices or tax policy targeted to supply rather than demand.

246. (C) Point a and point b are both on the same short-run aggregate supply curve, so this movement had to be caused by a change in the price level. Since point b lies below point a, the price level must have fallen and firms responded by reducing their production; collectively this reduces the nation's GDP.

247. (B) A movement from point e to point b indicates that the short-run aggregate supply curve has decreased, or shifted to the left. At the same price level, firms are willing and able to supply fewer units of their goods and services, so real GDP falls. Such a shift might occur due to higher factor prices across the economy.

248. (B) One of the explanations for why short-run aggregate supply curves are upward sloping is that wages (as well as other factor prices) rise more slowly than the aggregate price level. If the price of output rises and wage increases lag behind, a firm can increase their short-run profits by increasing output.

249. (A) If a firm notices that output prices are rising, they would not be able to increase output if the factor prices are rising at the same rate. However, if wage increases are delayed relative to the price increases, a firm can profit by increasing output in the short run. The theory that wages are unable to rise quickly is known as the sticky wage theory, and it explains why the short-run aggregate supply curve is upward sloping.

250. (D) The misperceptions theory asserts that producers see an increase in the overall price level and assume that the price is increasing only for their product. This misperception causes the firm to increase output in an attempt to increase profit. Because of this economy-wide behavior, there is a positive relationship between the price level and real GDP, and the SRAS curve is upward sloping.

251. (E) The two most common theories used to explain the upward-sloping short-run aggregate supply curve are the sticky wage theory and the misperceptions theory. The first theory assumes that firms will respond to a higher price level by producing more output because wages rise slower than prices. The second assumes that firms mistakenly assume that economy-wide inflation is increasing the price of only their products, and output rises accordingly.

252. (A) Energy sources (i.e., crude oil, natural gas, coal) are very important in the production process, and changes in prices for these energy sources can shift the SRAS curve. Higher energy prices make it more expensive to produce, so when energy prices increase, the SRAS curve decreases (or shifts to the left). However, energy prices will not cause the long-run aggregate supply curve to shift, as they do not fundamentally alter the economy's production potential.

253. (D) Commodities such as steel and copper are very important in manufacturing many goods. Therefore, changes in commodity prices can shift the SRAS curve. Lower commodity prices make it less costly to produce, so the SRAS curve increases (shifts to the right). However, changes in commodity prices will not cause the LRAS curve to shift, as they do not fundamentally alter the economy's ability to produce.

254. (E) Labor productivity improvements allow the nation to produce more real GDP both in the short run and in the long run. Higher productivity means that more output can be produced with the same amount of labor and capital, so both the SRAS and LRAS curves increase—shift to the right. In other words, higher productivity is both a temporary boost to output (SRAS increases) and a permanent increase in the nation's fundamental ability to produce (LRAS increases).

255. (C) Devastating natural disasters can greatly reduce a nation's ability to produce both in the short run and in the long run. When Texomabourg is afflicted with several disasters, we would see the SRAS curve decrease and the LRAS curve decrease. The decrease in LRAS tells us that the nation's potential output has permanently, or at least for a very long time, been diminished.

256. (B) Nearly every firm uses some amount of labor to produce their goods and services. Lower nominal wages will cause firms to be more willing and able to produce output at any price level, so SRAS increases. This will not cause the LRAS curve to increase, however, as the nation's potential output has not increased.

257. (A) Labor is a critical input in the production of goods and services. Higher nominal wages will cause firms to be less willing and able to produce output at any price level, and so SRAS decreases. This will not cause the LRAS curve to decrease, however, as the nation's potential output has not decreased.

258. (C) The long-run aggregate supply curve (LRAS) is vertical at the level of real GDP that corresponds to the nation's potential output. This level of real GDP is also called full-employment output, or the amount of GDP that can be produced when there exists no cyclical unemployment. If the LRAS has increased, the nation has experienced growth in the ability to produce goods and services.

259. (D) A nation can see an increase in long-run aggregate supply if something has caused the nation to become permanently more productive. Government tax credits for investment in new technology will allow firms to increase productivity; in other words, more output is possible for the same quantities of labor and capital.

260. (C) One of the key factors that allow a nation's productive potential to keep moving outward is the level of human capital (education and training) in the labor force. When a nation achieves more human capital, potential output rises. However, if a nation's students are graduating from high school at lower rates, this will actually decrease long-run productivity and reduce potential real GDP.

261. (E) The key words in this statement to pay attention to are "potential output." The vertical long-run aggregate supply curve marks the level of real GDP that equates to the nation's potential output. This level of output is sometimes referred to as "full-employment GDP" or the "non-accelerating inflation rate of unemployment" (NAIRU). This level of GDP corresponds to the natural rate of unemployment or the situation that would exist when cyclical unemployment was zero. If output were to increase further, and the unemployment rate were to fall further, inflation would accelerate. In this problem, potential output has decreased, so the LRAS curve must have shifted to the left.

262. (B) This difference in Keynesian and classical theory is why classical economists draw the aggregate supply curve as vertical and Keynesians draw it as horizontal. The classical belief is that the economy always returns to full employment at the vertical aggregate supply curve. If there is a recession, prices will quickly adjust downward and the economy returns to full employment. Keynesians, on the other hand, believe that a recession will not reduce prices, because they are sticky; the only thing that will happen is a large reduction in output.

263. (A) Classical economists see the aggregate supply curve as always vertical at full employment. This is consistent with the notion that free markets will quickly come back to equilibrium at full employment. Citing the Great Depression as evidence to the contrary, Keynesians believe that when output is very low, there is a huge surplus of labor in labor markets, and unemployment is rampant. If output begins to rise, wages and prices will not increase because of the surplus of labor. However, as output gets closer and closer to full employment, the surplus in the labor market is eliminated, and wages and prices must begin to rise. The Keynesian view therefore implies that the aggregate supply is horizontal at first but eventually becomes upward sloping as output approaches full employment.

264. (D) These statements are really hallmarks of classical economics. Product markets and the labor market will quickly adjust to equilibrium, and this implies that the macroeconomy will quickly adjust to the level of real GDP that is associated with full employment. If the government attempts to manipulate the economy to further lower the unemployment rate, the only outcome will be inflation. This implies a vertical aggregate supply curve and no role for the government in economic policy.

265. (C) As time has passed, most economists have merged the Keynesian and classical views of aggregate supply. At very low levels of output, the Keynesian view of aggregate supply is that it is essentially horizontal; output can rise without inflation. As output approaches potential GDP, some inflation will occur because labor markets are becoming tighter; this intermediate stage of aggregate supply is upward sloping. However, at full employment, output can no longer rise and the only outcome of attempts to raise output will be inflation; the classical view is a vertical aggregate supply.

Chapter 9: Macroeconomic Equilibrium

266. (D) The short-run macroeconomic equilibrium in an economy is the point at which the quantity of aggregate output supplied is equal to the quantity of aggregate output demanded. This intersection represents the quantity of goods and services that are actually produced and sold within an economy, and it is represented in the AD-AS model as the intersection of the short-run aggregate supply curve and the aggregate demand curve.

267. (B) When the short-run aggregate supply (SRAS) curve increases, or shifts to the right, at any given price level more aggregate output is supplied. Conversely, an alternate way of saying this is that for any given aggregate output level, the price level will be lower. When this occurs, the aggregate price level decreases and the aggregate output increases.

268. (A) An increase in the nominal wage rate would be an increase in the price of one of the factors of production. When this occurs, the short-run aggregate supply (SRAS) curve decreases (or shifts to the left). When SRAS decreases, this leads to an increase in the price level and a decrease in the aggregate output that is actually produced and sold in the economy in the short run.

269. (C) Exports are a component of aggregate demand, and when exports increase, the aggregate demand curve increases (or shifts to the right). This means that at any given price level, more aggregate demanded will be purchased. An increase in aggregate demand will therefore result in an increase in the real GDP (the output produced) and an increase in the price level.

270. (A) A decline in household income will lead to a decline in consumption, one of the components of aggregate demand. This will cause a leftward shift (or decrease) in the aggregate demand curve in the short run. As a result, the amount of aggregate output demanded in the economy will decrease, which would additionally cause the price level to decrease.

271. (D) A short-run macroeconomic equilibrium is the point where the aggregate output supplied is equal to the aggregate output demanded. This occurs where the short-run aggregate supply curve intersects the aggregate demand curve. In this graph, there are two different short-run macroeconomic equilibria, point q and point w. Note that neither point z nor point x represents any form of equilibrium.

272. (D) A short-run economic equilibrium represents the actual amount of output in an economy. Therefore, an intersection of the short-run aggregate supply curve represents an actual amount of output. The full employment output, however, represents a potential amount of output that the economy would be producing if it were at full employment. Therefore, Y_E represents a hypothetical amount of output.

273. (B) A decrease in investment will lead to a decrease in the aggregate demand curve. In Figure 9.1 this is represented by AD_1 shifting to AD_2. The short-run equilibrium changes from point w to point q. As a result the price level decreases from PL_1 to PL_2, and the aggregate output decreases from Y_1 to Y_2.

274. (C) The output gap refers to the difference between what an economy is actually producing and what it would be producing if it were producing at the full employment level of output. To find any output gap, first determine whether or not the amount that an economy is currently producing, let's call it Y^*, is above or below full employment output, let's call it Y_E. If the economy is producing above full employment output the output gap is $Y^* - Y_E$, and if the economy is operating below full employment output, the output gap is $Y_E - Y^*$. In the second period, the economy is producing an aggregate output of Y_2. However, full employment output is Y_E. Therefore $Y_E - Y_2$ represents the output gap.

275. (B) A *negative demand shock* is the term used to refer to when aggregate demand (AD) decreases, or shifts to the left, as is shown in Figure 9.1. A positive demand shock refers to when aggregate demand increases (or shifts to the right). A negative supply shock refers to when the short-run aggregate supply (SRAS) curve decreases (or shifts to the left), and a positive supply shock refers to when the SRAS increases (or shifts to the right).

276. (A) When aggregate demand increases, this results in an increase in the price level. As a result of this increase in aggregate demand, the aggregate output in this economy has returned to the full employment aggregate output, which means the unemployment rate will be equal to the natural rate of unemployment. Note, however, that this economy has *not* experienced economic growth. Economic growth is the ability to produce more goods and services, which would be reflected by a shift in the long-run aggregate supply curve, which has not occurred here.

277. (D) Figure 9.2 shows an initial short-run equilibrium where the economy is producing below the full employment level. The difference between what the economy was producing (Y_1) and what the economy should be producing (Y_E) is an output gap. Since the economy is producing less than the optimal level of output, the economy is in recession and therefore a gap such as this ($Y_E - Y_1$) is sometimes called a recessionary output gap.

278. (B) When the short-run aggregate supply curve decreases, as is shown in Figure 9.3, the aggregate output decreases and the price level increases. The natural rate of unemployment is associated with the long-run aggregate supply (LRAS) curve. When the LRAS curve shifts, the natural rate of unemployment will change. Since the LRAS curve has not shifted, there is no change in the natural rate of unemployment.

279. (C) To find the amount of the output gap, you subtract the current level of aggregate output from the full employment output. As a result of the decrease in SRAS shown, the actual current level of aggregate output is $70, but the full employment level of output is $100. Therefore, $100 − $70 = $30. This means that the economy would need to increase output by $30 to return to the natural rate of unemployment.

280. (E) A short-run equilibrium is where an aggregate demand (AD) curve intersects a short-run aggregate supply (SRAS) curve, which occurred at an aggregate output level of $100 before the shift in SRAS, so I is definitely true. A long-run equilibrium occurs when the current aggregate output is equal to the full employment level of output. Graphically, this is where AD intersects both SRAS and the long-run aggregate supply (LRAS) curve at the same point. Therefore, II is definitely true. Note that when an economy is producing the full employment level of output, the economy will be at the natural rate of unemployment, not zero unemployment, so III is also correct.

281. (B) If government increased government spending, aggregate demand would increase (or shift to the right). This could create a new short-run equilibrium at the full employment level of output. However, when aggregate demand increases, the price level increases. Therefore, any attempt to correct the negative supply shock shown will result in a worsening of the inflation that has already occurred.

282. (A) *Stagflation* is the term for a very special short-run macroeconomic outcome: the combination of inflation and stagnation. That is when the aggregate output of an economy decreases and the economy experiences a simultaneous increase in the price level. Stagflation is always caused by a negative supply shock, as is shown in Figure 9.3.

283. (C) When there is a negative supply shock (i.e., short-run aggregate supply decreases), output decreases, which means that unemployment increases, and prices increase as well. When there is a positive supply shock, output increases, which means that unemployment decreases and prices decrease as well. Therefore, the price level and the unemployment rate move in the same direction, and output moves in the opposite direction whenever there is a supply shock.

284. (A) When the price of an energy source such as natural gas increases, this causes the short-run aggregate supply curve to decrease (or shift to the left). When there is a negative supply shock such as this, inflation occurs. Each of the other options would lead to decrease in the price level rather than an increase in the price level.

285. (A) Negative supply shocks and positive demand shocks are both sources of inflation. If there is a positive demand shock, the aggregate demand curve shifts to the right and the price level increases. On the other hand, a negative supply shock will cause the short-run aggregate supply curve to shift to the left; however, this will also cause an increase in the price level.

286. (C) When an economy is in long-run equilibrium, the short-run aggregate supply curve and the aggregate demand curve intersect at a short-run equilibrium, and this short-run equilibrium is also at the full employment level of output. If there is a positive demand shock, the aggregate demand curve will shift to the right and aggregate output will be higher than the full employment level of output. This will drive the unemployment rate lower than the natural rate of unemployment in the short run. However, the fundamental ability of the nation to produce has not changed, so the long-run natural rate of unemployment will not change.

287. (D) When an economy is in long-run equilibrium, the short-run aggregate supply curve and the aggregate demand curve intersect at a short-run equilibrium, and this short-run equilibrium is also at the full employment level of output. If there is a negative demand shock, the aggregate demand curve will shift to the left. This will create a new short-run equilibrium at a lower level of output than the full employment rate, and as a result the unemployment rate will become higher than the natural rate of unemployment. The price level will also decrease as a result of the leftward shift in aggregate demand.

288. (C) At a long-run equilibrium, output is at the full employment rate of output. When there is a negative demand shock, aggregate demand will shift to the left and the result will initially be a decrease in output, an increase in the unemployment rate, and a decrease in the price level. However, the higher rate of unemployment will lead to a lower wage rate, lowering the price of labor. This will cause the short-run aggregate supply curve to increase, returning the output to the full employment level of output, which returns the unemployment rate to the natural rate of unemployment. The only change in the long run is that the price level will decrease compared to the price level at the initial long-run equilibrium.

289. (B) If there is a negative supply shock, the short-run aggregate supply curve will decrease (shift to the left). This will initially cause the output to decrease, the unemployment rate to increase, and the price level to increase. However, over the long run, the prices of the factors of production will adjust and short-run aggregate supply will return to its initial point.

290. (C) In the long run, demand shocks can change only the price level, not the natural rate of unemployment or the full employment level of output. The full employment level of output depends on the stock of the factors of production, and whenever there is a demand shock (whether positive or negative), the prices of the factors of production will change, but the stock of those factors will not.

291. (D) A critical distinction is the difference between an increase in output and economic growth. An increase in output can be temporary; economic growth is a permanent and sustained increase in output. Economic growth, therefore, is not reflected in an aggregate demand shock, but is represented only by an outward shift in the long-run aggregate supply curve.

292. (E) Figure 9.4 shows the segmented aggregate supply (AS) curve that appears in some textbooks. If aggregate demand (AD) increases in the C area of the curve, it will cause output to increase, but the price level will not increase. If AD increases in the B region, both output and the price level will increase. However, if AD increases in the A portion of the AS curve, then output will not change but there will be inflation.

293. (B) The segmented aggregate supply curve is sometimes used to represent the different macroeconomic theories in a single model. It incorporates the classical assumption that prices fully adjust in the long run, but output does not, and so the classical range is represented by the A region of the AS curve in Figure 9.4. The horizontal portion of the AS curve, labeled C, is called the Keynesian range. In this region of the aggregate supply curve, output is so low that increases in aggregate demand have no inflationary pressures. Region B on the curve is called the intermediate range, which is a hybrid of the two approaches.

294. (C) "Sticky prices" is a phrase that refers to the fact that prices, and wages in particular, tend to resist decreasing. This means that the aggregate supply curve is horizontal and the level of production is below the full employment level of production. Sticky wages are a feature of Keynesian theory. This means that even if output declines in this region, the price level will not be likely to decrease.

295. (D) If aggregate demand increases, the short-run impact is that the aggregate demand curve (AD) shifts to the right. This will cause an increase in output and an increase in the price level in the short run. However, in the long run, the increase in output will put inflationary pressures on the factors of production, in particular on wages. As a result, in the long run, the short-run aggregate supply curve will decrease. This will return the economy to the full employment output, but will place even further inflationary pressures on the price level.

296. (C) A shift of the production possibilities frontier (PPF), whether it is curved or linear, represents an increase in the ability to produce goods and services. A movement along a PPF represents only a change in the allocation of the factors of production, rather than an increase in technology or in the stock of the factors of production that are available. Therefore, a shift out of the production possibilities curve is akin to an increase in long-run aggregate supply: both are ways of illustrating economic growth.

297. (C) To find an output gap, first determine whether it is an inflationary gap or a recessionary gap. If the current level of output is less than the full employment level of output, then the gap is recessionary. To find a recessionary gap, solve: recessionary gap = full employment GDP – current GDP. Here, this is $240 − $200 = $40.

Chapter 10: Money and Financial Institutions

298. (C) Money is generally anything that is used to facilitate the transfer of goods and services between buyers and sellers. In general, anything that performs the three functions of money consistently can be considered money. While it is true that in many economies paper currency is a dominant form of money, this definition of money is too narrow. Similarly, a definition based on being made of (or even backed by) precious metals is not appropriate, as a number of economies have used moneys that do not fit this definition. Finally, although choice E is a tempting answer, it is not accurate. Indeed, in times of runaway inflation, even legal tender currencies will fail at the three functions of money and ultimately collapse regardless of government decree.

299. (B) Liquidity is the ability to convert an asset into goods and services, or cash, which can then be easily converted into goods and services. There are a wide variety of financial assets in an economy with varying degrees of liquidity. Cash is generally the most liquid asset, as it is effortlessly converted into goods and services. An asset such as a mutual fund, however, may need to go through several steps to convert its value into goods and services.

300. **(A)** A bond is a promise to repay, similar to an IOU, issued by a borrower of money. It is an agreement that the borrower will repay, at the end of the term of the agreement, the principal amount. Until that date, the agreement requires the borrower to also pay the holder of the bond a fixed amount of interest. Although they are both forms of borrowing, bonds as an asset have the advantage over loans in that loans are not standardized nor rated as easily as bonds are.

301. **(E)** The purpose of a financial system is to bring borrowers and lenders together in an efficient and effective way. To do this, a financial system must do three things well. First, it must reduce transaction costs, such as enabling borrowers and lenders to have accurate information about risk. Second, a financial system must help individuals and institutions minimize their risks. Finally, it must ensure that people are able to balance the need to hold illiquid assets and the need to have liquid assets as well.

302. **(A)** A bank is a financial intermediary that takes the liquid assets (cash and similar assets) and keeps them in the form of a bank deposit. The lenders of these liquid assets are able to access these funds to cover purchases of goods and services. The bank then uses these assets to finance investment spending needs of borrowers.

303. **(E)** Cash is the most liquid of financial assets. Bank deposits are also very liquid financial assets, as the holder of the bank deposit can generally access these funds and convert them to cash very easily. Bonds are less liquid than bank deposits or cash, but the nature of bonds make them easily tradable and thus fairly liquid compared to other forms of financial assets. A life insurance company is a financial intermediary, but is not itself considered a financial asset. Loans, however, are a financial instrument that are, by their nature, very illiquid.

304. **(C)** Anything that performs all three roles of money can be considered money. One of these roles is as a medium of exchange, meaning it must be an asset that can be used to trade for goods and services. Note that both commodity money and fiat money can serve as a medium of exchange. By buying Melanie flowers, Eric is engaging in exchange, and the money he uses to buy them is simply a means by which to do this.

305. **(A)** Margaret's pay is able to maintain its value. If it did not, Margaret would not be able to save it—she would immediately have to spend all of her money before its value disappeared. This is one of the reasons that some things, such as ice, would poorly serve as money. Even if it worked as a unit of account and a medium of exchange, it would be difficult for it to maintain its value.

306. **(D)** In Maxistan, people are paid in an asset that they can either consume or use to perform the roles of money. This is the very definition of commodity money: a form of money that serves the roles of money as well as has intrinsic value. Other commodity monies that have existed in history have been things such as gold and cigarettes.

307. **(A)** When there is hyperinflation, money loses its function as a store of value: goods and services may cost $100 dollars in the morning, but the same goods and services may cost $100,000 by that afternoon. In such a situation, you would have to immediately spend any money you received before it became worthless.

308. (D) Comparing cheese to saunas is not easy. If you knew how much each of these things was worth, however, the decision would be very easy. For instance, if you knew that Gary was offering you $200 worth of goods, but Patrick was offering you $250 worth of services, this comparison would be simple. Because we have no unit of account for the goods, however, it is difficult to assess their worth and make a transaction.

309. (B) A financial asset is an asset that gives the holder of that asset a claim on future income. For instance, a bond is a financial asset because the bond holder receives income from the issuer of the bond. A physical asset is a claim to an item with an actual physical presence. For instance, a title to a car is a physical asset: the holder of the title can use the object of value, the car, as the holder wishes.

310. (E) A financial system matches households, individuals, firms, and governments that have excess funds with households, individuals, firms, and governments who would like to use those funds to some investment end. In other words, a financial system is a type of market that matches savers with excess funds and borrowers with productive uses of those funds.

311. (A) The key to understanding why money is not, strictly speaking, a financial asset is to recall the definition of a financial asset: a claim to future income. Money is an asset because it functions as a store of value, but not a financial asset, because it does not entail a claim to future income.

312. (B) Commodity-backed money is a money that itself has no intrinsic value, but whose value is guaranteed with some commodity. In this case, since one may exchange the paper currency of Ile on demand for a commodity, silver, it would be considered commodity-backed money. If one could not exchange this paper currency for something of value on demand, it would be considered fiat money.

313. (B) Some people find it counterintuitive that money in checking accounts, and not just currency, are considered money. The reason that noncurrency items are counted as being part of the money supply is because they *are* money; that is, they are able to perform all three functions of money. Consider these in terms of a checking account. When you deposit a check into the account, the money you deposit stores its value until you use it. You can easily check your balance at any time and a firm amount of value is there (i.e., your balance is $200). Finally, you can write a check or use a debit card against the balance in your checking account to purchase goods and services.

314. (A) The money in Jack's checking account is counted as money. Note that for the first few transactions, both perform all three functions of money identically. However, eventually the savings account becomes less liquid. Because checking and savings accounts differ in terms of their liquidity, they are counted differently in the money supply. The money supply consists of two broad monetary aggregates, M1 and M2, where M1 is more liquid than M2. Jack's checking account would be counted in M1, and his less liquid savings account is counted in M2.

315. (D) The money supply in the United States comprises two monetary aggregates, that is, two categories of things that are counted as money, called M1 and M2. Small time deposits (less than $100,000) are similar to savings accounts, but have restrictions requiring them to be held at the bank for some period of time (these are sometimes called certificates of deposits, or CDs). Large time deposits are those over $100,000 in value. Prior to 2006, large time deposits were counted in a monetary aggregate called M3; however, not only has this monetary aggregate not been included in the official money supply, it isn't even tracked anymore.

316. (B) As the category of a monetary aggregate has a higher number, that aggregate is less liquid than the category that precedes it. M1 is, therefore, more liquid than M2, and M2 is more liquid than M3, and so on. Another way of thinking about this is that as the number gets higher, the definition of what exactly counts as money gets broader: M1 is a more narrow definition of money than M2.

317. (D) The present value of $Y reflects the amount of money that you would need to have today to be equivalent of receiving $Y at some point in time t years in the future if the interest rate is i. For instance, suppose you were offered $100 in 1 year from now and the interest rate is 10%. The current value of $100 in 1 year in the future is PV($100) = $100/(1 + 0.1)^1 = $90.91. The intuition behind this is simple: if you put $91 in the bank, and the bank paid 10% interest, it would be worth $100 in 1 year.

318. (E) To find the present value of a given dollar amount after a given amount of time at a given interest rate, you simply plug these values into the formula to find present value. Here, PV($500) = $500/(1 + 0.10)^1 = $500/1.1 = $454.55. Part of the intuition behind present value is that we prefer to have things in the present rather than the future. For instance, if you were offered the choice of $454.55 today or $454.55 in 1 year, getting the money today would be the obvious choice. We are willing to defer using money because we get interest to make up for this loss of immediate use. But if you were asked to choose between $454.55 today or $500 in 1 year from today, you would be indifferent between the two.

319. (C) This question is asking for the future value of a dollar amount. To find the future value of $Y, 1 year in the future, at an interest rate of i, use the formula FV($Y) = $Y(1 + i)$. Here, $1,000 is loaned at a 20% rate of interest, so FV($1,000) = $1,000 × (1 + 0.2) = $1,000 × 1.2 = $1,200. This means that in 1 year, Eric will pay Eli back the $1,000 principal (the amount that he borrowed) plus $200 in interest.

320. (B) Jane is essentially interested in obtaining a particular future value with her money, so to solve for the rate of interest she would need to get, we use the future value of money formula and plug in the information we are given: $130 = $100(1 + i)$. Now we simply solve for i to find the rate of interest that will give her $130 in 1 year from now if she deposits $100 in her bank: $130 = $100 + $100i$, which becomes $30 = $100i$, or $i = 0.30$, so she would need to get an interest rate of 30% to get $130 in 1 year.

321. (A) A common misperception is that the Federal Reserve System was created in response to the Great Depression when in fact it predates the Great Depression of the 1930s. In fact, the Federal Reserve System was created in response to a number of bank panics and crises that occurred just after the turn of the century (and the one that occurred in 1907 in particular).

322. (C) The Federal Reserve System was designed to have several key functions: maintain the stability of the financial system, oversee and regulate banks, provide financial services to depository institutions, and conduct monetary policy. Contrary to popular belief, it does not print money. Rather, the Treasury Department prints currency, and the Federal Reserve System distributes that money.

323. (A) The Board of Governors comprises seven members who are appointed by the US president and approved by the Senate, and is responsible for overseeing the entire system, including the Federal Reserve District banks. The 12 Federal Reserve District banks are primarily responsible for providing banking, supervisory, and regulatory services in their region. Additionally, district banks may have additional special tasks that they are responsible for.

324. (D) The Federal Open Market Committee (FOMC) is primarily charged with conducting monetary policy, which can be used to prevent, mitigate, or address macroeconomic fluctuations in the economy. The FOMC has a number of tools at its disposal to use the money supply to dampen macroeconomic fluctuations. Note, however, that this does not mean that the FOMC prints currency.

325. (A) Traditionally the Federal Reserve has used three tools in the conduct of monetary policy: the reserve ratio, the discount rate, and most commonly, open-market operations. More recently, the Federal Reserve has purchased securities more directly through a program called Quantitative Easing. Tax rates, however, are not an element of monetary policy but rather fiscal policy.

326. (D) Banks operate on what is known as a fractional reserve system. This means that banks do not keep every dollar deposited into accounts on hand, but rather some proportion of these. This means that if a large number of people suddenly start withdrawing all of their money, the bank may not have enough money on hand to meet those demands and may collapse. Such an event is called a bank run.

327. (A) Banks that operate on a fractional reserve system must have enough money on hand to meet the day-to-day requirements of depositors. As part of the banking regulatory system, the Federal Reserve sets a minimum proportion of money that banks must keep on deposit to meet those demands, known as the required reserve ratio.

328. (D) Not all money in a bank is counted as part of the money supply. In particular, money held as part of reserves is not included in the money supply. The intuition behind this is clear: the money supply includes things that can serve as all three functions of money. Reserves, however, must be kept on hand, meaning they cannot be used as a medium of exchange. Therefore, they are not counted in the money supply.

329. (C) A little more than half of M1 comprises currency in circulation. The next largest category of M1 is checkable deposits (such as checking accounts), which is close to half of M1. The remaining categories of M1 make up a very tiny proportion of the narrowest definition of money.

330. (C) The monetary base refers to a subset of moneys that are the most liquid. Near moneys refer to things that are basically almost money, but not quite. That is to say, they can't directly be used as a medium of exchange, but can be fairly easily converted to cash or a checking account deposit. Near moneys are, therefore, counted in M2.

331. (E) One of the goals of the design of the Federal Reserve System is to try to insulate members against short-term political concerns, which could destabilize the system. The presidential election cycle is 4 years, which means that even though members of the Board of Governors are chosen by the president and then confirmed by the Senate, a 14-year term helps insulate them from political pressures.

332. (D) The Federal Open Market Committee (FOMC) is designed to straddle the two main bodies of the Federal Reserve System: the Board of Governors and the Federal Reserve District Banks. The FOMC comprises all of the members of the Board of Governors and five of the presidents of the district banks. Of those five slots, one is always held by the president of the Federal Reserve Bank of New York, and the other slots rotate among the remaining 11 banks.

333. (B) The Glass-Steagall Act of 1933 was one of the regulatory responses to the Great Depression. It is designed to reduce the amount of risk that certain kinds of financial institutions can take to help prevent future banking failures like those that occurred during the Great Depression. It separates banks into commercial banks, whose deposits were covered by deposit insurance, and investment banks, which were not insured and engaged in riskier behavior.

334. (C) Salt, gold, silver, and cigarettes are all forms of commodity money (salt was used as payment during the Roman Empire and is where the term *salary* comes from). Metal coins (like American quarters), however, are not commodity money. While coins do contain metals with intrinsic value, the value of the metal contained in a coin is far less than the face value of that coin.

335. (B) As the number of the monetary aggregate increases, the measure is not only less liquid than the previous aggregate but also includes the previous aggregate. This means that M2 is less liquid than M1, and M2 contains M1. When it was tracked, M3 was less liquid than M2 and also contained M2 (which means M3 also contained M1).

336. (A) To solve this problem, we apply the present value formula: $PV(\$x) = \$x/(1 + i)^t$. We are told that the present value is $400 in 1 year, and the interest rate is 10%, so this formula becomes $400 = \$x/(1 + 0.1)$. Now we merely need to solve for $\$x$ to find the amount of money 1 year from now that would be equivalent to having $400 today. The result of solving this equation for $\$x$ is $440.

337. (E) When commercial banks borrow from the Federal Reserve, they pay the discount rate. The discount rate is a rate set by the Federal Reserve, usually about 1% higher than the federal funds rate, the rate that banks charge each other for very short-term loans. The Federal Reserve sets the discount rate slightly higher than the federal funds rate to discourage banks from seeking loans from the Federal Reserve and instead seek them from other banks.

Chapter 11: Monetary Policy

338. (D) Monetary policy is the use of the money supply to affect macroeconomic variables such as aggregate output, unemployment, and the price level. The money supply is used to affect interest rates, which in turn affect the investment component of aggregate demand. Understanding monetary policy therefore requires an understanding of the money market and how interest rates are determined.

339. (E) In most economies, some form of central bank is generally the agency responsible for conducting monetary policy. In the United States, the Federal Reserve Bank is the agency responsible for a number of tasks, among which is determining when, how, and if monetary policy should be used to affect macroeconomic variables.

340. (B) A T-account is a way of representing the assets and liabilities of a bank. On one side of the "T" are the liabilities of a bank: the amount of money that can be demanded from the bank (such as checkable deposits). On the other side are the assets of the bank: the financial instruments of value such as cash or loans that the bank holds.

341. (A) Under a fractional banking system, a bank is required to keep only a certain percentage of any checkable deposits on hand. In this case, there is $100,000, of which they must keep 20% on hand. Therefore, the bank must hold onto only $0.20 \times \$100,000 = \$20,000$ in cash in their vault on reserve. The bank is free to do a number of things with the remaining $80,000. It can keep it in the bank vault as well, or it can lend the money out and earn interest from the loan. It cannot, however, lend out more than $80,000, since it must keep at least $20,000 in reserve.

342. (E) When a bank has excess reserves, this means that it is keeping more than the reserves that it is required to keep on hand. We are told, however, that this bank has no excess reserves, so it is holding on reserve only the amount it is required to. The dollar amount that they must keep on hand is the reserve ratio (RR) multiplied by the amount of checkable deposits, in this case, $\$50,000 = \$200,000 \times RR$. To find the required reserves, we simply solve for RR, which yields 0.25, or 25%.

343. (C) If the required reserve ratio is 10%, then the Bank of Fredonia must keep 10% $\times \$200,000 = \$20,000$ on hand. However, the bank has $50,000 on hand, which is $30,000 more than it is required to keep to meet the day-to-day needs of depositors. The bank can continue to hang on to these excess reserves, or it can make up to $30,000 in additional loans.

344. (C) When cash deposits are made into the banks, those deposits actually cause the money supply to expand. The money supply includes cash that is being circulated throughout the economy and also the money that is deposited in the checking accounts at the nation's banks. Because banks are required to keep only a fraction of checking deposits in reserve, the majority of checking deposits (the excess reserves) can be lent to borrowers who need money to pay for homes, cars, or other expensive items. The process of cash deposits, loans to borrowers, and the redeposit of those funds into new checking deposits creates a multiplier effect that expands the money supply.

345. (C) The money supply comprises cash not held in reserves, cash in circulation, and checkable deposits. Consider an economy with only $10,000 in cash in it; so the money supply (MS) is $10,000. Now consider that if $10,000 is deposited in a bank, the MS is still equal to $10,000 (cash in circulation = 0 and checkable deposits = $10,000). If the bank is required to keep 20% in reserve, it must keep only $2,000 in the vault and now has $8,000 in excess reserves. If it lends that money out to someone, the bank's assets go down by the amount of cash that is lent ($8,000) and increases by the value of the loan ($8,000), so there is no change to the asset side of the bank's T-account. Note, however, that now cash in circulation is $8,000 and there are still $10,000 in checkable deposits, so MS = $18,000 as a result of the loan.

346. (D) The money multiplier (MM) is the maximum amount that a money supply will increase by as a result of an increase in the amount of excess reserves available, and it is dependent on the reserve ratio (RR). The MM is found using the equation MM = 1/RR. So for Fredonia, MM = 1/20% = 1/0.2 = 5. This means that if there are suddenly $100 in excess reserves, the money supply will increase by up to five times that amount (5 × $100 = $500).

347. (E) We cannot tell from the statement the dollar amount of reserves in either country, as we would need to know the dollar amount of checkable deposits in each country to determine this. Likewise, we cannot tell which country has a higher amount of excess reserves. We can, however, determine the money multiplier (MM) for each country. In Jacksonia the money multiplier is MM = 1/0.10 = 10, and in Amandania the money multiplier is MM = 1/0.2 = 5. Therefore, Jacksonia has a larger money multiplier.

348. (B) To determine the maximum amount that a money supply (MS) will increase, we multiply the amount of the injection of money by the money multiplier (MM), or (maximum increase in MS = $ injected × MM). Note that this reflects an upper limit on the amount that the money supply will increase. The MM of Maxistan is MM = 1/0.25 = 4, so for a $100,000 increase, $100,000 = injection × 4 means that if $25,000 is injected, the money supply will increase by up to $100,000. Therefore, there needs to be an injection of *at least* $25,000 to obtain this increase in the money supply.

349. (E) When the money multiplier is multiplied by the amount of the monetary injection, the resulting number represents the maximum potential increase. It is not possible for the money supply to increase by more than that amount. It is also not likely that the money supply will increase by exactly that amount due to leakage: banks may choose to keep some excess reserves, and people may choose to not deposit all of their money.

350. (B) Technological innovations that enable people to have ready access to cash, like ATMs (or at least use deposits for transactions, like debit cards), mean that people need to keep less cash on hand to carry out purchases of goods and services and can keep more in checkable deposits and other accounts. Note that the demand for money does not change in response to changes in the interest rate, but rather the quantity of money demanded responds to changes in the interest rate.

351. (D) If the reserve ratio is decreased, then a bank would suddenly have excess reserves that it could loan out, which would then increase the money supply. An increase in the reserve ratio, however, would result in a decrease in the money supply. Another way the money supply can be increased is if the Federal Reserve buys bonds, which injects money into the economy and starts the process of the multiple expansion of deposits.

352. (E) If real GDP increases, more money is necessary to conduct transactions and the demand for money will increase, which would increase the interest rate. An increase in the price level also increases the demand for money. If the reserve ratio is increased, this would decrease the money supply, which would raise interest rates. If the Federal Reserve buys bonds, however, the money supply will increase and the equilibrium interest rate will decrease.

353. (E) If any of these events occur, the process of the multiple expansion of deposits will stop. If people stop depositing money, banks will not have excess reserves to lend. If banks do not lend to borrowers, the expansion stops immediately. Finally, if the reserve requirement is raised, banks may even have insufficient reserves and will stop lending.

354. (A) With the initial money supply curve and the money demand curve given, the money market is in equilibrium when the interest rate is i_1. However, when the money supply increases, the quantity of money supplied exceeds the quantity demanded at interest rate i_1. As banks seek to lend excess funds, they will lower interest rates to attract more borrowers until the surplus of excess reserves clears.

355. (C) The Federal Reserve has traditionally had three main tools of monetary policy: open market operations (buying or selling bonds), raising or lowering the reserve ratio, and raising or lowering the discount rate. The Federal Reserve has almost exclusively used open market operations to conduct monetary policy. If the Federal Reserve wants to increase the money supply, it buys bonds, and if the Federal Reserve wants to decrease the money supply, it sells bonds.

356. (B) When the Federal Reserve announces changes in the interest rate, it announces the changes in terms of "basis points," which are 100ths of a percentage point. Therefore, a decrease in interest rates of 50 basis points is 0.5% (or one-half of a percentage point). To decrease the interest rate, the Federal Reserve will buy bonds, which increases the money supply. This causes the equilibrium interest rate in the money market to decrease.

357. (B) When monetary policy is used to affect macroeconomic aggregates, the primary target is the investment component of aggregate demand. Investment (I) is the creation of capital and other productive goods, and it is typically done by firms that borrow money to do so. Therefore, if the cost of borrowing money is lower, firms will be more likely to invest, which will increase aggregate output and decrease the unemployment rate.

358. (D) If the Federal Reserve sees a combination of low unemployment and high inflation, it may use monetary policy to decrease aggregate demand to alleviate inflationary pressures on the economy. To do this, it will sell bonds, which will lower the money supply. This results in an increase in the interest rate, which will cause investment to decrease. As a result, aggregate demand will decrease, aggregate output will decrease, the price level will fall, and the unemployment rate will increase.

359. (C) A common misperception is that the Federal Reserve sets interest rates, and in fact the phrase "the Federal Reserve set interest rates today" incorrectly appears in many media reports. The Federal Reserve uses open market operations to affect macroeconomic variables, which means it buys and sells bonds. To increase investment, the Federal Reserve will need to buy bonds to lower interest rates, making investment more affordable for firms.

360. (B) Figure 11.2 shows an economy that has experienced a decrease in aggregate demand from full employment to a level of output below full employment. When the economy is producing below the full employment level of output, the Federal Reserve may act to increase aggregate demand and bring output back to the full employment level. To do this, it will buy bonds, which will increase the money supply. This will lower the interest rate and increase investment, which shifts aggregate demand to the right.

361. (C) The Taylor rule for monetary policy is that the federal funds rate should have a target that takes inflation and the percentage of the output gap into consideration: federal funds rate = 1 + 1.5 × inflation rate + 0.5 × output gap. In Figure 11.2, the output gap is $(100 - 95)/100 = 5\%$, or -5% because the economy is operating below full employment (a recession). If inflation is 10%, then according to the Taylor rule, federal funds rate = 1 + 1.5 × 10% + 0.5 × (−5%) = 13.5%.

362. (E) The Taylor rule is a proposed way of using monetary policy to dampen economic swings, but without using the discretion of policy makers. It is a way of setting the federal funds rate (the rate at which banks loan money to each other) in such a way to take into account both inflation (which drives up the federal funds rate in the Taylor rule) and negative output gaps (which would drive down the federal funds rate).

363. (B) Traditionally open market operations are the primary tool of monetary policy: if output is too low, the Federal Reserve (or any other central bank) can increase the money supply to lower the interest rate and stimulate investment. However, an interest rate can go only so low—once the interest rate is at or near 0%, open market operations cannot be used to stimulate the economy, because a negative interest rate is impossible. This situation is called a liquidity trap.

364. (A) The demand for money is downward sloping based on a concept called liquidity preference. This is simply the idea that people prefer to keep some of their assets in the form of illiquid assets, as these tend to earn interest, but still need some amount of assets in cash to exchange for goods and services. The amount that they keep on hand will depend on their individual preferences, as well as the opportunity cost of holding money (i.e., the forgone interest when you hold an asset in the form of cash instead of another asset).

365. (D) Suppose you had the choice of keeping $1,000 in your checking account, where you could easily access it to buy goods and services, or in a certificate of deposit, which would make the value of the money more difficult to use but you would get 10% interest on it. By holding onto $1,000 in your checking account, you are giving up 10% × $1,000 = $100. If the interest rate goes up to 15%, you are giving up even more by holding it as cash.

366. (D) When the Federal Reserve sells bonds, this will decrease the money supply, which will drive interest rates up. This will have a dampening effect on the economy: lowering investment, which will decrease aggregate demand, decrease aggregate output, and raise unemployment. The Federal Reserve has a dual mandate to have stable prices and maintain employment. So the only reason that the Federal Reserve would increase unemployment is if prices had become unstable and there is high inflation.

367. (B) The quantity theory of money is a way of describing the relationship between output, price level, and the money supply in an economy. In the quantity theory, M represents the money supply, V represents the velocity of money (i.e., how many times currency changes hands), P represents the price level, and Y represents the amount of output in the economy.

368. (D) To solve this we can apply the quantity theory of money. There is $600 in the money supply, so M = $600. There are 1,200 oranges, so Y = 1,200. The oranges sell for $2 each, so P = $2. Therefore, MV = PY becomes $600 × V = $2 × 1,200, where V is the velocity of money, or how many times the currency changes hands. Solving for V yields V = 4, so each dollar bill in Ergo will change hands an average of four times.

214 〉 Answers

369. (E) The classical school in macroeconomics assumes that output is fixed. The velocity of money does not change either (or only very rarely), as it reflects more the spending habits of a population, the technology of money used, and other features that tend not to change often. Therefore, in the classical quantity theory of money, MV = PY, but V and Y will not change even if other variables do. This means, according to this school of thought, that if the money supply (M) increases, the only result will be an increase in the price level (P).

370. (D) If there is an increase in the demand for money, the demand curve for money will shift to the right. This leads to an increase in the interest rate. If the Federal Reserve wanted to maintain interest rates at the same level, it would have to increase the money supply at the same time, lowering the interest rate. In fact, there are different parts of the year when something very similar to this happens: people want to spend more money than usual (e.g., during holidays), and the Federal Reserve anticipates this and increases the money supply to prevent an increase in interest rates.

371. (A) If there is a financial innovation that allows people to keep fewer of their assets liquid, such as the invention of ATM machines or debit cards, then the demand for money will decrease. If the demand for money decreases, interest rates will decrease if the Federal Reserve takes no action. If the Federal Reserve wants to increase interest rates above what they already were, it will have to lower the money supply by a larger amount than the decrease in the demand for money.

372. (E) Figure 11.3 shows an increase in aggregate demand. This could occur if the investment component of aggregate demand increased. If the Federal Reserve wanted to stimulate investment, it would need to lower the interest rate, which it would do by increasing the money supply. If the Federal Reserve either lowered the reserve ratio or bought bonds, the money supply would increase.

373. (B) The Federal Reserve is said to operate under a dual mandate: maintain price stability and maintain full employment. In Figure 11.3 we see that the economy was experiencing a recessionary gap, so expansionary monetary policy was required to increase employment. Note that this does not mean that the objective of the Federal Reserve is to maintain an unemployment rate of zero or an inflation rate of zero. Indeed, if the Federal Reserve wanted to lower inflation, it would have to increase the unemployment rate to achieve this.

374. (A) When a bank is fully loaned out, it has exactly the amount of reserves that it is required to have on hand: any less and it would be violating banking regulations. When a customer withdraws money at this point, the bank must increase what it holds in its now depleted reserves. It has a number of options available to it, such as calling in loans, borrowing from other banks, or even as a last resort borrowing from the Federal Reserve. It cannot, however, lower its own required reserve ratio, as this is set by the Federal Reserve.

375. (A) If there is an increase in exports, this will increase aggregate demand in Cam, which will increase output, but also cause inflation. If the Central Bank of Cam wants to counteract this, it could take an action that would decrease aggregate demand, such as raising interest rates to discourage investment. If the Central Bank of Cam uses open market operations similar to the Federal Reserve, it would need to sell bonds to decrease the money supply, which would raise interest rates.

376. (B) When the central bank buys securities, it injects $100 million into the banking system. If this was a deposit from a large firm, the banking system must keep 20% of this (or $20 million) on hand as required reserves. But since this is essentially a deposit from the central bank, the entire $100 million is excess reserves that can be lent to borrowers. The final maximum impact of a $100 million injection will be $100 million × (1/20%) = $100 million × 5 = $500 million.

377. (C) If the central bank is buying securities, it is trying to increase the money supply to lower interest rates to stimulate the investment component of aggregate demand. This means that the economy is currently operating at less than full employment output. When an economy is operating at less than full employment, the unemployment rate is higher than the natural rate of unemployment.

Chapter 12: Fiscal Policy

378. (D) The marginal propensity to consume (MPC) describes the proportion of an additional dollar of income that people will spend. In this case, the MPC = 0.75, meaning that if someone receives an additional dollar of income, he or she will spend $0.75 of that dollar and save $0.25 of that dollar, so that for every additional dollar in income, some of it is saved and some of it is spent.

379. (E) Every dollar of additional income can only be saved or spent, so $1 = (the amount of the dollar spent) + (the amount of the dollar saved). Rephrased in terms of proportions of $1, 1 = (proportion spent) + (proportion saved). So the marginal propensity to consume (MPC) plus the marginal propensity to save (MPS) must equal one, or 1 = MPC + MPS. The government spending multiplier is the total change in GDP in proportion to the increase in government spending, or M = ΔGDP/ΔG. To find this amount, the formula for the government spending multiplier (M) is M = 1/(1 − MPC). Note, however, that since 1 = MPC + MPS, if we rearrange this we get 1 − MPC = MPS, so M = 1/MPS is equivalent to M = 1/(1 − MPC).

380. (D) If the marginal propensity to consume (MPC) is 0.8, then the government spending multiplier M is M = 1/(1 − 0.8) = 1/0.20 = 5. The multiplier is also represented by M = ΔGDP/ΔG. Therefore, to find the change in GDP that will result if there is no crowding out effect, we plug in the numbers we have (M = 5 and G = 20) to get 5 = ΔGDP/$20 million. Solving for ΔGDP yields $100 million. Therefore, if there is no crowding out, an increase in $20 million dollars of government spending will increase GDP by $100 million.

381. (C) Just as there is a government spending multiplier, there is a tax multiplier (Tm). The tax multiplier, however, tends to offset the government spending multiplier (M), which depends on the marginal propensity to consume (MPC). To find the tax multiplier, we use the formula Tm = −MPC × M. In this case, Tm = −0.8 × 5 = −4. This means for every $1 in higher taxes, GDP will decrease by $4. So if there is $20 million in new taxes, GDP will decrease by $80 million. The tax multiplier is often expressed as a negative value (as in this question) because a change in taxes causes a change in GDP in the opposite direction; higher taxes reduce GDP and lower taxes increase GDP.

382. (E) To find the effect on GDP of a change in government spending (G) and new taxes, we need to add these two effects together. The change due to the government spending is the amount of new government spending multiplied by the government spending multiplier; $\Delta GDP = \$20$ million $\times 5 = \$100$ million. The decrease in GDP due to the new taxes is the tax multiplier multiplied by the amount of new taxes, or $\Delta GDP = -4 \times \$20$ million $= -\$80$ million. Therefore, the total change in GDP is $\$100$ million $- \$80$ million $= \$20$ million. Note that the net effect on GDP is exactly the increase in government spending. Because the budget was balanced, the increase in government spending was paid for by an equivalent increases in taxes. This is known as the balanced budget multiplier: the balanced budget multiplier is always equal to 1, regardless of the MPC or the dollar amount.

383. (E) Whenever government spending is decreased, GDP will decrease. Whenever taxes are increased, GDP decreases. So if both of these are done simultaneously, it will result in the largest decrease in GDP. If the government increases spending with no changes in taxes collected, this will increase GDP by the largest amount, since there is no offsetting effect of taxes at all. Increasing spending with an increase in taxes by the same amount will also increase GDP.

384. (D) Fiscal policy refers to the use of either government spending or taxes to change macroeconomic variables such as unemployment, output (or GDP), and inflation. Either government spending exclusively, tax policy, or a combination of these two would be considered fiscal policy. Using the money supply, however, to manipulate macroeconomic variables would be considered monetary policy.

385. (A) In any given period of time (but usually considered over a year), a government may have more government spending than it takes in through tax revenues. When this occurs, it is called a budget deficit, and the deficit is the amount of the shortfall during that period. On the other hand, it is also possible for a government to collect more tax revenues than it spends. If it does so, this situation is called a budget surplus.

386. (B) In each of the previous 20 years, Maxistan has collected less in tax revenue than it spent, meaning that in each of the 20 years, it has run a budget deficit. For instance, in year 1 Maxistan overspent by $2 million, and in year 2 Maxistan overspent by another $2 million, thus overspending a total of $4 million over those two years. As deficits are financed using borrowing over time, the government accumulates national debt.

387. (B) Contractionary fiscal policy refers to using either government spending or tax policy to reduce the size of the economy, that is, using lower government spending, higher taxes, or both to lower output and raise unemployment, usually to lower the rate of inflation. Using the money supply to increase or decrease inflation would be different types of monetary policy.

388. (C) Expansionary fiscal policy refers to using higher government spending or lower taxes to increase the size of the economy. That is, expansionary fiscal policy is using fiscal policy tools to increase output and decrease unemployment; as a result, this may lead to an increase in the price level. For instance, if the government increases government spending, this is designed to increase output and decrease unemployment, which may also lead to an increase in the price level. Policy makers in this situation are attempting to reduce the unemployment rate and are willing to trade off some inflation for a stronger labor market.

389. (C) If the unemployment rate is higher than the natural rate of unemployment, GDP is below the full employment output. If the government decides to address this, it would need to engage in expansionary fiscal policy. To engage in expansionary fiscal policy, the government could either increase government spending or decrease taxes. Either will increase output and decrease the unemployment rate.

390. (D) Automatic stabilizers are changes that occur to fiscal policy that do not require any action on the part of the government, that is to say, they happen automatically and no discretion is needed to determine whether or not something changes. For instance, when unemployment is high, expansionary fiscal policy is appropriate. If government spending will go up automatically when expansionary fiscal policy is appropriate, this would be an example of an automatic stabilizer.

391. (B) A progressive tax is an example of an automatic stabilizer. When incomes increase during an economic expansion, more incomes get pushed into higher marginal tax brackets, effectively acting as contractionary fiscal policy. On the other hand, when incomes decrease, people move into lower tax brackets, effectively acting as expansionary fiscal policy. Both occur without any action from the government.

392. (D) The market for loanable funds describes the market in which savings become investment. The supply of loanable funds comes from those who save and earn interest in exchange for their savings. The demand for loanable funds comes from those who wish to use those savings by borrowing money for either deficit spending by the government or firms and individuals borrowing money in exchange for paying interest. Thus the interest rate (the price of borrowing) will change to bring the quantity demanded of loanable funds in line with the quantity supplied of loanable funds.

393. (A) In the market for loanable funds, if demand increases, the equilibrium interest rate will also increase. This occurs because when borrowers want to borrow more money, the borrowers will bid up the interest rate to attract more money to borrow. If this does not occur, lenders will not be willing to supply any more money, and a shortage of loanable funds would exist.

394. (D) Figure 13.1 shows an increase in the demand for loanable funds. This can come from two possible sources. First, firms may perceive that there will be improved business opportunities in the future. This increases their incentive to invest, and thus the demand for loanable funds will increase as a result of their desire to borrow to fund investment spending. Second, this increase in the demand for loanable funds may be because of an increase in borrowing by the government.

395. (E) This question is asking you how changes in capital inflows and outflows affect the market for loanable funds. If savers in Maxistan see higher interest rates in Ile, they will save their money in Ile, thus increasing the supply of loanable funds in Ile. This will simultaneously decrease the supply of loanable funds in Maxistan. As the interest rate in Ile falls, and the interest rate in Maxistan rises, this flow of financial capital will equilibrate interest rates in both nations.

396. (B) The idea of the crowding out effect is that when government increases deficit spending, the resulting effect on interest rates will offset increases in aggregate demand. When governments engage in additional government spending, this causes aggregate demand to increase. However, if they engage in deficit spending, the government must borrow to pay for this spending. By borrowing, the government drives up the interest rate, thus crowding out private investment and consumption spending, which will decrease aggregate demand.

397. (B) If an economy is initially producing at AD_A, an increase in government spending will increase aggregate demand because of an increase in the G component in aggregate demand, as represented by the curve AD_G. However, if this government spending is not paid for out of tax revenues, the government will have to borrow money. This will increase the interest rate in the market for loanable funds. As a result of the increase in the interest rate investment spending (the I component of GDP) falls, and the increase in aggregate demand will be somewhat reduced, as shown by the slight shift to the left of AD to AD_X.

398. (E) The shift from AD_A to AD_G is an expansion, but the subsequent shift back to AD_X is the result of the crowding out effect. Crowding as a result of deficit government spending can come from two sources. First, an increase in interest rates can crowd out private investment. Second, the increase in interest rates will make purchasing securities (which earn that higher interest rate) more attractive to foreign investors. Suppose this represented the United States, and Treasury bills are now more attractive to foreign investors. However, to buy those securities, foreign investors will need to have US dollars. When foreign investors purchase dollars, it drives up the value of the dollar. This will in turn make our exported goods more expensive, and so exports may decrease.

399. (B) The Fisher effect states that an increase in the expected rate of inflation will have no effect on real interest rates. For example, suppose initially there is no expected inflation, so the current real rate is the same as the nominal rate of interest and is equal to 5%. In response to expected inflation of 10%, the demand for loanable funds will increase (shift up) by a 1% increase in the nominal rate for every 1% increase in inflation. The supply of loanable funds will also decrease by a 1% decrease in the nominal rate for every 1% increase in inflation. Therefore, a new equilibrium nominal interest rate will exist at 10% higher than before, or 15%. However, the real rate of interest = nominal rate of interest − inflation, so here 5% = 15% − 10%, so the real rate of interest has not changed.

400. (A) The crowding out effect offsets the positive impact of deficit government spending on the GDP. When governments must borrow, this drives up the interest rates, which discourages investment (I) by private firms. As a result, even though the G category of aggregate demand increases, the I category decreases, partially (or even completely) offsetting the increase in GDP due to the expansionary fiscal policy.

401. (A) When economies are in recessions, they tend to automatically run deficits, because automatic stabilizers tend to increase government spending during recessions and decrease tax revenues during recessions. When economies are in expansions, they are more likely to experience surpluses, since government spending decreases during expansions and tax revenues increase during expansions. Therefore, it may be of more interest as to whether an economy has a balanced budget on average over the course of the entire business cycle, rather than having a balanced budget regardless of where an economy is in the business cycle.

402. (D) According to Keynesian theory, expansionary fiscal policy is useful to fight recessions because on the Keynesian portion of the segmented aggregate supply curve, this will lead to increases in aggregate demand and no corresponding increase in inflation. According to classical economics, however, no discretionary policy of any kind should ever be used, since prices will always adjust in the long run and output will return to full employment on the vertical long-run aggregate supply (LRAS) curve. The modern consensus says that discretionary fiscal policy to affect the business cycle is probably not a good idea unless circumstances are exceptional (such as particularly severe recessions), as problems such as policy lags may cause more harm than good in the long run.

403. (B) The effect of decreasing government spending on the macroeconomy is that aggregate output would decrease, unemployment would increase, and the price level may decrease. However, increasing the money supply would decrease the interest rate, which would increase investment, increase aggregate output, decrease unemployment, and increase the price level. Therefore, these two actions, if they occurred simultaneously, might counteract each other.

404. (C) If the Federal Reserve wanted to control inflation, it would act to increase interest rates by decreasing the money supply. If the government decreased government spending, this would also lessen inflationary pressures, perhaps by increasing tax rates. However, if the government paid down debt with a budget surplus, the demand for loanable funds would decrease. This would drive the interest rate down, which would increase the investment component of aggregate demand and put upward pressure on the price level.

405. (C) The larger the marginal propensity to consume (MPC) is, the larger both the spending multiplier (M) and the tax multiplier (Tm) will be. The formula for the spending multiplier is $M = 1/(1 - MPC)$, and the formula for the tax multiplier is $Tm = -MPC \times M$. If the MPC is 0.75, then M is 4 and Tm is -3. However, if the MPC is 0.8, then M is 5 and Tm is -0.8×5, or -4. If people save more and therefore spend less of each additional dollar of income, the MPC is lower and thus so is Tm.

406. (B) When governments run a balanced budget, that is, the amount of tax revenue is equal to the amount of government spending, then all else equal, there is no effect on the interest rate. However, if the government runs a deficit, it must borrow money, which drives up interest rates. On the other hand, if the government runs a surplus and uses this to pay down debt, this will decrease interest rates.

407. (C) Most economists believe that discretionary fiscal policy can have an effect on unemployment in the short run. However, the long-run rate of unemployment is tied to the full employment level of output, which is tied to a country's stock of the factors of production. Without changing one of these directly, discretionary policy would have no effect on employment in the long run.

408. (D) If the marginal propensity to save in Teragram is 0.2, then the marginal propensity to consume is 0.8, the spending multiplier is 5, and the tax multiplier is -4. Therefore, if the government pays for spending by raising taxes (i.e., a "balanced budget" policy), this will not increase interest rates and drive down investment, but will only increase GDP by $20 million. On the other hand, the government spending is paid for by borrowing, and the spending multiplier of 5 will magnify this effect to eventually increase gross domestic product by $100 million. However, the crowding out effect (rising interest rates in the market for loanable funds) due to the borrowing will dampen the total impact of the expansionary fiscal policy by reducing investment spending.

409. (C) If government spending is $100 million and the marginal propensity to consume is 0.5, this means that the multiplier (M) = 1/(1 − 0.5) = 2 and the tax multiplier is Tm = −0.5 × 2 = −1. Therefore, if this policy is financed solely through deficit spending and borrowing, the net effect on GDP will be the difference between the initial $200 million increase in GDP and the crowding out effect. If the crowding out effect were larger than the multiplier, the net effect on GDP would be negative (i.e., GDP would decrease rather than increase). If Ile financed increased taxes by $50 million, the net effect on GDP would be ($100 million × 2) − (1 × $50 million) = $150 million, less the impact of the crowding out effect. Therefore, only the third option is possible.

410. (C) There is no national statute in the United States that requires a balanced budget. Many state and local municipalities, however, do have such legal requirements. This means that while automatic stabilizers can allow the federal budget to run at a deficit, state and local governments with such laws cannot. Therefore, even if the federal government cuts taxes to stimulate spending during a recession, local cash-strapped governments may be increasing taxes (or decreasing spending) and offset some of the increase in GDP from government spending.

411. (B) At the national level, the marginal propensity to consume (MPC) is the change in consumption spending divided by the change in national income, or $\Delta C/\Delta NI$. Table 12.1 shows us that for every $100 increase in income, that consumption rises by $75 so the MPC = $\Delta C/\Delta NI$ = $75/$100 = 0.75.

412. (A) Using Table 12.1, we determine that the marginal propensity to consume (MPC) is equal to 0.75. This allows us to compute the spending multiplier (M) of 4 and the tax multiplier (Tm) of −3. An increase in GDP of $2,400 could be the result of three policy options. First, there could be an increase of government spending equal to $2,400 with a corresponding increase in taxes of $2,400. Because the balanced budget multiplier is equal to 1, this would increase GDP by $2,400. Second, because the tax multiplier is −3, we could decrease taxes by $800, which would multiply by a factor of 3 to increase GDP by $2,400. Finally, we could increase government spending by $600, which would multiply by a factor of 4 to increase GDP by $2,400.

413. (E) An inflationary gap means the economy is currently producing $1,800 more than full employment GDP. If government policy makers wish to return the economy to full employment, they must reduce aggregate demand with higher taxes, lower government spending, or both. Because the MPC is 0.75, the spending multiplier is 4 and the tax multiplier is −3. A reduction in government spending of $450 would reduce GDP by $1,800 (4 × $450) or an increase in taxes equal to $600 would reduce GDP by $1,800 (3 × $600).

414. (D) Economic data gathering is always months behind the business cycle, so the beginning of a recession is always dated in hindsight. If the recession has already begun, and economists have not yet recognized it, this recognition lag can hinder the effectiveness of fiscal or monetary policy. By the time the political decisions are made and spending programs are implemented, these further lags reduce policy effectiveness.

Chapter 13: The Relationship Between Inflation and Unemployment

415. (C) The short-run Phillips curve (SRPC) is a downward-sloping curve that illustrates the short-run relationship between inflation and unemployment. According to the SRPC, as the rate of inflation increases, the unemployment rate decreases, and likewise, as the unemployment rate increases, the inflation rate decreases. The SRPC has its origins in the observations of the apparent relationship between wages and unemployment in several countries. Similar to the difference between short-run aggregate supply and long-run aggregate supply curves, you should consider what is actually occurring at the SRPC in relation to what can potentially happen (the LRPC).

416. (D) When there is a decrease in investment spending, which is a component of aggregate demand, there is a decrease in output and as a result a decrease in employment. Note that in the aggregate demand/aggregate supply model, there is also a decrease in the price level when aggregate demand decreases. Therefore, when aggregate demand shifts to the left, there is a decrease along the short-run Phillips curve.

417. (B) The long-run Phillips curve (LRPC) is derived from the fact that the long-run aggregate supply curve is vertical at the natural rate of unemployment, and as a result the LRPC is also vertical at the natural rate of unemployment. This LRPC also represents the rate of unemployment that is associated with a stable rate of inflation.

418. (D) When an economy is in long-run equilibrium, this is represented on a Phillips curve graph as a point that is at the intersection of the long-run Phillips curve (LRPC) and the short-run Phillips curve (SPRC). When an economy is in recession, output decreases and as a result, unemployment increases above the natural rate of unemployment. When a recession results from a decrease in aggregate demand, there is also a decline in the price level. Therefore, a point in a Phillips curve graph that represents an economy in recession must be to the right of the long-run Phillips curve (so that unemployment is higher than the natural rate of unemployment) and moving along the SRPC to a lower level of inflation.

419. (A) The long-run Phillips curve (LRPC) is vertical at the natural rate of unemployment. In Figure 13.1, the LRPC is vertical at 5%. The acronym *NAIRU* stands for *non-accelerating inflation rate of unemployment*, meaning the rate of unemployment that is consistent with inflation not permanently increasing. The NAIRU, therefore, is the same as the natural rate of unemployment.

420. (B) If the economy is at full employment on the graph, then the point that represents the current state of the economy is on the short-run Phillips curve (SRPC) as well as on the long-run Phillips curve, which would be point B in Figure 13.1. If the unemployment rate decreases 1%, we move along the SRPC to a point that is 1% lower, which would be point A. Point A is associated with an inflation rate of 11%, which is 2% higher than at point B.

421. (B) Movements along the short-run Phillips curve (SRPC) are associated with changes in aggregate demand, and shifts in the SRPC are associated with changes in short-run aggregate supply (SRAS). Recall from the AD-AS model that when SRAS decreases (or shifts to the left), output decreases and the price level increases. This means that when SRAS decreases, unemployment increases and inflation increases. Therefore, a decrease (or leftward shift) in SRAS is associated with an increase (or rightward shift) in the SRPC. An increase in the price of oil would cause a decrease in the SRAS and therefore would cause a rightward shift in the SRPC.

422. (E) Rational expectations theory says that people anticipate future inflation. That is to say, if people expect there to be inflation in the future, they will take actions to protect themselves from future inflation. For instance, people may make purchases today instead of next year if they anticipate prices to be higher next year, and they will negotiate higher wages so that their real wage will not decrease. Of course, by taking these actions, the price level is driven up, making these expectations self-fulfilling.

423. (D) *Stagflation* is a term for when output is decreasing and inflation is increasing. In the AD-AS model, this occurs when the short-run aggregate supply shifts leftward. When output is decreasing, but inflation is going up, this can be represented on the Phillips curve model only as a rightward shift in the short-run Phillips curve.

424. (D) Figure 13.2 shows a rightward shift of the short-run Philips curve (SRPC). Consider point Y on the initial SRPC: it is associated with an inflation rate of 8% and an unemployment rate of 1%. However, when the SRPC shifts, point Z represents a point where inflation is still 8%, but unemployment is higher. This means that in the AD-AS model, something must have happened that would be associated with decreased output and an increased price level, which can only happen when SRAS decreases, which occurs when the price of a factor of production increases.

425. (C) The movement from point X to point Y is a movement along the short-run Phillips curve (SRPC), which is associated with an increase in inflation and a decrease in unemployment (and implicitly an increase in output). This would be associated with an increase, or rightward shift, in aggregate demand (AD). Leftward movements up an SRPC curve are associated with positive AD shocks, and rightward movements down a SRPC curve are associated with negative AD shocks.

426. (D) The move from point Y to point Z in Figure 13.2 is the result of a shift in the short-run Phillips curve from $SRPC_1$ to $SRPC_2$. Recall that a rightward shift in SRPC is associated with a decrease in short-run aggregate supply (SRAS). Decreases in SRAS are associated with an increase in the price of any of the factors of production, or even an expectation of an increase in the price of the factors of production, so either I or II could have caused the change shown.

427. (A) The non-accelerating inflation rate of unemployment (NAIRU) is the rate of unemployment that will not lead to expectations of future inflation. The NAIRU in Figure 13.2 is 4%. If the government attempted to keep the rate of unemployment below 4%, inflation would increase. As people come to accept this new higher rate of inflation (and thus their expectations have incorporated higher price), the short-run aggregate supply curve will shift to the left. As a result, the short-run Phillips curve will shift to the right, returning the unemployment rate back to the NAIRU in the long run and with a permanently higher rate of inflation.

428. (C) It is important to note that the *y*-axis on a Phillips curve model is a *rate* of inflation, not a price level. At the new equilibrium after the shift in the short-run Phillips curve, the rate of inflation is 8%, meaning that prices are increasing 8% every year. While choice D is tempting, it is incorrect because for there to be deflation, the inflation rate must be negative showing a *decrease* in prices, rather than a decrease in the rate.

429. (E) After the shift in the short-run Phillips curve, the new equilibrium at the natural rate of unemployment is associated with a permanently higher rate of inflation of 8%. If the government wanted to decrease the rate of inflation, in the short run it would have to make policies that would also lead to an increase in the unemployment rate above the natural rate of unemployment. In this case, the higher rate of unemployment would be at 7%, rather than 4%.

430. (D) If an economy experiences a sudden increase in net exports, this would result in an increase in the aggregate demand (AD) curve in the AD-AS model. This increase in AD would lead to a movement up along the short-run Phillips curve, as an increase in AD will lead to higher output (and thus lower unemployment), but also create inflationary pressure on the price level.

431. (A) If the current rate of unemployment is equal to the natural rate of unemployment, then the current rate of unemployment is equal to the NAIRU, or the non-accelerating inflation rate of unemployment. That means that this level of unemployment is not associated with increases or decreases in the rate of inflation. Moreover, if the level of inflation was expected, there would be no reason for people to adjust their expectations and shift the short-run Phillips curve.

432. (E) Whenever policies are used to keep the unemployment rate below the NAIRU, the result will be unanticipated inflation. As people adjust their expectations of inflation, the short-run Phillips curve will shift out. Further attempts to keep an artificially low level of unemployment will only continue this cycle, leading to a "ratcheting" effect as inflation rates continue to increase.

Chapter 14: Growth and Productivity

433. (D) Economic growth is defined as the sustained ability to produce more goods and services. Economic growth can be illustrated in both the production possibilities frontier (PPF) model and the AD-AS model. In a PPF model, growth is shown by a shift out of the PPF curve. In an AD-AS model, economic growth is represented by an increase in the long-run aggregate supply curve.

434. (E) Note that while all three graphs show an increase in output, not all three of the graphs show economic growth. A common misperception is that an increase in output, or GDP, is economic growth: the key here is how sustainable this increase is. In the second graph (II), this shows an economic expansion and increase in output. However, the economy has not had a change in its ability to produce goods and services, and it will eventually return to the initial level of output.

435. (C) One could go through the tedious process of calculating growth year by year: after 1 year, the GDP would be $100 million + ($100 million × 0.05) = $105 million: then after 2 years, the GDP would be $105 million + ($105 million × 0.05) = $110.25 million and so on. However, there is a handy shortcut called the "rule of 70" that can be used instead. This rule says that if you divide the number 70 by the rate of growth, this gives you the doubling time of the economy. Here, the rate of growth is 5% per year, so 70/5 = 14 means that the economy will double in size in 14 years.

436. (C) This question is another application of the rule of 70. Note that $375 billion is one half of $750 billion, so the economy of Ile has doubled. Recall that this rule says that if you divide the rate of growth by 70, you get the annual rate of growth, so if the economy of Ile doubled in 10 years, let *x* represent the rate of growth: 70/*x* = 10. Solving for *x* yields *x* = 7; therefore, the annual rate of growth was 7%.

437. (A) Economic growth is represented by an increase (outward shift) of the long-run aggregate supply (LRAS) curve. Recall that the LRAS will increase whenever there is an increase in the stock of the factors of production. Consumption, however, is a component of aggregate demand. While an increase in consumption might lead to an increase in the aggregate demand curve and a short-run increase in output, it would not increase LRAS and therefore would not be growth.

438. (D) Capital depreciates over time, meaning that if capital is not replaced, the stock of capital will start decreasing. Maintaining a capital stock, therefore, requires enough investment to maintain the stock of capital. If there is inadequate investment, the stock of capital will eventually decline, and this would cause a decrease in the long-run aggregate supply curve.

439. (A) When economists use the term *technology*, they are referring to the ability to combine the other factors of production into the goods and services. Therefore, an improvement in technology is an ability to produce more given the same amount of resources. Of course, technology can increase at the same time as any (or all) of the other factors of production, but an increase in technology alone can lead to an increase in output.

440. (B) Growth economists have identified two key drivers of growth in modern history: improvements in human capital and technological change. Human capital refers to not just the physical stock of labor (i.e., the quantity of labor), but also the effective quantity of labor. That is, human capital doesn't count just people but also the abilities of a workforce, including their health, education, and skills. Most analysis of growth accounting has identified improvements in human capital as one of the major drivers of growth.

441. (A) A decrease in literacy rates would be a decrease in the stock of the human capital in the country, decreasing the productivity of the country. All else equal, an increase in immigration would lead to an increase in growth as the stock of labor is larger. The same would be true of an increase in the technology available or the discovery of a new source of energy. A decrease in taxes on investment would stimulate investment in capital, which would increase growth.

442. (B) If there is a tax on consumption of nondurable consumption goods, this will discourage spending on these goods. Since income can be only spent or saved, this will increase savings, which will increase investment and increase the stock of capital. An additional income tax on immigrants would discourage immigration and lead to a lower labor supply. A tax on health or education would also decrease the stock of human capital.

443. (A) The crowding out effect is when government spending is increased without a corresponding increase in taxes. The government finances this spending by borrowing, which drives up the interest rate. When the interest rate increases, the incentive to invest decreases and there will be less investment in capital. If capital is not replaced, the stock of capital will decrease, which will decrease the rate of growth.

444. (C) An increase in economic growth means that there is an increased ability to produce goods and services, and it is represented by a shift in the long-run aggregate supply curve to the right. Such a shift will increase the full employment rate of output to move to a higher level. This means that if Maxistan has an increased ability to produce more, but does not produce more, it does not employ all of its resources.

445. (E) Figure 14.2 shows a production possibility frontier (PPF) of a country that has experienced economic growth, as evidenced by the shift of the PPF. If the economy is initially at point X, any change to a point on the new PPF would represent economic growth, and therefore a move to either point U or Z would represent economic growth.

446. (A) The shift in the PPF shows that there has been an improvement in the ability to make one of the goods, Snads. This is evidenced by the rotation out of the production possibilities frontier (PPF) on the Snads axis. If there was an improvement in the ability to produce all goods and services, which would be caused by an increase in land (including energy) and labor that could be used to produce any good, then the PPF would have shifted out on both axes.

447. (B) A change from producing at point T to point W is an increase in output. It is not, however, economic growth. Economic growth is the ability to produce goods and services, and moving from point T to point W is not representative of an increase in ability, but rather representative of moving from underemployment of resources to full employment of resources.

448. (D) Gross domestic product (GDP) is generally accepted as being a good measure of a country's standard of living, and sustained increases in GDP reflect economic growth. However, there are different measures of GDP. Nominal GDP does not account for inflation; so an increase in nominal GDP may reflect increases in the price level and not necessarily increases in the production of goods and services. Real GDP does account for price changes; however, if the population of a country is growing faster than real GDP is increasing, the country may experience a decline in the standard of living. Increases in real GDP per capita (per person), however, would capture all of these factors.

449. (A) While both human capital and technological change have been identified as more significant contributors to economic growth than changes in the stock of physical capital, stock of labor, or stock of land, growth accounting measures have demonstrated that improvements in technology have been the major driver in economic growth. One of the reasons that growth patterns differ between countries is that some countries have accumulated and, just as important, have applied new technologies to improve their productive capacities, which allows output to expand even with the reality of diminishing marginal returns to capital.

450. (E) As the capital stock of a nation grows, it will have more capital per worker (if all else equal, the stock of labor does not also grow), which will increase the real GDP per capita of the country. In other words, more capital per worker will lead to economic growth. However, because there are diminishing returns to capital, each additional unit of capital will not generate the same increase in output, leading to a lower rate of economic growth.

451. (C) Maxistan is currently experiencing a very rapid rate of growth compared to Ile. One of the reasons that the rate of growth of some less-developed nations is very rapid compared to more-developed nations is that the more developed nations already have fairly well developed stocks of human and physical capital. As a result, less-developed countries will not experience the same magnitude of decreasing returns that more-developed countries will face.

452. (D) If the population of Maxistan will double in 16 years, then real GDP will also need to double in 16 years to maintain the same standard of living. According to the rule of 70, the doubling time of an economy is equal to $70/x =$ doubling time in years, where $x =$ annual rate of growth. Therefore, $70/x = 16$ yields 4.375, so Maxistan will have to grow at a rate of 4.4% during this period to maintain the same standard of living. Note that this is true regardless of the initial starting point: whether the economy is currently producing $1 million in real GDP or $100 million, the time it takes to double will be the same.

453. (D) To solve this problem, we must first determine the growth rate for each country. In Ile, ($210 − $200)/$200 = 5%, and in Maxistan, ($25 − $20)/$20 = 25%. Therefore, even though Ile grew by a greater amount (Ile grew by $10 million, twice the dollar amount as Maxistan), Maxistan is growing at a faster rate than Ile (Maxistan had a 25% rate of growth and is growing 5 times as fast as Ile). According to the rule of 70, the doubling time (the time it will take for Ile to double its GDP from $200 million to $400 million) of Ile is 7 years and the doubling time of Maxistan (the time it will take for Maxistan to double its GDP from $20 million to $40 million) is only 2.8 years.

454. (C) Figure 14.3 shows a decrease in long-run aggregate supply (LRAS). This can occur when the stock of one of the four factors of production has declined. Policies that restrict pollution can lead to decreased output and growth. Policies that encourage education and immigration increase the stock of human capital in a country, and policies that encourage investment would lead to increases in physical capital. If a plague devastated a population, however, this would cause a decrease in human capital.

455. (D) Decreasing investment in human capital, creating restrictions on growth, and limiting the workforce would all serve to further damage the productive capacity of this economy. While it is tempting to say that improving consumption would improve this situation, this is not correct. Increasing consumption may lead to a short-term increase in output as aggregate demand increases, but it does not improve the productive capacity and may in fact damage it: if people consume more and save less, this may lead to less investment. Creating ways of improving human capital, however, would increase the stock of human capital.

456. (A) Shift number 3 shows a decrease in the ability to produce both consumption goods and investment goods. If a country chooses allocation R on its initial production possibilities frontier, it is choosing to produce only consumption goods. Because investment goods depreciate, the stock of its capital will decrease and in the future it will be able to produce less of either type of good.

457. (C) Shift number 2 shows the largest increase in growth, as it is the largest shift outward of the production possibilities frontier (PPF). This implies that, all else equal, an initial allocation that produced more investment goods than consumption goods must have been chosen. On the initial PPF, allocation X represents the larger allocation of production to investment goods.

458. (D) There is a trade-off associated with investment and consumption. While a country that would like to grow at a very rapid rate would like to allocate as much production to investment goods as possible, there is a limit to the amount that an economy could divert from consumption to investment. Similarly, one of the reasons for different rates of growth between countries is different institutions and political systems, which includes differences in political stability. If consumption in a country were cut back too drastically, this could lead to further political instability, which would further undermine growth.

459. (B) Human capital refers to the amount of knowledge, skills, and health status of a population that can be used to do labor. It is a more complete description of the labor of a country than just the labor supply. For instance, if two countries both had a labor supply of 10 people, but in one country all 10 people were literate and in the other all 10 were illiterate, we would expect the labor productivity of the literate country to be higher because it has a greater stock of human capital.

460. (E) An important, but often overlooked, factor that promotes growth is a nation's system of transportation and communications infrastructure. Good roads, bridges, and ports allow for goods and services to be moved around the nation more efficiently and for greater international trade. A reliable communications infrastructure facilitates commerce and investment in new technologies.

Chapter 15: Balance of Payments and Foreign Exchange

461. (C) A country's balance of payments account tracks the flow of currency from that nation to other nations. The current account tracks short-term payments on goods and services, factor income payments, and other cash transfers. The financial account tracks the long-term payments on physical assets, buildings, stocks, and bonds. The sum of the balance in the current account must equally offset the balance in the financial account.

462. (A) One of the largest sources of international payments is in the exchange of goods and services. A nation exports goods and services to other nations and receives currency payment in return. A nation also imports goods and services from other nations and sends currency in return. If the value of a nation's exports exceeds the value of the nation's imports, it is said to have a trade surplus. It is important to distinguish between the value (measured in currency) of imports and exports and the simple quantity (measured in cars, computers, shirts, etc.) of imports and exports. A nation's balance of trade considers the value of the goods being traded. For example, if the United States exports 1,000 cars to Europe and each car is worth $20,000, then the United States has exported $20 million worth of cars.

463. (B) A nation exports goods and services to other nations and receives currency payment in return. A nation also imports goods and services from other nations and sends currency in return. If the value of a nation's imports exceeds the value of the nation's exports, it is said to have a trade deficit, or a negative trade balance. Similar to the computation of GDP, it is important to keep in mind that trade balances are computed using the *value* of the goods and services, not just the *quantity* of goods and services.

464. (D) The Canadian current account records the inflow (additions) and outflow (subtractions) of currency for the purchase of goods and services or factor payments to and from other countries. If a firm in Canada sells a product to a consumer in foreign countries, like any nation in Europe, currency will flow from Europe to Canada. The key difference between the current account and the financial account is that the financial account records the inflow and outflow of financial transactions (like the sale of shares in a mutual fund) and capital asset sales (like the sale of a corporation or building) between nations.

465. (E) When a firm in Texas sells products (like beef) to consumers outside the United States, the value of the exported beef will be recorded as an addition to the current account in the United States because currency from Mexico will flow into the United States and the product will eventually reach Mexico. In the Mexican current account, this will be recorded as an imported good and would be subtracted from the value of all exported goods.

466. (C) When a physical or financial asset like a corporation is sold to a foreign firm, the entry appears in the financial accounts of both nations. The ownership of the asset (chain of restaurants) is going to Mexico, but the currency is coming into the United States, so this will be an addition to the financial account in the United States and a subtraction from the financial account in Mexico.

467. (E) Government bonds are frequently bought and sold between nations as financial assets. If the Canadian government needs to borrow money, it will issue government bonds, and investors in other countries (like Japan) will buy them, lending Canada money in the process. This is recorded as an inflow of currency to Canada's financial account and a subtraction from Japan's financial account.

468. (D) When interest rates are higher in Britain than they are in the United States, investors (or savers) will withdraw money from the US markets and invest (or save) them in the British financial markets. This creates an inflow of funds into Britain and puts downward pressure on interest rates. The outflow of funds from the United States allows the interest rates in the United States to rise. This flow of financial capital will cease when interest rates are equal in both nations.

469. (D) When interest rates are higher in the United States than they are in Japan, investors seeking higher returns will withdraw money from the Japanese markets and invest them in the American financial markets. This creates an inflow of funds into the United States and puts downward pressure on interest rates. The outflow of funds from Japan causes the interest rates to rise. This flow of financial capital between nations ceases when interest rates are equal in both nations and equilibrium is reached.

470. (D) Foreign consumers need US dollars to purchase goods made in the United States. All else equal, if inflation in the United States is low relative to other countries, foreign consumers will find US-made products to be relative bargains, thus increasing the demand for those goods. When there is stronger demand for the US goods, there will be stronger demand for the US dollar.

471. (C) When consumers outside of Japan acquire a stronger preference for Japanese products, they will need to also acquire more Japanese currency, the yen, to make those purchases. A stronger demand for Japanese products causes a stronger demand for the yen and the demand curve for the yen will shift to the right.

472. (A) Higher interest rates in Iceland, all else equal, will attract more financial investment from foreign firms and banks because they will see Iceland's financial markets as providing a better return. In this situation, interest rates in Iceland are falling, so demand for the króna will fall as investors will seek other nations that are offering higher interest rates on their bonds.

473. (B) A huge influx of foreign tourists for an event like the Olympics or World Cup tournament will require foreign visitors to exchange their domestic currencies for the host-nation's currency. In this case, there will be an increase in the demand for the Brazilian real, shifting the demand curve to the right. One way to think about this is that when a nation receives tourists, that nation also receives the currency of those tourists.

474. (A) The American possesses US dollars but must acquire euros to travel within Europe and pay for goods and services. Basically the American must purchase euros with her dollars, and this purchase, or exchange, acts as an increase in the demand for the euros. The exchange of dollars for euros simultaneously increases the supply of dollars.

475. (C) A clothing manufacturer in the United States will sell clothing in exchange for US dollars, whether the customer is from the United States or from Japan. The Japanese customer possesses yen, so to acquire dollars, the firm must increase the supply of yen to the currency markets. At the same time, there is an increase in the demand for dollars.

476. (B) A recession in Europe causes fewer tourists to come from Europe to the United States. A tourist to the United States must exchange euros for dollars, because firms in the United States will wish to be paid only in dollars. Reduced tourism therefore decreases demand for the US dollar and decreases the supply of the euro to the currency markets.

477. (D) When the US government borrows and issues bonds, many foreign governments will purchase those bonds, but the bonds must be purchased in US dollars. The Chinese purchase of US bonds increases the demand for the US dollar, but the dollars must be acquired by increasing the supply of the Chinese yuan.

478. (E) The student is essentially using his euros to buy dollars. The exchange rate can be expressed a couple of different ways; the exchange rate tells us how many dollars can be bought with 1 euro, or how many euros can be purchased with 1 dollar. If it takes 50 euros to buy $30, then 50 euro = $30. We then divide both currencies by 50 euros, and we find that 1 euro buys $0.60 ($30/50 euro). Equivalently, we can divide both sides of the equation by $30 and find that 1 dollar would buy 1.67 euros (50 euro/$30).

479. (D) An American tourist can buy 0.50 euro with his 1 US dollar, so it will take him $2 to buy 1 euro. If the hotel room in Germany is priced at 75 euros, and it takes $2 to buy just 1 euro, then it will take him $150 to buy the hotel room.

480. (A) While this graph shows the market for the US dollar, the vertical axis represents the price of a dollar in terms of how many units of a foreign currency (in this case, the Japanese yen) that it takes to buy 1 dollar. This equilibrium price P_2 would also be referred to as the yen price of a dollar or how many yen you would receive if you exchanged dollars for yen.

481. (C) The price of P_3 lies below equilibrium. At this price of a dollar (measured in yen) the quantity of dollars demanded at point d exceeds the quantity of dollars supplied at point e. Because there is a shortage of dollars in the exchange market, the price of a dollar must rise. This would be seen as an increase in the number of yen it would take to purchase 1 dollar in currency markets.

482. (B) The initial equilibrium in the market is at point c and price of P_2 yen per dollar. At point a, the price of a dollar is higher, P_1 yen per dollar. Because it now costs more yen to purchase a dollar, the dollar is said to have appreciated. Because each dollar is now worth more yen, each yen is now worth fewer dollars; hence, the yen has said to have depreciated in value.

483. (D) The initial equilibrium in the market is at point c and price of P_2 yen per dollar. At point e, the price of a dollar is lower, P_3 yen per dollar. Because it now costs less to purchase a dollar, the dollar is said to have depreciated. Because each dollar is now worth fewer yen, each yen is now worth more dollars; hence, the yen is said to have appreciated in value.

484. (C) If Canadian customers find European goods more popular, the Canadian demand for these imported goods will rise. This increased demand for European goods must increase the demand for the euro and the dollar price of the euro rises (it appreciates). At the same time, the supply of Canadian dollars must increase, lowering the euro price of the dollar (it depreciates).

485. (E) A recession in the United States reduces demand for Mexican goods and reduces imports from Mexico. With reduced demand for Mexican goods, there is a reduced demand for the peso and the dollar price of the peso falls (it depreciates). Simultaneously, the supply of dollars falls, increasing the peso price of the dollar (it appreciates).

486. (A) At the current price of 10 pesos per dollar, a hotel room priced at 1,200 pesos would require that Stan pay $120 for the room (1,200 pesos/10 pesos per dollar). While the room rate in Mexico hasn't changed from June 1st to July 1st, the value of Stan's tourist dollars from America has changed. Now that the exchange rate is 12 pesos per dollar, Stan would need to provide only $100 for the room (1,200 pesos/12 pesos per dollar).

487. (B) Political instability in Russia decreases the flow of tourists from European nations into Russia, thus decreasing the demand for the Russian ruble. When the demand for the ruble falls, the euro price of a ruble falls, depreciating the ruble. At the same time, the supply of euros is falling, increasing the ruble price of a euro, appreciating the euro.

488. (C) If net exports in the United States are falling, it means that the United States is exporting fewer goods to foreign nations, importing more goods from other nations, or both. All else equal, this translates into fewer foreign currencies flowing into the US economy and a decreased demand for the US dollar; therefore the dollar's value falls (the dollar depreciates).

489. (E) All of these statements are correct. When the value of the dollar is low, it means that foreign consumers find that goods made in the United States will be relatively inexpensive. The United States will start to export more goods to foreign countries, and net exports will rise. If the dollar is rising in value, American consumers will find that foreign goods are relatively inexpensive, and the United States will start to import more goods from foreign countries, and US net exports will fall. If the trade deficit is getting larger, it means that net exports are falling (becoming more negative). Because the United States is exporting fewer products and importing more products, there is a weaker demand for the US dollar and a greater supply of the dollar. This combination of events will lower the value of the dollar in currency markets.

490. (D) If foreign investors increase their deposits of foreign currencies in Canadian banks, this increases the demand for the Canadian dollar and increases the supply of foreign currencies in Canada. An increase in the supply of foreign currencies would depreciate the foreign currency relative to the Canadian dollar, which means that the Canadian dollar would appreciate relative to other currencies.

491. (A) A widening trade deficit means that the United States is exporting fewer goods to Mexico and importing more goods from Mexico. Declining exports means that the demand for the US dollar is falling; this depreciates the value against the peso. Increasing imports means that the supply of the dollar is rising, which also causes it to depreciate against the peso. The opposite is happening in the market for the peso; demand is rising and supply is falling, and this increases the value of the peso against the dollar.

492. (B) As the central bank of Portlandia increases the money supply, interest rates in Portlandia will begin to fall. This should spark domestic capital investment, as borrowing is less expensive, but it should depress incoming financial investment from abroad, as the return on saving in Portlandia is lower. As the inflow of financial investment decreases, demand for the currency decreases and it will depreciate in value.

493. (C) When the central bank of Portlandia decreases the money supply, interest rates will rise. This is designed to slow domestic capital investment to fight inflation, but at the same time it will attract more financial investment from abroad as the return on savings in Portlandia is rising. As the inflow of financial capital increases, the demand for the currency also increases and the currency will appreciate.

494. (D) When the government borrows to finance deficit spending, we expect the domestic interest rates to rise. Higher interest rates will attract foreign savers to invest their financial capital into the domestic financial system, increasing the value of the domestic currency. An appreciating currency will give domestic consumers more purchasing power when they buy imported products. At the same time, this will make domestic products more expensive to foreigners, dropping exports. The combination of falling exports and rising imports causes net exports to fall.

495. (C) An open market purchase is designed to lower interest rates and spur capital investment in the US economy. However, lower interest rates will decrease demand for the US dollar because foreigners will find it less attractive to save in the US financial markets. In the market for the dollar, we expect to see a movement from point V to point III as the demand curve shifts to the left.

496. (E) An open market sale is designed to raise interest rates and reduce capital investment in the US economy. Higher interest rates will increase demand for the US dollar because foreigners will find it more attractive to save in the US financial markets. In the market for the dollar, we expect to see a movement from point V to point II as the demand curve shifts to the right.

497. (A) Because of the rapid hyperinflation in Argentina, Brazilian consumers will find products from Argentina to be very expensive relative to domestically produced substitute goods. Brazilians will reduce imports from Argentina, and Brazilian firms will export more products to Argentina. The increased demand for the Brazilian goods increases demand for the real, and it appreciates against the peso.

498. (B) Contractionary monetary policy is designed to slow down the inflation of an overheating economy by raising interest rates. While this may reduce investment in physical capital and borrowing, higher interest rates will make financial investments in the nation more attractive to foreigners. More foreign currency will flow into the domestic market, increasing the demand for the domestic currency, appreciating its value against other currencies.

499. (D) When the dollar appreciates against the rupee, it means that a dollar can buy more rupees in the currency markets. This means that any good produced in India (and therefore priced in rupees) takes fewer dollars to purchase. For example, if the dollar is exchanged for 54 rupees, a Mumbai hotel room priced at 5,400 rupees would cost $100 to a tourist from America. If the exchange rate changes to a dollar being worth 60 rupees, the same hotel room would cost an American tourist only $90.

500. (C) Foreign currencies, like US dollars, European euros, Mexican pesos, and Japanese yen, are exchanged just as any other commodity can be exchanged in a market. For a Japanese consumer to buy an American car, she must first demand American dollars and supply her Japanese yen. A German artist selling a painting to a Mexican museum will expect to be paid in euros, so the museum must first supply pesos and exchange them for euros. These transactions occur in the foreign exchange markets.